The Pubs of
St. David's, Fishguard
and
North Pembrokeshire

The Pubs of
St. David's, Fishguard and
North Pembrokeshire

by

Keith Johnson

Logaston Press

LOGASTON PRESS
Little Logaston, Woonton, Almeley,
Herefordshire HR3 6QH
logastonpress.co.uk

First published by Logaston Press 2010
Copyright © Keith Johnson 2010

ISBN 978 1 906663 50 6

Set in Times New Roman by Logaston Press
and printed in Great Britain by
Bell & Bain Ltd., Glasgow

Contents

Newport Castle

Acknowledgments

And so we come to the end of what has been a mammoth historical pub crawl around Pembrokeshire. It started in Angle in 2003 and now, four books later, it staggers to an end in Llanfyrnach. Perhaps one day I'll count up how many pubs there were along the weary way – it must be well over 2,000.

This fourth book in the series has been the most difficult to research, not least because of the geographical spread from St. Bride's Bay right round the northern coast and over the hills to far-flung reaches of the county, places such as Clydey and Henfeddau that I didn't realise were even in Pembrokeshire until I began my researches. The main problem has been that the sources I usually rely on proved to be rather patchy for the north of the county. Trade directories and early newspapers tended to concentrate on the few main settlements and all but ignored the smaller villages; census enumerators rarely bothered to give the names of inns and ale-houses (and the 1861 census is missing altogether for several parishes), while the records for the Fishguard and Goodwick licensing division from about 1910 to 1980 have disappeared.

As a result of these gaps it has sometimes proved impossible to build up a chain of evidence linking an early reference to a village pub to a later one, so that while I may be convinced in my own mind that the Anchor Inn mentioned in an ale-house recognisance of 1828 is the same place as the Anchor Inn recorded in the 1851 census and the Anchor Inn mentioned in a trade directory of 1875, there is often no way of proving it. So if I appear to be hedging my bets sometimes, with phrases such as 'seems to be' and 'appears to be', then that is the reason.

Fortunately, while the records are a little thin on the ground, this is made up for by the fact that there is a wealth of material to be found in books about the north of Pembrokeshire, from the early journals of often grumpy travellers such as Malkin and Millicent Bant through to the excellent series of local history titles published by Peter Davies. Solva and St. David's have been particularly well covered in this respect, with local historians such as F.W. Warburton and Dr. George Middleton including much valuable information about local hostelries in their writings. Dillwyn Miles' history of Newport contains a useful section on the old pubs of the township (although he does get a little confused in some cases), while the books by E.T. Lewis are invaluable for the Llanfyrnach and Crymych area. More recently, the heritage societies in Cilgerran and

Eglwyswrw have produced excellent books on their local communities, and I am grateful to them for permission to use material from these publications. On a smaller scale, I particularly enjoyed Evan Raymond's *Memories of Letterston* and John Miles Thomas' *Looking Back,* both marvellous evocations of times gone by and well worth seeking out. The surprising thing is that there appears to be no comprehensive history of Fishguard, because while countless books continue to be written about the French invasion, and while the building of the ferry port at Goodwick has been well documented, the town itself has been rather neglected. At least now the pubs have been recorded.

As ever, I owe a particular debt of gratitude to all the staff at the Haverfordwest Reference Library and the County Records Office for their help and forbearance; they will be relieved not to see me for a while. Thanks also go to Andy Johnson and Ron Shoesmith of Logaston Press for their guidance and patience throughout this project and to Katy Shoesmith who once again produced the maps.

Very many people have provided information and illustrations for this book and it would be impossible to list every one; my thanks go to them all. In particular I would like to thank Glen Johnson of St. Dogmael's, Dr. Reginald Davies of Newport and Rex Harris of Dinas for casting an expert local eye over the relevant chapters in the book and offering invaluable suggestions.

Thanks also to Mike Bennett, Eurfron Bowen, Meyrick Brown, Beatrice Davies, Philip Davies, Sheila Doherty, Sybil Edwards, Dai Griffiths, Peggy Jones, Roy Lewis, Tom Lloyd, Charlotte and Jason Morell, Julian Orbach, Christine Page, Robert Scourfield, David Stephens, Owen Vaughan, Yvonne Thomas, Cilgerran Language and Heritage Committee, Eglwyswrw and District Heritage Society, and to all the licensees and pub regulars who gave up valuable serving and drinking time to answer my daft questions.

> You true honest Britons who love your own land,
> Whose sires were so brave, so victorious and free,
> Who always beat France when they took her in hand,
> Come join honest Britons in chorus with me.
>
> Let us sing our own treasures, old England's good cheer,
> The profits and pleasures of stout British beer.
> Your wine-tippling, dram-sipping fellows retreat,
> But your beer-drinking Briton can never be beat!
>
> The French with their vineyards are meagre and pale,
> They drink of the squeezings of half-ripened fruit.
> But we who have hop-yards to mellow our ale
> Are rosy and plump and have freedom to boot.
>
> (Traditional song)

CHAPTER ONE

Introduction

Almost as long as the history of boozing in Pembrokeshire is the history of opposition to boozing, or at least to over-indulgence in drink. As far back as the 6th century, St. David himself – a confirmed teetotaller long before the word was invented – was forced to issue the following edict to his fellow monks: 'Those who get drunk through ignorance must do penance 15 days; if through negligence, 40 days; if through contempt, three quarntains' (a quarntain – from which we get the word 'quarantine' – being a period of 40 days).

Many centuries later, the north Pembrokeshire homeland of the patron saint became a battlefield in the war between the drinking man and the temperance movement. If you carry on reading this book, you will notice that one of the main themes to emerge is the endless campaign by the Rechabites, the Band of Hope and the Nonconformist church to close as many pubs as possible, apparently in the belief that reducing supply would also reduce demand. All it did, of course, was drive the drinkers from properly regulated and policed public houses into unlicensed 'shebeens' of which there were large numbers dotted about the countryside and which stayed open all hours. For example, Herbrandston didn't have a pub in 1899 but it did have a thriving shebeen run by a widow named Mary Sutton; on one occasion a watching policeman counted 23 men – locals and militia – entering the cottage for an illegal pint of home brew. And so popular was a shebeen in St. Dogmael's that it nearly put a nearby pub out of business!

Ironically, perhaps, it was the shrine of St. David which brought many thousands of pilgrims flocking to the county in the Middle Ages, resulting in numerous hostelries being opened up along the pilgrim ways. But the concept of the inn can be traced back to a period long before the Age of the Saints. It is thought that the Romans introduced the idea to Britain, setting up *tavernae* along their network of roads where travellers could rest and perhaps enjoy alcoholic refreshment. Home-brewed beer and cider were already being produced in these islands, but this did not appeal to the refined Roman

1

palate – as the Emperor Julian famously remarked: 'Wine smells of nectar, beer smells of goat' – so the Romans imported wine from other parts of their empire for the benefit of their legions in Britain.

Then came the Angles and Saxons, beer-drinking tribes from northern Europe, who not only gave England its name but also its national beverage. Soon the Roman wine-bars were a thing of the past and there were houses in every village where the men would gather to hold petty courts and to quaff ale out of drinking horns – the real fore-runner of the modern pub.

The earliest ale-houses in Pembrokeshire would probably have been fairly primitive affairs, thatched wooden huts where the inhabitants owned a cauldron capable of boiling up a brew of sweet ale. None of these would have been 'full-time' pubs; they would simply have rustled up a brew when there was a demand – perhaps for a feast day. By the 6th century these ale-houses had become slightly more sophisticated, to the extent of offering a choice of alcoholic beverages. Mead – made from fermented honey – was a well-established favourite of the Celtic people; one early Welsh law specified that a cask of mead should be nine palms high and wide enough to serve as a bathtub for the king and one of his court. And in Wales there were two types of ale – *cwrwf*, which was an everyday kind of ale, and the highly-flavoured (and more expensive) *bragawd* which was spiced up with cinnamon, ginger and cloves.

By AD 745, ale-houses were widespread – and had gained such a low reputation that the Archbishop of York had to issue a Canon: 'That no priest go to eat or drink in taverns'. There were so many inns by the time of King Edgar (959-975) that he tried to limit them to one per village.

The arrival of the Normans in Pembrokeshire and the creation of castle towns such as Pembroke, Tenby, Haverfordwest and Newport meant the establishment of permanent ale-houses in the county. These were often found alongside the market square and close to the church – the historic link between the monasteries and the brewing industry being a strong one. Outside the protection of the towns there were fewer ale-houses – especially in the disputed countryside. These were sometimes known as 'hedge ale-houses' because, with their thatched roof and low walls made out of 'clom' (mud or clay strengthened with straw), they were barely distinguishable from the surrounding vegetation. But as time went by and St. David's began to gain a reputation as a shrine of international importance, so rather

A 14th-century inn with its pole and bush sign

2

more substantial wayside inns were opened to provide hospitality for the pilgrims and later for travelling merchants.

Moves to regulate the pub trade began at an early date. The *Magna Carta* included a decree designed to standardise the measurements of wine, ale and corn throughout the land, while in 1266 the Assize of Bread and Ale recognised that these items were the necessities of life and sensibly linked their retail price to the current price of grain. Breaking the assize of ale became an offence which was to keep the manorial courts busy for centuries to come. In 1606, for example, Caria Tanner, a resident of Newport, Pembrokeshire, 'broke the Assize of Ale, selling small measures in illegal measures, therefore she is in mercy 12d'.

The widespread introduction of hops in the 15th century meant that ale slowly began to give way to a new, bitter drink called beer. Despite considerable opposition to this 'pernicious weed' – its use was even prohibited for a while – the hop proved very popular with brewers and eventually with drinkers; beer having a sharper flavour and better 'keeping' qualities than the traditional ale. There seems to be no record of large scale hop-growing in Pembrokeshire, although hops were grown in the Carew area at one time (as the name Hop Gardens testifies) while the name Hopshill at Saundersfoot might indicate another area where the vines were cultivated successfully.

As the number of common ale-houses increased, so did the number of regulations controlling them. It was Henry VII – a son of Pembrokeshire – who introduced Acts in 1495 and 1504 giving local Justices the power to suppress ale-houses which were badly run or which were responsible for keeping men from their all-important archery practice. A further Act in 1553 made a legal distinction between the different kinds of hostelry; ale-houses sold only ale and beer, taverns were restricted to towns and cities and sold only wine (though later they sold beer as well), while inns also offered accommodation. Most of these places would have brewed their own beer, although in the smaller houses, where the part-time ale-house keeper had a trade which occupied most of his day, it was the practice to buy beer from better-equipped inns and later from full-time brewers.

A 16th-century brewer

3

Although both Tenby and Haverfordwest were notable wine-importing centres at one time, it seems unlikely that there were too many taverns in Pembrokeshire that offered only wine – ale and beer were the order of the day for the Welsh lower classes. However a complaint to the Star Chamber in 1602 stated that an Irish priest who visited Pembroke was 'a comon haunter of alhouses and wintaverns', so there must have been wine bars in the town 400 years ago. Even so, most of the wine that the merchants shipped into the county was destined for the castles and manor houses of the gentry; according to the bards who sang his praises, Tomas ap Phylip of Picton Castle once took delivery of a shipment of 20 tuns of wine – about 5,000 gallons.

Despite this impressive statistic, the Elizabethan historian George Owen thought that heavy drinking was rare in Pembrokeshire. However he did concede that an influx of Irish settlers into the county in the days of Henry VIII had given the locals a taste for whiskey. As Owen explained:

> Those Irish people here do use their country trade in making of Aqua Vitae in great abundance which they carry to be sold abroad the country on horseback and otherwise, so that weekly you may be sure to have Aqua Vitae to be sold at your door, and by means thereof it is grown to be an usual drink in most men's houses instead of wine.

By the beginning of the 17th century, there were plenty of licensed alehouses in Pembrokeshire – and more than a few unlicensed ones as well. In 1606, the Court Leet and View of Frankpledge in Newport dealt with the case

A mid-18th century brewhouse

of a tailor named Richard ap Ievan and ten others who 'kept taverns in their houses and sold ale without licence'.

In the towns, the inns and ale-houses tended to cluster around market squares and harbours where there was always a lively trade. Bridge End in St. Dogmael's, the Parrog in Newport and the area around Fishguard harbour all had their share of rough and ready 'sailortown' pot-houses, while the pubs on Fishguard Square, Narberth Square and the East End of Pembroke came alive on market days and fair days. Out in the country-side, wherever there was hard work to be done, ale-houses – legal and otherwise – sprang up to provide refreshment for the labouring man. Bread, cheese and 'table beer' – as opposed to strong ale – sustained the quarryman and labourer, ploughman and collier throughout the long working day.

One of Pembrokeshire's longest-surviving coaching inns, the Mariners Hotel in Haverfordwest. The illustration shows the famous occasion when the local hounds chased a fox onto the roof

Many of the smaller country ale-houses had names designed to encourage the passer-by to enter – some of which live on in the name of Pembrokeshire localities. There were several ale-houses called 'Step Inn', as well as a 'Venture Inn' (now Venterin) near Lampeter Velfrey, the 'Stop-and-Call' at Goodwick and the 'Step Aside' near Kilgetty. With the Cleddau River carving its way through the heart of the county there were numerous ferry crossings, and all of these had an ale-house on at least one side of the river – usually run by the ferry-man and his wife and usually called 'Ferry Inn' or 'Waterman's Arms'.

In the towns, inns of a more substantial nature had been established, perhaps following the dissolution of the monasteries when pilgrims could no longer seek shelter in abbeys and other religious houses. The sadly-demolished Swan in Haverfordwest was said to date from the 16th century, while there are references to both the King's Arms in Pembroke and to the King's Arms in Tenby in 1617. These inns offered reasonable accommodation for travellers, stabling for their horses, and a ready meal, but the golden age of the inn – the era of the stage coach – had yet to arrive, and they were far from the bustling establishments they were to become.

16  99

Whereas by the Laws and Statutes of This Realm

NOTICE

IS HEREBY GIVEN TO ALL

INN KEEPERS, ALEHOUSE KEEPERS, SUTLERS, VICTUALLERS

and other Retailers of

ALE and BEER

AND EVERY OTHER PERSON or PERSONS KEEPING A PUBLIC HOUSE
IN ANY
CITY, TOWN CORPORATE, BOROUGH, MARKET TOWN, VILLAGE, HAMLET, PARISH,
PART or PLACE IN THE *Kingdom of England*

That, as from the **24**th *day of* **JUNE, 1700**

THEY SHALL BE REQUIRED TO RETAIL and SELL THEIR ALE & BEER

by the **FULL ALE QUART** or **PINT**

According to the Laid Standard

IN VESSELS DULY MARKED *with* **W. R** *and* **CROWN**

be they made of

WOOD, GLASS, HORN, LEATHER or **PEWTER** etc.

Any Person Retailing Ale or Beer to a **TRAVELLER** *or* **WAYFARER** *in Vessels not
signed and marked as aforesaid will be liable to a* **PENALTY** *not exceeding*

FORTY SHILLINGS

FOR EVERY SUCH OFFENCE

By Act of Parliament ~ at WESTMINSTER
In the Reign of Our Sovereign ~ WILLIAM III by the Grace of God, King,
Defender of the Faith &c

*In 1700 it became a legal requirement that vessels in which ale and beer
were served should be accurate and marked*

The 18th century saw a further development with the arrival of purpose-built public houses. Where ale-houses were basically cottages with a room in which refreshments could be enjoyed, the public houses might have several rooms to cater for the different classes of drinker (but without offering the accommodation which would have turned them into inns). This competition had the effect of dragging many ale-houses 'up-market', although this increased respectability didn't prevent the criminal classes – the pickpockets, prostitutes, smugglers and highway robbers – from continuing to frequent the seedier houses at the bottom end of the scale.

Another change in the 18th century was in the amount of spirits being consumed, particularly cheap brandy and gin. While duty had to be paid on beer, spirits remained exempt for a good many years, so that the consumption of spirits increased from about half a million gallons in 1684 to eight million gallons in 1743 – an increase of well over a gallon per person per year! It took a succession of 'Gin Acts' to curb the dram shops and gin palaces and persuade people to turn back to the relatively healthy consumption of beer, ale and – increasingly – porter.

Porter was a specially blended mild beer which took its name from its popularity among London's market porters, and porter breweries soon sprang up all over the country – notably that of Samuel Whitbread in Chiswell Street in the City of London. This also led to another new development – the brewer's dray. Where once the ale-house keeper would have been expected to fetch the casks from the brewery himself, now the brewer made regular deliveries to all the pubs on his patch – a practice which eventually led to the 'tied house'. Although brewery-to-pub delivery was initially confined to the larger centres of population, horse-drawn brewer's drays inevitably found their way onto the streets and country lanes of Pembrokeshire.

Up to this time, and for many years to come, the easiest way to travel to Pembrokeshire was by sea, and little in the way of coaching inns had developed in the county. This changed in the late 18th century with the establishment of a packet service to

A horse-drawn dray delivers casks for local wine and spirit merchant James Williams in Church Street, Narberth, in the 1930s.

(Picture courtesy of the Narberth Museum)

Ireland from Hakin Point and also the emergence of Tenby as a fashion-able sea-bathing resort. The coach road to Hakin Point ran by way of St. Clears, Llanddowror, Tavernspite, Narberth and Haverfordwest, and several coaching inns were established as posting stages along this route including the Picton at Llanddowror, the Plume of Feathers at Tavernspite, the Golden Lion in Narberth, the Coach and Horses in Robeston Wathen and the Castle in Haverfordwest. On the road which branched south to Pembroke, there were the Milford Arms in Saundersfoot, the White Lion in Tenby and the Golden Lion and Green Dragon in Pembroke itself. These were all substantial build-ings with good rooms and plenty of stabling, and as often as not had been built at the instigation of the local squire.

Many coaching inns were well-run establishments; some weren't. According to John Byng, writing in the 18th century:

> The innkeepers are insolent, the hostlers are sulky, the chambermaids are pert and the waiters are impertinent; the meat is tough, the wine is foul, the beer is hard, the sheets are wet, the linen is dirty and the knives are never clean'd!

It is to be hoped that Pembrokeshire's inns were run to a better standard, though most late 18th-century travellers settled for describing them as 'middling' or 'tolerable' at best.

While the number of larger, well-appointed inns and public houses continued to increase, approved and licensed by the magistrates, there were also growing numbers of smaller and humbler houses which operated in the grey area between ale-house and unlicensed 'shebeen'. In 1779, several people in Steynton, Pill and Hubberston were convicted of 'selling ale and strong beer without being licensed so to do', and as time went by it became apparent that gin drinking was once again on the increase and that the dodgier ale-houses were turning into dram-shops.

Various Acts were passed in the 1820s in an attempt to reverse this trend, culminating in the 1830 Beer Act. This was designed to encourage the consumption of beer at the expense of spirits – a move which would boost the country's agriculture and brewing industries and also improve health. Beer was widely considered to be a wholesome and health-giving drink, much more so than water which was often of a dubious quality – especially in the towns. For example, when Milford Sunday School held a New Year's Day treat in 1818, nearly 200 children enjoyed a meal of roast beef and plum pudding 'and afterwards ale supplied by Mr. G. Starbuck and Mr. R. Byers' – Byers being the local surgeon.

The 1830 Beer Act duly abolished all duty on beer and brought into being the 'beer-shop' or 'beer-house'. For the cost of two guineas, any householder could obtain a beer-house licence which would permit the sale of beer and cider only – as opposed to the fully licensed public houses which could also sell wine and spirits. The result of this new legislation can be easily imagined – beer-houses by the thousand opened up all over the country. Former 'shebeens' entered the fold of legitimacy, while masons and black-smiths, farmers, coopers and carpenters took the opportunity to sell beer as a sideline to their regular trade. Within a year of the Act coming into force there were 24,000 new beer-houses in Britain and the figure had reached 46,000 by 1836. In the twin towns of Pembroke and Pembroke Dock there were 45 beer-houses in 1840 while Milford Haven had 24. 'Everybody is drunk', reported Sydney Smith soon after the Beer Act came into force. 'Those who are not singing are sprawling'.

These new drinking premises were often called 'Tom and Jerry shops' after a pair of dissolute characters in Pierce Egan's serialised novel *Life in London,* or sometimes 'Kiddleywinks'. They were often badly run, and as the Haverfordwest weekly newspaper *Potter's Electric News* noted: 'Beer-shop owners prey upon labouring men who earn their money like horses – and then spend it like asses'. They also attracted a seedy clientele.

> The beer-shop keeper collects about him the very dregs of society. It is in these places that robberies are planned and crimes committed. The beer-shop keeper is too frequently the banker of the thief.

Because of their very nature, beer-houses are difficult to research. The Beer Act made no provision for the keeping of records of licences, and numerous 'Kiddleywinks' came and went without leaving any trace other than a vague folk memory. Several of these were *ad hoc* affairs which opened to take advantage of such things as the arrival of gangs of navvies to build a road or railway and which closed again following their departure. Others lasted much longer, and there was hardly a street in Pembroke Dock which didn't have a beer-house or three to cater for the town's hard-drinking popula-tion of shipwrights, seamen and soldiers.

Running parallel with the spread of the beer-shop came the rise of Nonconformity and also the growing influence of the temperance movement. This movement had become organised as far back as 1828, and – ironically perhaps – had strongly supported the Beer Act and its aim of getting people to stop drinking gin. Its members pledged themselves to abstain from all spirits – except for medicinal purposes – and only to drink beer and wine 'in modera-tion'. This wasn't enough for some of the hard-line reformers who went even further and advocated total abstinence. These teetotallers, who often clashed with their more 'wishy-washy' temperance colleagues, embarked on a high-profile campaign aimed at persuading people to give up the demon drink

DRUNKARD'S CATECHISM

1. Q. What is your name?
   A. Drunken sot.
2. Q. Who gave you that name?
   A. As drink is my idol, Landlords and their wives get all my money; they gave me that name in one of my drunken sprees, wherein I was made a member of strife, a child of want, and an inheritor of a bundle of rage.
3. Q. What did your Landlords and Landladies promise for you?
   A. They did promise and vow three things in my name; first, that I should renounce the comforts of my own fireside; second, starve my wife and hunger my children; third, walk in rags and tatters, with my shoe soles going flip flap, all the days of my life.
4. Q. Rehearse the articles of the belief.
   A. I believe in the existence of one Mr. Alcohol, the great head and chief of all manner of vice, the source of nine-tenths of all diseases; lastly, I not only believe, but am sure when my money is all gone and spent, the Landlord will stop the tap and turn me out.
5. Q. How many commandments have ye sots to keep?
   A. Ten.
6. Q. Which be they?
   A. The same which the Landlord and Landlady spoke in the bar, saying, We are thy master and mistress, who brought thee out of the paths of virtue, placed thee in the ways of vice, and set thy feet in the road which leadeth to New South Wales.

   I. Thou shalt use no other house but mine.
   II. Thou shalt not make for thyself any substitute for intoxicating drinks, such as tea, coffee, ginger pop, or lemonade; for I am a jealous man, wearing a coat that should be on thy back, eating thy children's bread, and pocketing the money which should make thee and the wife comfortable all the days of thy life.
   III. Thou shalt not use my house in vain.
   IV. Remember that thou eat but one meal on the Sabbath day, for six days hast thou been drinking, and nought else wouldst thou do; but the seventh is the sabbath day, and thou canst have no trust; therefore thou skulketh on the seventh day and abominates it.
   V. Thou shalt honour the Landlords and Landladies and Gin-shops with thy presence, that thy days may be few and miserable in the land wherein thou dwellest.
   VI. Thou shalt commit murder, by starving, and hungering, and beating thy wife and family.
   VII. Thou shalt commit self-destruction.
   VIII. Thou shalt sell thy wife and children's bread and rob thyself of all thy comforts.
   IX. Thou shalt bear false witness when thou speakest of the horrors, saying thou art in good health when thou art labouring under the barrel fever.
   X. Thou shalt covet all thy neighbour is possessed of, thou shalt covet his house, his land, his purse, his health, his wealth, and all that he has got, that thou mayest indulge in drinking, help the brewer to buy a new coach, a pair of fine horses, a new dray and a fine building, that he may live in idleness all his days: likewise to enable the Landlord to purchase a new sign to put over his door, with 'Licensed to be drunk on the premises', written thereon.

An 1850s Temperance Society Tract based on the Ten Commandments

The Railway Temperance Hotel opposite the station in Haverfordwest. It
later became a pub, taking over the name and licence of
the Masons' Arms alongside.
(Picture courtesy of Rosemary Bevan)

altogether. Meetings were held up and down the country at which reformed drunkards in their Sunday best were paraded in front of the audience as living examples of the benefits of total abstinence.

One such character who addressed a meeting in Ebenezer Chapel, Haverfordwest in January 1839 was introduced as 'a reformed drunkard from Milford'. He gave what was described in the *Welshman* newspaper as 'an exciting, though melancholic' account of himself, explaining that for 17 years he had 'served the monster intemperance'. During this time he had been notorious for his habitual drunkenness, but he had signed the pledge 12 months before and was now 'in every respect more happy than when he was in the habit of indulging in the intoxicating draught'.

In Narberth, a Total Abstinence Society was formed in 1837 and in 1841 the *Welshman* reported that there were 'numerous' total abstainers in the town of Pembroke whose battle-cry was: 'Honour to the Welsh water-drinkers! Destruction to the publicans and sinners of Cymru!' To begin with they were fighting a losing battle. The number of pubs and beer-houses continued to grow, and although the coaching inns were badly hit by the arrival of the railway, this was more than offset by the number of pubs created to serve the new form of transport, with Railway Inns and Railway Taverns being opened in every town and nearly every village on the line – from Johnston and Wiston to Jameston, Lamphey and Penally. Quarrying villages such as

West Williamston, Ludchurch and Cilgerran were awash with pubs and beer-houses and it was said that every house in Hakin that wasn't a licensed pub was an unlicensed one.

Gradually, however, the tide began to turn. The Lord's Day Observance Society had been founded in the same year as the British and Foreign Temperance Society, and the two movements soon found plenty of common ground on which to campaign. They achieved some early success with the passing of the Lord's Day Act of 1848 which prevented pubs from opening before 1pm on a Sunday. Attempts to restrict Sunday opening still further in 1855 led to street riots in London; even so an Act was passed soon afterwards restricting Sunday opening to the hours of 1pm to 3pm and 5pm to 11pm. In Pembrokeshire, as in the rest of Wales, the campaign against Sunday drinking was spearheaded by the Nonconformists. Each wave of religious revival which swept across Wales was accompanied by a wave of temperance activity – in Cilgerran it was claimed that the thunder of one revival had turned the beer sour.

In 1860 came the first movement towards 'early closing' – a laudable scheme designed to give shop-workers in the towns a mid-week half-day holiday. Sports clubs – most famously Sheffield Wednesday – were formed in many places to provide 'healthful and innocent amusement' for young men with time to kill. Cricket clubs were formed all over Pembrokeshire; as one of the founders of the Pembroke club pointed out:

> If these young men are not on the cricket field, there will probably, many of them at least, be found in the pursuit of some vice or sensual pleasure – perhaps guzzling like brute-beasts in the pot-houses with which the town of Pembroke unfortunately abounds.

By the end of the 1860s there was a growing consensus that the beer-house had long outlived its usefulness and that the number of pubs in the country needed to be curtailed. The 1869 Wine and Beer-house Act brought all licensed premises under the control of the magistrates. This effectively meant that no new beer-houses were opened while many of the existing ones closed down, their trade not being sufficient to warrant the cost and effort of applying for a justices' licence. The Aberdare Act of 1872 added to the burden of legislation on the drinking trade, curtailing drinking hours, increasing fines for licensing offences, prohibiting the sale of liquor to under 16s and generally making life difficult for the landlord. (This Act was so unpopular that it was blamed for the fall of Gladstone's government two years later; Disraeli's administration increased the opening hours by 30 minutes as a mark of appreciation).

In Wales, Sunday opening remained the biggest bugbear of the temper-ance brigade. In Calvinist Scotland the pubs had been closed on the Sabbath since 1853, and when Ireland introduced Sunday closing in 1878, the Welsh campaigners were determined to be next. Temperance and chapel leaders claimed (with some justification) that the majority of people in Wales were behind them – although a public meeting held in Tenby in February 1880 to press for Sunday closing was 'miserably attended'. In the industrialised areas of Wales, the sabbatarians received powerful support from the iron-masters and the coal-owners who were fed up with half their workforce turning up for the Monday morning shift still drunk from the excesses of the previous day. Wales was ripe for Sunday closing, and when a private member's Bill, introduced by Flint MP John Roberts, received its third reading in August 1881, the Welsh Sunday Closing Act duly entered the statute books.

An Act to prohibit the Sale of Intoxicating Liquors on Sunday in Wales.
[27th August 1881.]

WHEREAS the provisions in force against the sale of fermented and distilled liquors during certain hours of Sunday have been found to be attended with great public benefits, and it is expedient and the people of Wales are desirous that in the principality of Wales those provisions be extended to the other hours of Sunday:

Be it therefore enacted by the Queen's most Excellent Majesty, by and with the advice and consent of the Lords Spiritual and Temporal, and Commons, in this present Parliament assembled, and by the authority of the same, as follows:

1. In the principality of Wales all premises in which intoxicating liquors are sold or exposed for sale by retail shall be closed during the whole of Sunday. — *Premises where intoxicating liquors sold to be closed on Sundays in Wales.*

2. The Licensing Acts, 1872–1874, shall apply in the case of any premises closed under this Act as if they had been closed under those Acts. — *Application of Licensing Acts. 35 & 36 Vict. c. 94. 37 & 38 Vict. c. 49.*

3. This Act shall commence and come into operation with respect to each division or place in Wales on the day next appointed for the holding of the general annual licensing meeting for that division or place. — *Commencement of Act.*

4. Nothing in this Act contained shall preclude the sale at any time at a railway station of intoxicating liquors to persons arriving at or departing from such station by railway. — *Sale of intoxicating liquors at railway stations.*

5. This Act may be cited as the Sunday Closing (Wales) Act, 1881. — *Short title.*

The 1881 Welsh Sunday Closing Act

In Pembrokeshire, many of the big landowners were also active supporters of temperance – among their tenants, if not on a personal level. As a result, estates like Stackpole, Marloes and Lawrenny were without a public house for many years – to the great benefit of pubs in villages like Dale, Hundleton and Landshipping which were just over the border in neighbouring estates.

Towards the end of the 19th century and in the first part of the 20th century, efforts continued to be made to reduce the numbers of public houses and also to standardise their lay-out. Magistrates found themselves with the power to take away licences for petty offences or because the lay-out of a pub did not meet their approval. And since many of the magistrates were chapel deacons and temperance-supporting landowners themselves, they did not hesitate to use this power.

It has to be said that statistics were on their side. A survey carried out in 1899 revealed that Pembrokeshire had exactly 500 pubs out of a Welsh

Published for Bettering the Condition and Increasing the Comforts of the POOR.

CAUTION

To Alehouse Keepers, & their Guests.

It is better that Offences against the Laws should be Prevented, than that Offenders should be Punished.

THE PROPER USE OF INNS, &c.

THE proper use of Inns and Alehouses, is to furnish Refreshment and Lodging to Travellers, upon a reasonable profit; to accommodate persons meeting on *necessary* business; Soldiers in his Majesty's service; and some whose occupations require a frequent change of residence, or who cannot provide themselves with meat and drink in a more convenient manner.

The neighbouring Justices of the Peace have the Power of granting a License for keeping a Publick House, and they have the like Power of refusing to grant a License, without giving any reason whatever for such refusal, which is entirely at their discretion; it is therefore the Interest as well as the Duty of an Alehouse keeper to take care, that he conduct himself and his House in a becoming manner, lest he forfeit the good opinion of the Justices and be deprived of his License.

A principal duty of an Alehouse keeper is to prevent Artificers and Labourers from drinking more than for their necessary Refreshment; and not to allow them to lose their time and spend their money to the injury of themselves and their families: therefore, almost all debts (commonly called Ale Scores) are incurred in an improper manner; and are such, as the lawful means (if any) of recovering such debts would often discover bad conduct in the Alehouse keeper, and hazard the loss of his License.

The Law protects the Alehouse keeper from losses, by giving him the power of detaining the Person of any Guest who refuses to pay the reasonable charges for the meat and drink which have been furnished him: Debts are seldom incurred by Travellers, who are generally Strangers, and when they are incurred by Artificers and Labourers, great blame will attach to the Alehouse keeper from the manner in which such Ale Scores must have been contracted.

An Alehouse keeper is liable to heavy penalties for allowing Tippling, Drunkenness, or disorderly behaviour in his House, extending to the Forfeiture of his Recognizance, and that of his Surety or Bondsman, and the loss of his License.

The Guests who are guilty of Tippling, Drunkenness, and disorderly Behaviour are also liable to heavy penalties; and Artificers and Labourers who waste their time and their money at Publick Houses, ought to consider that although they may avoid punishment from the forbearance with which the Laws are executed, yet their Wives and their Families cannot escape from the miseries of Poverty, the certain consequence of their Husband's misconduct; and that the wholesome restraint which the Law lays upon a man in this respect, gives the best assurance of protection to his Family and to Himself, when it forbids him to waste his time and his money in a Publick House, and disturb the peace of others by his intemperance and bad example.

To   *Alehouse keeper.*

You are desired to have this Paper pasted up in your Kitchen, or some other usual place where your Guests take their Refreshment.

SIGNED

Many notices of this nature were published in the 19th century

total of 8,124. Neighbouring Cardiganshire had 314 licensed houses and industrial Carmarthenshire had 782. However the real significance of these figures became apparent when the number of pubs was set alongside the population figures of each county, because with one pub for every 164 inhabitants, Pembrokeshire was firmly at the head of the Welsh drinking league. (By comparison Merioneth had one pub for every 450 inhabitants, and it was calculated that Glamorgan would need an extra 2,000 pubs to match Pembrokeshire's ratio).

In 1904 a new Act was passed which established the principle of compensation for any publican whose house was considered 'redundant' and whose licence had been suppressed through no fault of his or her own (although in practice most of the compensation went to the owner of the property rather than to the publican, who was usually a tenant). The first pub in Pembrokeshire to be axed under the compensation scheme was the St. Dogmells in Hakin, and the Act was eventually responsible for the closure of nearly 100 pubs in the county, among them noted houses like the Mariners in Solva, the Tower Inn in St. David's, the Plough in Eglwyswrw and the Sailors' Arms in Lower Fishguard. However, the publicans did not go down without a fight. Pembroke Dock Licensed Victuallers Association was formed in 1909 'for combination to combat the forces acting against them' and the Pembrokeshire LVA followed a year later with about 50 members. One of their aims was to obtain an 'impartial bench of magistrates' to adjudicate on the renewal of licences. All too often the magistrates would instruct the police to object to a certain licence, and then rule on the objection themselves – a 'disgraceful' situation according to Mr. S. McCulloch, the first president of the Pembrokeshire LVA.

The Defence of the Realm Act – DORA – took a toll on Pembrokeshire pubs following the outbreak of the First World War. The Act meant the introduction of even tighter licensing laws aimed at preventing drunkenness among servicemen, dockers, munitions workers and the like. In Lloyd George's opinion: 'Drink is doing us more damage in the war than all the German submarines put together' – but as someone who had once pressed for total prohibition in Wales, he might not have been entirely objective. Opening hours were curtailed, while one of the daftest rules brought in by the Act was the 'no treating' law. Under this rule no-one was allowed to buy a round of drinks or even buy his mate a pint; such actions were thought to encourage excessive drinking. In 1916 James Gray, landlord of the eminently respectable Avondale in Hakin, was fined ten shillings for allowing 'treating' in the pub.

He was lucky not to lose his licence. With a mass of new rules and regulations to fall foul of, it was inevitable that many landlords found themselves in court. And when they appeared before the bench there would be the inevitable clamour from the temperance brigade for the pubs to be shut.

A convivial gathering outside the Cambrian Inn in Solva

Many were, and when the troops returned from the trenches it was often to find that their favourite local had been forced to close. Wartime 'casualties' in Pembroke Dock alone included the Foresters' Arms, the Albert, the Sun and the Duke of York.

Licensing restrictions were gradually lifted following the end of the war – although Sunday closing remained sacrosanct. The number of pubs continued to fall, both as a result of the still-active redundancy committee and the economic depression, while changing social habits (and weaker beer) meant the number of drunks on the street dropped dramatically. In 1908, 99 people had been convicted of drunkenness in Pembroke Borough; by the 1930s the figure was down to half-a-dozen each year.

As attitudes changed, so people began to look upon the pub as a convivial social centre rather than a den of iniquity. The 1931 Royal Commission on Licensing encouraged brewers and publicans to turn their pubs into places 'where the public can obtain general refreshment of whatever variety they choose in decent, pleasant and comfortable surroundings', and many an old and dingy drinking den was given a makeover which involved introducing such novelties as separate toilets for men and women.

While the temperance movement, which tolerated drinking in modera-tion, tended to support the improvement of pubs, the teetotallers actively opposed the measures, realising that it was much easier to persuade magistrates to close a grubby dive than a clean and smartly furnished establishment. But

These wartime customers at the Sloop in Sandy Haven seem to be showing the good effects beer had on morale

by this time, support for the hard line anti-drink movement was beginning to wane. By the time the Second World War came, the tide had turned to the extent that calls for a return to the licensing restrictions of 1914 were dismissed out of hand. In his excellent history of brewing in Wales, *Prince of Ales*, Brian Glover quotes Quintin Hogg (later Lord Hailsham) as stating in 1939:

The Temperance Council must clearly understand that the national emergency is not a moment to introduce temperance propaganda under the cloak of national necessity. Beer is the innocent pleasure of many millions, especially those who bear the brunt today.

Such a sentiment – a million miles from that of Lloyd George 25 years earlier – shows how much attitudes had changed. The temperance movement was in retreat, although the redundancy committee continued to pick off pubs well into the 1950s – the Crown and Anchor and the Bell and Lion in Pembroke Dock were both closed in 1953.

With the post-war growth of tourism, inns began to be seen as an amenity and Sunday closing in Wales became increasingly regarded as an anachronism and a hindrance to the industry. A new Licensing Act in 1961 paved the way for each county to decide by a referendum (held every seven years) if it wanted Sunday drinking. The three west Wales counties of Pembrokeshire, Carmarthenshire and Cardiganshire voted to stay 'dry' in 1961, but in November 1968, alone of the three, Pembrokeshire voted to become 'wet' – thereby causing a Sunday trading boom for any pub fortunate enough to be just this side of the border.

The late 1960s and early '70s also saw the opening of a number of new pubs in the tourist areas of the county – the Lobster Pot, the Lawrenny Arms, the Galleon and the Miracle Inn among others. Others, such as the Wolfe in Wolfscastle and the Mariners at Nolton reopened after a long period of closure, while many others were enlarged and refurbished. Sadly, this refurbishment was often at the cost of the character of the old inn, and a pub guide of the

*The results of a typical Pembrokeshire pub makeover in the 1960s/'70s.
This is the Drovers' Arms at Puncheston*

time called *The Inn Crowd* shows (unintentionally) the widespread damage
that was caused by the over-enthusiastic application of formica, leatherette
and fake beams covered with equally fake horse-brasses.

Fortunately a good number of old Pembrokeshire pubs managed to
avoid this kind of tasteless 'scampi in the basket' 1970s makeover, so that
the county still has a wide range of unspoilt taverns – from 'Bessie's' in
the Gwaun Valley to the Castle in St. Dogmael's and the Masons' Arms in
Cwnce. And although well-established pubs continue to close – the Barley
Mow in Narberth, the Horse and Jockey in Haverfordwest and the Caledonia
in Pembroke Dock are all recent victims – a glance at the pages of this book
will show that this is simply part of an on-going process that has seen pubs
come and go throughout the centuries as taste and economic circumstances
changed with the passing years.

CHAPTER TWO

The Cardigan Road

CRUNDALE, CLARBESTON ROAD, AMBLESTON, TUFTON

Unlike the three previous Pembrokeshire titles in this series, where the pubs were situated predominantly in towns and villages, this book deals with a large and often sparsely-populated area, much of it farmland rising to the rolling Preseli moors. Except for the northern coast there are few centres of population and many of the pubs in the early chapters of this book would have been isolated roadside hostelries offering refreshment to travellers on the long journey to or from Haverfordwest markets and livestock fairs. The St. David's Road, the Fishguard Road, the Newport Road and the Cardigan Road were spokes on a wheel which had Haverfordwest as its hub, and all had pubs at irregular intervals. The last named of these ancient trackways, the Cardigan Road, was the longest and most gruelling, so it is no surprise that it should have been well supplied with hostelries. Some were well-appointed coaching inns, others were more humble ale-houses catering for the waggoners and drovers; nearly all have vanished.

Heading out of Haverfordwest, the first pub the traveller would have encountered not long after leaving the oddly-named suburb of Tangiers would have been the **Ivy Bush** where Thomas Morgan was landlord in 1828. This was a short-lived establishment, unlike the much more durable **Boot and Shoe** at Stephensford near the Crundale fork which survived for some 200 years until disappearing almost overnight early in 2010. William Owens was the landlord from 1807 until the 1830s and shoemaker Thomas Richards kept this roadside ale-house from 1841 to 1861. For some reason the pub at this time was nick-named 'The Rand' and the landlord was always known as 'Tom the Rand'. It was a popular haunt of poachers during the period that William Morgans was landlord; indeed Morgans himself was fined for 'taking conies' in 1866. (He had left the pub by this time to run the Fountain in Prendergast).

By the 1870s one half of the building was a public house and the other half was a grocer's shop, the proprietor being David Harries, 'a hard-working and industrious man' who had six sons, one of whom, William Harries, was

The Boot and Shoe, Crundale, which for a number of years went under the sign of General Picton. It has recently been demolished

landlord from 1901 until his death, aged 43, in 1914. His widow Mrs. Mary Jane Harries took over and one of her first jobs was to apply to change the name of the pub. There was another Boot and Shoe not too far away, near Camrose, the reputation of which was not entirely spotless, and Mrs. Harries was concerned that people might confuse the two establishments. She applied to the Poyston Estate, which owned the pub, for permission to change the name, and it was the landowners who suggested **General Picton** in honour of the local hero of Waterloo, General Sir Thomas Picton. Mrs. Harries later bought the property from the Poyston Estate and remained licensee until her death, aged 78, in May 1948. Her daughter Florence Adams took over, her husband Robert farming the 30 acres of land which went with the pub. Mrs. Adams remained in charge until the night before decimal currency was introduced, handing over the task of running the business (and dealing with the pesky new coinage) to her daughter, Mrs. Mary Harries. When Mrs. Harries retired in about 1980, the pub was taken over by a consortium of local businessmen and run by various managers.

Thereafter the pub changed hands several times, one of the licensees changing the name back to Boot and Shoe, but sadly no-one seemed able to make a real go of this historic little inn. It closed in 2006 and after standing empty for some years was completely demolished in March 2010, along with the farm buildings adjoining. A small housing estate is planned for the site.

The road forks at the **Boot and Shoe**, the right-hand route – the Maenclochog Road – passing through the villages of Crundale and Clarbeston Road *en route* to Maenclochog. A scattering of pubs existed along the way, few of them very well documented and some of them only open for a short span of years to cater for the navvies building the nearby railway. A mile or so beyond Crundale is New Bridge where Thomas Howells was the landlord of the **New Bridge Inn** from 1809 to 1828, while nearer to Clarbeston Road was the **Railway Tavern** where Martha Phillips was the licensee in 1860; the exact location of this pub is unknown, although there may be a clue in the fact that the hill leading up from the railway bridge at Ram's Wood is still known as 'Tavern Hill'. No doubt this was a haunt of navvies, as was the **New Inn** at Pentyparc Cross.

Before the coming of the railway, Clarbeston Road did not exist – it was simply a cluster of thatched cottages on a lonely crossroads north of Wiston, with a tiny courthouse where the petty sessions took place. It was only after the railway arrived in the 1850s that the name Clarbeston Road was concocted as a sign for the station, despite being nowhere near Clarbeston village.

Thomas Lewis ran the **Clarbeston Road Hotel** next to the station in 1861. This seems to have become the **Picton Inn** where John Reed was the landlord from 1871 until 1906, also farming a fifty-acre holding. There is a story that a Captain Penn from Camrose, while hunting in the vicinity, once rode his horse in through the door and up to the bar for a drink. Joseph Morris was landlord in 1914 and Mrs. Florence Morris kept the pub from 1923 to 1926 when Mrs. Mary Lloyd took over. She handed over to Olive Lloyd in 1931 and she was followed by Elizabeth Davies and then Mr. and Mrs. David Lewis, formerly of the Prescelly Hotel in Rosebush, who were tenants of this James Williams house from 1939 to 1948.

Licensee in 1955 was James Gordon Lewis and Harold Manning was in charge from 1958 to 1973 followed by Larry Evans in the 1980s. After a major revamp, the Picton was taken over by Adrian Jones and Jane Lewis who soon began winning awards for outstanding food. They were succeeded by Dai Rees, a well-known figure in local horse-racing circles. The pub became part

The Picton Inn, Clarbeston Road, pre-First World War
when Joseph Morris was licensee.
(Picture courtesy of Mr. John Stevenson)

This photograph is thought to show police and other officials gathered for a sitting of the petty sessions in the Picton Hall behind the Picton Inn. The Hall superseded the old courthouse near the Cross Inn

The Picton Inn as it looked in 2002

of Celtic Inns at some stage and the new licensees in January 2006 were Dennis James and Delyth Ride. Sadly, and somewhat surprisingly, the Picton closed in 2008 and shows no sign of reopening.

The **Cross Inn** – the village's original inn, and now its sole survivor – lies on the other side of the railway line. At one time the railway bridge was half-way between the two village pubs and in the 1880s was said to be the nightly gathering place of 'roughs' – young men who 'used obscene language' and even 'threatened the lives of passers-by', especially those attending chapel.

The Cross Inn stood next to the courthouse at the heart of the pre-railway community; indeed, before becoming Clarbeston Road, this remote little hamlet was usually called 'Cross Inn'. James Phillips is known to have been the innkeeper in 1807 and the landlord from 1812 until at least 1828 was William Evans. The pub was kept by Mr. Evans' widow Jane from 1841 to

1866 when she was in her 90s; it was also the home of the Loyal Dungleddy Lodge of Odd Fellows. Evan Jenkins kept the pub from 1871 to 1881 and also farmed 18 acres.

Mr. and Mrs. H. J. Clapp were there in the early 1890s; he was from Somerset and appears to have moved to the area to work as a gardener at Pentypark mansion. The licensee from 1895 until his death in 1925 was a butcher named Thomas James, whereupon the licence passed to John Morris Crook who remained until 1931. Joseph Watts was there in the 1930s and Charles and Annie Thomas were mine hosts from 1955 to 1962, by which time it was a James Williams house.

The old courthouse outside the Cross Inn has long been demolished.
(Picture courtesy of the Cross Inn)

The Cross Inn, Clarbeston Road in the 1960s.
(Picture courtesy of the *Western Telegraph*)

In the late 1960s, with the creation of the nearby Llysyfran Reservoir and its associated leisure facilities, the area enjoyed a minor tourism boom and the licensees of the Cross – Bert and Mary Gibbs from Monmouthshire – were quick to take advantage. According to *The Inn Crowd* – a guide to Pembrokeshire pubs of the time:

> In the lounge they are serving scampi in a basket, chicken in a basket, curries, salads etc. On the lawn at the rear there are tables under decorative umbrellas where mum and dad can go with the children and spend a very pleasant evening.

Other plans for the pub included 'a restaurant and petrol pumps' and it seems to have been around this time that the ancient courthouse was demolished, having long been disused for judicial purposes; in fact, for a time it served as the gents' toilets. Keith and Anona Wells were in charge in the

1980s, and they too made a few structural alterations without harming the character of this historic inn. For the past ten years the pub has been owned by Mr. Jason Slater and overseen by various managers, and it remains very much at the centre of village life.

Tradition has it that a property called 'Holmes' on the way to Clarbeston was once a pub, while nearer Wiston there was a short-lived pub called the **New Inn** which appears on the 1841 census but is otherwise unrecorded.

Back-tracking to the site of the Boot and Shoe and turning sharp right to follow the Cardigan road northwards, there was once a pub in Crundale village called the **Fox and Hounds**. This was run by butcher Thomas Philpin in 1841, while Joseph Philpin was there from 1851 to 1861 and William Lewis was occupant from 1868 to 1871. How much it operated as a pub in the latter years is hard to determine.

Also in the village, on the right-hand side, the house now known as 'Mistral' was once called 'Forest' and is believed to have housed the ale-house known by the sign of the **Forest Arms**. John Morgan ran a pub of this name in Rudbaxton parish between 1822 and 1827, while according to a report in the *Welshman* newspaper in 1853, the Forest was then kept by John White who may have reopened the old ale-house to cater for the navvies working on the line. If so, it was a big mistake. One bright May morning Mr. White set off for market in Haverfordwest leaving his wife in charge of the pub. He returned that evening to discover that she had run off with one of the customers – a navvy. The aggrieved husband pursued the couple on horseback as far as Tavernspite but was there obliged to give up the chase as they had boarded a coach bound for Swansea and were many miles down the road.

Outside the village, on the right of the roadside between the two Spittal turnings, was the **Step In**. This would have been an early 'hedge ale-house', so called because with its low walls made from 'clom' and its unkempt thatch it would have been all but indistinguishable from the adjoining hedgerow. It is long gone.

Jezreel Evans kept the **New Inn** at Scollock Cross from 1819 to 1828, while just up the road was the **Cross** at Woodstock Cross. Research by Nikki Bosworth of the Pembrokeshire Record Office has revealed that this pub was built by Benjamin Jones of Ambleston and his wife Margaret in 1836 and they remained innkeepers and shopkeepers at this crossways pub for some 15 years.

North of the Cardigan Road are the neighbouring moorland villages of Ambleston and Wallis, the latter being an important centre of the local woollen industry with a mill in operation for two centuries. Just off the footpath that runs between the two villages, sheltering below a rocky outcrop, was the **Farmers' Arms** kept by innkeeper William Myles in 1861. It had become the **Rock Cottage** pub by 1871 when the landlord was William Morris who

Many a weary weaver must have stopped for refreshment at Rock Cottage near Wallis

also ran a small shop. Thomas Young kept the Rock Cottage in 1875 and William Rees was the innkeeper in 1881. In 1889 the landlady Elizabeth Rowland was robbed of eight shillings in copper which she kept in a box on the chimney piece. The pub closed in the 1890s.

There is a tradition that a house in Ambleston village called Gwalia was also a pub at one time; possibly this was the unnamed 'tavern' run by James Phillips at the time of the 1881 census.

Back on the Cardigan Road at Woodstock there was a village alehouse kept by Thomas Thomas from 1795 until his death in 1828 and thereafter by Dinah Thomas. The licensing records all refer to it as **Woodstock Slop**, an odd name for a pub. ('Slop' is a Pembrokeshire dialect term for a gap in a hedge).

Further north, the impressive **Tufton Arms** was at one time part of the Trecwn estate and seems to have derived its name from Lady Caroline Tufton, daughter of the Earl of Thanet, who was the second wife of Joseph Foster Barham of Trecwn. It was first recorded in 1836 and was being kept by John Bateman in 1841. In the 1840s and 1850s, this moorland inn was the regular venue of coursing matches. One such event in 1854 attracted 300 gentlemen of the county and during the day over sixty hares were put up. And after the 'toils and pleasures of the day' there was always an excellent dinner to be enjoyed at the Tufton Arms.

Farmer and innkeeper Mrs. Hannah Thomas was landlady from 1851 until her death at the age of 79 in 1863, after which her son Thomas Thomas took charge until at least 1875. The unmarried Sarah Thomas was there from 1881 to 1891; staying with her from time to time was her brother Benjamin who must have felt slightly uncomfortable at being on licensed premises since he was a Calvinistic Methodist minister. A widow named Mrs. Mary Morris held the licence from 1901 to 1906 and John Owen was the landlord from 1914 to 1929 when he handed over the reins to his son James who was still there in 1938.

Hugh Harries Davies was licensee in 1939, although his wife Gertrude – always called 'Gertie' – was the main presence behind the bar until 1957

*The Tufton Arms is one of the few pubs still open on
the old Haverfordwest to Cardigan road*

when their son William and his wife Ivy took charge. Following in her mother-in-law's footsteps, Ivy Davies welcomed customers to the Tufton Arms for 38 years before retiring in 1995; she still has vivid memories of harsh winters when the pub would be cut off for days on end due to the heavy snowfalls.

For the past 15 years the pub has been run by Ivy's daughter and son-in-law, Laura and Emyr Edwards, and although changed somewhat over the years and no longer a farm, the Tufton Arms remains a classic, old-fashioned Welsh country pub, much appreciated by the hill-farming community which it serves.

Beyond the village of Tufton – which took its name from the pub – the Cardigan road continues over the hills past New Inn and Tafarn-y-Bwlch towards Eglwyswrw; the roadside pubs on the northern slopes of the Preselis will be considered in a later chapter.

CHAPTER THREE

The St. David's Road and the Crow Hill Road

PELCOMB, KEESTON, CAMROSE, HAYSCASTLE

It has been said that there are '17 hills and 16 miles' from Haverfordwest to the cathedral village of St. David's. This route – the St. David's Road – probably began life as one of the early pilgrim ways to the shrine of the Welsh patron saint, later becoming a busy thoroughfare connecting the county town with the coal mines of Newgale, the harbour at Solva and thence the St. David's peninsula. The road is marked on a 1762 map, and an Act for its improvement was passed in 1791. As with all these roads fanning out from Haverfordwest, it was at its busiest on fair days and market days. Francis Kilvert, who set off along this road one morning in 1871, noted: 'Droves of black cattle and sheep were pouring along the muddy road. Most of the men wore blue coats and the women long blue cloaks'.

John Miles Thomas, who was born and brought up in north Pembrokeshire, recalled the market-day droves in his wonderfully evocative book *Looking Back – A Childhood in St. David's.*

> Father and other farm hands had regularly to walk in to and back from the market in Haverfordwest, driving the cattle or sheep destined for, or bought at, the market. He often described for me the day-long journey begun at dawn, the slow progress, keeping the animals herded together, the misery of wet days with sacking covering head and shoulders, and the long trek home after a tiring day. The Rising Sun was the first, most welcome stop, the Victoria Inn the next, then the Ship in Solva with the last lap in sight.

The **Rising Sun** which Mr. Thomas mentions is still a welcome stop at Pelcomb Bridge. At one time this was a thatched cottage ale-house, popular with anglers, and half a century ago its only form of lighting was by Tilley lamp. Kilvert is unlikely to have seen the pub, since the first

The original Rising Sun public house at Pelcomb Bridge.
(Picture courtesy of the Rising Sun)

licensee was probably Benjamin Rees who was there in 1881. William Laugharne was landlord from 1884 to 1891 and his widow Martha kept the pub from 1901 to 1914, followed briefly by James Adams and then the oddly-named Mr. Orchard Hedden. George Evans was running the pub in 1923 after which a few licensees came and went before Thomas Roch stabilised things by being landlord from 1932 to 1939. Robert Evans was there during the 1940s and Ron and Ethel Davies were tenants of this Ansells pub from 1952 to 1978, by which time it boasted its own camping and caravan site. Former professional footballer Bobby Brown took over in 1984 and the original building was more or less demolished at this time, with a new pub-cum-restaurant being built on the site. Mr. Brown is still the licensee.

A recent view of the modern Rising Sun

At nearby Sunnyhill was the **Lark** which Thomas Lawrence ran in 1817-1818. Thomas Young also ran a pub somewhere in the Sunnyhill area in 1817 but no name has survived; he is merely described as a farmer in the 1841 census.

Further along the road is Pelcomb Cross where the **Cross Inn**

The Pelcomb Inn at Pelcomb Cross

was being run by labourer John Davies in 1871; he had lived at Pelcomb Cross since 1851 but there is no indication when the pub opened. In 1881 the Cross was being run by Ellen Davies, her husband – a first mate in the merchant navy – being away at sea. This was George Davies, son of the previous licensees, and he returned to dry land to be the long-serving landlord from 1884 to 1927, helped latterly by his son Wilfred. Matthew Philpin was landlord between 1928 and 1932 and Thomas Goodridge was there from 1934 to 1938. William Evans then ran the pub for a dozen years. At this time it was little more than a cottage with outbuildings alongside, but a major fire in the early 1950s led to the pub being rebuilt in rather more modern roadhouse style. It also took a new name, the **Pelcomb Inn**, and Hubert Davies was landlord from 1953 through to the 1970s. John Lewis was landlord in the 1980s and former miner Alun Pugh and his wife Eryl took over in 1990 and increased the emphasis on food, most notably by opening a new restaurant extension. Further improvements, including a new conservatory, were made by current licensee Geraint Jenkins when he took over four years ago.

Moving further along the road, there was a time when the long haul up Keeston Hill could be broken at the **King's Arms** where Thomas Hancock was publican between 1808 and 1816, or at the **Old Inn** where John Jones was in charge from 1809 to 1841. By 1861 the inn was being kept by Mary John, a blind woman of 33 who also ran a grocery. Two years later she married John Lloyd and he became the licensee in 1870 when Mary died. Lloyd soon remarried and moved to Roch, after which the Old Inn is not heard of again.

Soon afterwards, in September 1874, one Jacob John Jones was granted permission to open a new pub being built on Keeston Hill. Unimaginatively called the **New Inn**, it was run by Vincent Morris in 1881, by William Griffiths, farmer and publican in 1891, and by a widow named Martha Adams in 1892. By the time William Lewis was landlord in 1895 the name had been changed to **Hill Arms** and the licensee between 1898 and 1906 was George Edwards,

formerly of the Stag in Bridge Street, Haverfordwest. He was an artificer on HMS *Blake*, which meant that his wife Florence was usually left to run the pub. Florence and her husband divorced in 1910 and she then married John White, a Haverfordwest butcher, who ended up running the pub. However the Hill Arms was on its last legs and closed in about 1916, Mrs. White claiming this was due to 'hardships' caused by the war. It opened again briefly but closed for good in 1921; for some reason the dormant licence was kept up in the name of Florence White until at least 1939.

The Hill Arms was once a welcome place to rest for travellers toiling up Keeston Hill

Returning to Haverfordwest, the next route north is the Mathry Road, the winding lane which leads out of town via Crow Hill. This is said to have been an old drovers' trail, the route by which livestock was taken to Haverfordwest Mart from the Croesgoch and Strumble Head area without the need to pay the tolls on the turnpike roads. There being no laws against drinking and droving, this trail was abundantly served with ale-houses, licensed and otherwise, along its entire length.

The first of these was possibly **Tafarn Diod Vain** which B.G. Charles has found a reference to in 1797. It was apparently located near Crow Hill Bridge and the name means 'small beer tavern'. A later hostelry at Crow Hill Bridge was the **Fisherman's Arms**. From the 1850s to 1871 this was kept by John John and his wife Anne, the landlady usually going by the nickname of 'Nanny Prush'. The pub had only two rooms and a little cellar at the back and seems to have closed in the 1870s.

The **Boot and Shoe** was a little further along, a simple cottage pub in a little valley between Barnsley and Red Hill. John Devereaux was the landlord in 1808 and Daniel Jenkins was licensee from 1811 to 1828; his widow Elizabeth Jenkins was in charge from 1831 to 1841. Anne Roberts was licensee in 1861 and Richard Absalom was in charge from 1871 to 1881 followed by Army pensioner Edward Pearce. The tenancy changed at Michaelmas 1892 when Pearce left and Miss Hannah Edwards became the landlady; she was still there in 1906. Alfred Griffiths took over in 1913 and seems to have been the landlord when the Boot and Shoe was closed under the redundancy ruling in February 1919, with £155 compensation being paid to the owner of the premises, Mr. Louis Thomas of Haverfordwest. Still standing, it is now a private dwelling called 'The Vale'. A short distance up the road is Cutty Bridge where Elias Williams was innkeeper in 1841. This was probably the **Lark** which was run by Thomas Watts from 1861 to 1863.

The Boot and Shoe at Barnsley on the Mathry Road a century ago

James Adams ran the **Carpenters' Arms** at Calf Field in 1812 and '13. This may have later become the **Old Inn**, because in 1861 the Old Inn at Calf Field was being run by Scotsman James Scrymiger who was being helped by his daughter, Martha Mabe. She was the wife of local farm labourer Mark Mabe and by 1871 the Mabes were running the pub; their home-brewed beer apparently enjoyed a wide reputation. Mabe was still there in 1881, by which time the pub was commonly called 'Mark Mabe's House'. It was reported at the time that the property was just a two-room cottage, and that there was a bed in each of the rooms – probably a 'put up'. At this time it was a popular pub with anglers, and later with anyone from Haverfordwest who fancied a drink on a Sunday. The pub was just outside the 'three mile limit', so that anyone who made the journey duly qualified as a '*bona fide* traveller' and could be served, moderately legally, with a pint. William Adams ran the pub in 1891 and William Penry was there in 1895. The landlady from 1901 to 1914 was Mrs. Mary Ann Lloyd and from 1923 until his death, aged 79, in November 1948 the pub was 'ably conducted' by David Thomas. The 1950s saw a steady turnover of licensees before David Solomon arrived in 1964 and stayed for at least five years. William Hodgson and Malcolm Willis were in charge in the early 1980s, followed by Ken Barlow from Cheshire who was landlord for some 20 years. For the past six years this popular village local has been run by Kevin Chaffey.

The Old Inn is one of Pembrokeshire's more haunted pubs, with two resident spooks. One is young and called Ianto and is fond of practical jokes,

The Old Inn near Camrose has a couple of resident ghosts

while the other is a much more mysterious figure which roams the pub in an apparently endless quest to find a person (or fellow ghost) called Eileen.

Camrose is a substantial village and had two fairs a year in the 1790s, although there doesn't seem to have been a pub in the village itself. Continuing on the old Mathry Road, the **New Inn** was just beyond Camrose, to the north of Folly Cross and opposite Camrose North School. The 'New Inn Homestead', Camrose, is mentioned in a list of property for sale in June 1832 and David Poyntz, who farmed at nearby Wolfsdale Mill, seems to have been connected with the inn on and off from 1838 to 1874 – the last date it is recorded as being open. James and Rebecca Berry were the only other recorded licensees; they were there in the 1850s when the pub had a reputation for 'rows'. The **Masons' Arms** was three-quarters of a mile beyond the New Inn on Cold Blow hill and was a favourite stopping-off point for farmers trekking home from Haverfordwest with their livestock. Stonemason John Griffiths gave the pub its name and was its only landlord between 1851 and 1881.

The next chance travellers had to break their journey was at the **Cross** at Hayscastle Cross. It is believed that this pub was opened in about 1861 by Ebenezer Phillips who handed over to his brother William Phillips a couple of years later. It was the start of a marathon stint behind the bar for William who was licensee for over 60 years until his death in January 1930. He also farmed on quite a large scale, while the pub also served as a shop, bakery and post office; at his death, William Phillips was the oldest sub-postmaster in the county. The licence passed to one of William's sons, Albert, and he remained in charge until 1956, despite being a lifelong teetotaller. During the last war, Land Army girls became the first women to frequent the pub – and to the horror of some locals they even drank beer! Albert's daughter Anna

The Cross Inn at Hayscastle in the days when William Phillips was licensee.
He can be seen standing outside the pub with his daughter Maud.
(Picture courtesy of Mr Philip Davies)

'Nan' Stephens succeeded her father as licensee and she handed over to her sister Mrs. Mona Harwood in about 1965. The pub passed to the next generation in 1982 when Mrs. Harwood's daughter Dawn Gerlach and her husband Derek took over from her mother. They ran the pub for 25 years, adding a restaurant extension, and in 2007 Dawn's cousin Wayne Phillips and his wife Angela took over. They are planning a celebration in 2011 to mark the 150th anniversary of the pub – and also the remarkable fact that it has remained in the same family since the day it opened.

Still in the same family, the Cross Inn has been greatly extended
in recent years

Artist's impression of the Llandeloy Arms in its hey-day.
(Image courtesy of Mr. Ken Rees)

North of Hayscastle Cross the old drovers' routes fork left and right, fanning out towards the coast. On the route to Strumble Head was the **Weary Traveller**, now a farm called Weary, while the final watering hole on the road before Croesgoch was the **New Inn** cottage ale-house near Llanreithan, although when this was operating as a pub is unclear.

A left turn off the road to Croesgoch brings one to Llandeloy, where John Roch ran a pub in 1784; local tradition has it that this pub was near the church. Of more recent vintage was the **Llandeloy Arms** in the village; presumably this was the unnamed ale-house where a mason's widow called Martha Jones was licensee from the 1860s to the 1890s. George Thomas and his wife Mary then ran the Llandeloy Arms for many years, he being the landlord from 1901 to 1948. George was succeeded by his son Llew Thomas who ran this typical Pembrokeshire country pub until his death in early 1976. The pub stayed in

the family, passing to a cousin Brenda Rees and her husband Ken who were licensees for 20 years until the pub closed on the last day of March 1996. It is now a private house. A widow named Sarah Morgan ran a pub at Treffynnon, Llandeloy, in 1851, but there is no record of the sign.

The Llandeloy Arms is now a private house

CHAPTER FOUR

The Fishguard Road

SPITTAL, TREFFGARNE, WOLFSCASTLE

The turnpike road north of Haverfordwest is still known as the Fishguard Road and has long been an important routeway linking the north coast with the county town by means of the narrow gap in the ridge of hills known as the Treffgarne Gorge. It is said that stage coaches operating between Haverfordwest and Fishguard offered first, second and third class fares. The difference in status only became apparent at the first hill – the first class passengers remained seated; the second class travellers climbed down and walked beside the coach; those with third class tickets were expected to push.

In 1801, cabinet-maker John Llewellyn of Spittal married Margaret Tucker 'of Cornerpiece, innkeeper'. This appears to be the first recorded reference to a pub on the triangle of land at the junction of the Fishguard Road and the Spittal Road known as 'Three Corner Piece'. The pub's official sign was **Square and Compass**, but most people seem to have called it **Corner Piece**, and the original name is now long forgotten. John Llewellyn was the licensee until 1821 and from 1822 into the 1840s his widow Margaret carried on the business. She may have been there when the pub hit the headlines in 1843. Describing it as 'a small roadside pothouse called the Three Corner Piece', the *Carmarthen Journal* of September 1843 went on to reveal that the pub had been the gathering place for a large group of Rebecca rioters. Their target was the tollgate at Prendergast in Haverfordwest, and after a few drinks, some rabble-rousing speeches and a few more drinks the men set off from the ale-house suitably disguised as 'Rebecca and her daughters'.

Unfortunately, the time they had spent depleting the stocks of the Corner Piece had given a spy in their ranks time enough to slip away and warn the authorities in Haverfordwest what was happening. Consequently the Rebeccaites were met in Prendergast not by a quaking tollgate keeper but by a large number of special constables. The rioters were forced to beat an undignified retreat, two of 'Rebecca's daughters' were captured by the constables,

*Thomas and Mary Llewellyn and their daughter
Rosaline outside the Corner Piece.*
(Picture courtesy of the Corner Piece)

and the only person to benefit from the whole affair was the landlady of the Corner Piece who enjoyed her busiest night of the year.

Margaret Llewellyn's blacksmith son, William, was the next innkeeper and he remained in charge from 1851 until his death in 1878 at the age of 74. He also ran the smithy alongside the pub, where a bungalow now stands.

William's nephew Thomas Llewellyn inherited the pub; he was a Chelsea Pensioner, having served for 20 years in the Fusiliers in India and Canada. Thomas remained licensee until his death in 1915, after which his daughter Mrs. Rosaline Richards was the licensee from 1923 to 1938. Sarah Harries took over in 1939 and Mansel Victor Harries was there from the mid 1950s (when it was still known in official records as 'Square and Compass, Corner Piece') through to 1967.

As a James Williams house, the pub was given a makeover when the Harries family gave up the licence. Dai and Jean Phillips were tenants in 1973 followed by Dave Saunders and later by Thomas Edwards who was there from 1979 to 1984. Tenants came and went, eventually becoming a revolving door

The Corner Piece as it looks today

36

of licensees – six in two years, one of whom only lasted a week. This did little for this landmark hostelry, but fortunately Mike and Paula Davies came to the rescue six years ago, providing good food and returning the pub to its former glory – a fact no doubt appreciated by the resident ghost, thought to be the wandering shade of Thomas Llewellyn's only son Austin who died in 1894.

Taking the right-hand fork at the Corner Piece, along the old Newport Road, the Victorian traveller would have passed the **Old Cross** which stood on the left-hand side, just past the crossroads to the west of Spittal village. James Thomas was landlord of this cottage inn from 1809 to 1841 and shoe-maker William Williams kept the Old Cross from 1851 to 1881, for much of that time with the help of his wife Martha. In 1852 their four-month-old son Isaac was tragically killed, an inquest concluding that he had 'died from suffocation from being accidentally shut up in a turn-up bed'. The couple raised seven other children without mishap. The pub seems to have closed in the 1890s; it is believed that the building was subsequently used as a cow-shed by a neighbouring farmer before becoming derelict.

Further along the Newport Road there were a couple of ale-houses in the Triffleton area, one of them being the short-lived **Bridge End Inn** which was kept in the 1850s by a family named Vaughan. Thomas Edwards, yeoman, of Spring Wells, Ambleston, opened the **Farmers' Arms** in 1826, but by 1828 the landlord was John Gibby. The property, between Triffleton and Glandwr, is later recorded as a farm with a widow named Hannah Gibby as the occupant; when it stopped being a pub isn't known but the name has since reverted to Spring Wells.

The Pump on the Green in Spittal, not long after it opened in the 1970s

A more recent view of The Pump on the Green

Spittal village itself does not seem to have had a pub until fairly recently. The present-day **Pump on the Green** in the middle of the village was a former shop, chip-shop and petrol station, converted into a comfortable and modern pub in 1972 with beer pumps replacing petrol pumps. 'Tapper' John was the first licensee and George and Brenda Williams were there in the late 1980s, having arrived from the Royal at Broad Haven in 1984. Despite changing licensees every few years, the Pump remains the popular social centre of this large village.

Returning to the cross-roads at the Old Cross, the lane straight ahead drops down under the railway line to the Fishguard Road and to Treffgarne Bridge where there were a couple of roadside ale-houses at different times. The **Fox and Hounds** was run by Thomas Bowen from about 1805 to 1820, while the oddly-named **Three Taverns** was kept from 1841 to 1861 by boot- and shoemaker Charles Allen. Sarah Allen – presumably his widow – was there in 1867 and in 1880 Seth Allen was in charge. He seems to have given up innkeeping for farming, running a 60-acre holding at The Kell in the 1880s.

From Treffgarne Bridge the road winds northwards through the wooded Treffgarne Gorge – once a haunt of footpads - to the village of Ford where travellers would no doubt have been pleased to find the **Commercial Inn**. Before the 1850s this had been a tailor's shop run by James Edwards, and it was his son John – a draper by trade – who was the first innkeeper. John Edwards ran the pub for over 40 years, helped by his sisters Elizabeth and Anne. A third sister, Mary, ran a 15-acre smallholding, selling the produce at the grocery shop attached to the inn. In coaching days the Commercial came to be recognised as a busy 'half-way house' on the road from Haverfordwest to Fishguard, but the passing trade fell off with the building of the railway.

At some stage in the 1890s the Commercial changed hands, the new landlord being William Thomas who was described in the 1901 census as 'auctioneer, grocer and innkeeper'. The following year he found himself in the bankruptcy court with debts of over £1,000, prompting a clear-out sale of all livestock, furniture and shop goods. Frank Thomas then held the licence

The Wolfe at Ford in the days when it was still the Commercial.
(Picture courtesy of Mr. Peter Wheeler)

from 1903 until 1918; in 1916 he was one of the first licensees in the county to be fined for serving outside the restricted wartime opening hours of 6pm to 9pm on weekdays. Two years later the local magistrates were presented with a petition drawn up by the nearby Congregational Church and signed by over 100 local people who wanted to see the pub closed; the magistrates duly obliged.

The Wolfe in post office clothing

The building became a post office and shop and wasn't licensed again until February 1964, when Mrs. Dorothy Clavier of Tucking Mill, Treffgarne, applied to reopen the old Commercial as the **Wolf Inn**. To back up her application she too produced a petition, this time signed by 196 people who were in

39

A recent view of the flower-bedecked Wolfe Inn

favour of the pub re-opening – 76 of them residents of nearby Wolfscastle. Opposing the application, the Rev. John Roberts produced a petition of his own, signed by 57 objectors to the pub. 'There is no desire in the village for a public house and as a citizen I think it is morally wrong', said Mr. Roberts. But after hearing that Mrs. Clavier proposed running the Wolf as an eight-bedroom inn, and that the county Tourist Association was keen to see more holiday accommodation in the area, the magistrates gave the Wolf the go-ahead – a classic illustration of how attitudes had altered in half a century. Since then the inn has changed hands a few times while establishing a reputation for fine food; it has also gained an 'e' to become the **Wolfe Inn** – why, nobody seems to know.

In Wolfscastle itself was the **Sealyham Arms** which was mentioned in the 1851 census when Joseph and Mary Phillips were innkeepers; presumably this was the unnamed inn kept by John Griffiths at the time of the 1861 census. The pub seems to have occupied the site of the present **Wolfscastle Country Hotel**. Outside the village, the **Rising Sun** was at Danbarch near Sealyham mansion and was probably connected with Sealyham slate quarry, although very little is known about this cottage ale-house.

CHAPTER FIVE

Letterston, Little Newcastle, Puncheston, Scleddau

At one time the roadway south of Letterston was bleak and lonely and became notorious for its highway robberies. The perpetrators weren't the romantic mounted highwaymen of legend, but were more akin to modern muggers. One safe refuge for travellers was the **Harp,** the original of which (according to one account) dates back to the 1500s. Perhaps the name can be traced to Llain Delyn, a local place-name meaning 'land in the shape of a harp'. The present Harp seems to have been opened by stonemason and farmer Thomas Rowlands in 1821 and he was still there in 1841. It appears that the running of this pub-cum-farm then passed to a neighbouring stonemason called Richard Owen for a few years, and in 1845 it was reported in the press that the True Britons Friendly Society was to meet at the house of Mr. Richard Owen, innkeeper, parish of Letterston.

The Harp Inn was originally a farmhouse pub.
(Picture courtesy of the Harp)

Thomas Rowlands' widow Jane was running the Harp and farming the land in 1861 and their son Samuel Rowlands was landlord in 1876 when he was fined for serving after time and allowing a donkey to stray onto the highway. Charles Phillips was in charge in 1881 and William Phillips, farmer and postman, was landlord from 1891 to 1895. He drove a pony and red-painted trap with the words 'Royal Mail' emblazoned on it, his daily round taking him to Mathry and Trefin. Local farmer Arnold Henry Lewis held the licence in 1901, with Mrs. Lewis taking over in 1903, while Mrs. Martha Phillips was the landlady from 1906 to 1933. James Lewis George held the licence in the 1930s; his son Tommy George was a keep-fit fanatic who ran a training gym at the pub – the Harp Physical Culture Club – and claimed to be the third strongest man in the world. (To prove it he once towed a bus across a bridge in Haverfordwest using his teeth). Hubert Thomas was licensee from 1947 to 1960 followed by Axa Thomas. Harold J. Phillips ran the Harp in the 1970s as a tenant of Allied Breweries Ltd. which sold the pub to Jack Sandall in 1981. Mr. Sandall then began the transformation of what had hitherto been a small farmhouse pub into a smart, modern roadhouse, complete with restaurants, conservatory and large car-park, ideally situated to catch the Irish ferry traffic heading into and out of Fishguard. Nowadays much more of a licensed restaurant than a pub, the Harp is run by Mr. Sandall's son Giles and his wife Rebecca.

A working farm until 1972, the Harp once boasted a range of white-washed sheds and stables which have now been completely renovated and incorporated into the new-look inn. It is said that on one occasion in the distant past a travelling circus stabled its animals here *en route* from Haverfordwest to Fishguard and that an elephant was taken ill in the night and died, being buried in a nearby field. Since similar legends are attached to several other pubs in Wales (in Begelly they claim to have a buried camel), the tale needs to be taken with a goodly pinch of salt.

A recent view of the much-altered and renovated Harp

In the village itself, carpenter Peter Williams ran the **New Inn** from about 1861 to 1876; it was close to Saron Chapel and later became a grocery shop. And local tradition has it that the large building facing the village green was once the **Red Lion**, although no record of such a pub appears to exist. Across the road, and still going strong, the **Jubilee** seems to have taken its name from Victoria's anniversary shindig in 1887. It was probably opened in response to the news that the newly-constituted North Pembrokeshire and Fishguard Railway Company intended routing its line past Letterston; although the village station was eventually built some distance away, the Jubilee was handily placed to catch the passing trade of people from the St. David's peninsula heading to and from the trains. A pub-cum-hotel, it was run from 1891 to 1895 by auctioneer Joseph Watts, by which time it had become the headquarters of the local lodge of Foresters. George James took over, being succeeded by William Hart, W. John James and John Eynon. Peter Williams, hotelier and occasional rabbit dealer, held the licence from 1916 to 1933 and Sarah Ann Richards was the long-serving licensee from 1933 to 1962, followed by Mr. and Mrs. John Askwith. Mrs. Iris Davies was licensee in the early 1980s while John Morgan was there for nearly 20 years, his successors including Roland Mansell and current licensee James Gwilt.

West of Letterston, at Pontfelin Morris on the way to Mathry, was the **Bridgend**. Farmer Thomas Jones and his wife Hannah ran this pub in 1877, and Hannah was still going strong in 1914 despite the occasional brush with the law for serving on a Sunday. In November 1919 Dewisland magistrates

The Jubilee is thought to have been built for the railway trade

ruled that the pub was surplus to requirements and paid owner and occupier David Morris Jones £200 for the loss of the licence. Described at the time as 'doing a considerable trade with passing traffic', it is now a private house.

The road to Mathry continues through Castle Morris where it crosses the old drovers' route from Strumble Head to Haverfordwest. Ann Davies kept an ale-house here in 1851 and this may well have been the **Castle Inn**. Now called Castle House, it stands overlooking the village green where the animals would have grazed while the drovers had a well-earned rest and a pint. The **Gwesty Bach** on the crossroads was a successful restaurant in the 1970s, run by Mr. and Mrs. Ken Blake. Following the death of his wife, Mr. Blake converted it into the present attractive pub in the 1980s.

North of Letterston Square, the road from Haverfordwest to Fishguard remains as busy as ever. Responsibility for the roadway from Wolfscastle to Fishguard rested at one time with the Fishguard Turnpike Trust, formed in the early 1790s, and it was minuted in 1793 that 'a new gate be set up at Scleddy, of the breadth ten feet ... with two keys and a lock'. At some stage, probably in the early 1850s, a pub was opened at Scleddau Gate called the **Ivy Bush**. The first licensee was farm labourer Thomas Nicholas. When he died in the 1860s his widow Jane took over and she remained in charge for some 20 years. Margaret Harris was innkeeper at the Ivy Bush by 1891, although by the turn of the century the more usual name for the pub was the **Gate**.

In March 1905, several carriages of Rechabites left Fishguard Square to travel to Eglwyswrw petty sessions in order to voice their objections to the

The Gate Inn as it looked in 2004,
a century after it was almost forced to close

renewal of the pub licence. Mrs. Harris had died a couple of months earlier and the occasion was the application for the transfer of the licence to her son-in-law William Jenkins. The Great Revival was in full swing, the local temperance brigade needed a target and the tiny, two-room ale-house fitted the bill. 'There are no upstairs rooms and no stable', chuntered a spokesman for the teetotal Rechabites, adding: 'This belongs to the class of public house which ought to be done away with!'

In the inn's defence, it was pointed out that the mail-cart from Haverfordwest to Fishguard called there every day, while farmers from Pencaer broke their journey to Letterston Fair by stopping at the pub. It was also stated that the owner, Mrs. Davies of Glancleddy, intended rebuilding the house. To the annoyance of the assembled Rechabites, the magistrates voted to renew the licence on condition that the pub was completely rebuilt within six months, which was apparently done, because William Jenkins was running the pub – now officially renamed the Gate – in 1907. It subsequently became the Thomas family pub, with David Thomas and William Thomas both having stints in charge, followed by Alun and Bessie Thomas in the 1960s. It was Bessie who did most of the work in the pub, Alun running the adjacent Shell petrol station and also working as a carpenter. The Gate has changed hands a few times since the Thomases left, being modernised in the process and adding a restaurant; the current licensee is Lesley Llewellyn.

There are brief mentions of two pubs in the Llanstinan / Trecwn area in the 1870s. B.G. Charles has discovered a reference to the **Trecwn Arms** in 1873, while a slateworker called William Jenkins ran the **White Gate** on the road to the Gwaun Valley at around the same time. Neither enterprise seems to have lasted very long.

The road east of Letterston Square heads into the sparsely populated hills, passing through a couple of farming villages. There were two alehouse keepers in Little Newcastle in 1780, Elizabeth Watts and Griffith David, while William Lamb was the village innkeeper from 1795 to 1805. This was probably the **Cross** inn where Joseph Thomas was in charge from 1807 to 1813. Thomas Nicholas appears to have run the **Lion** or **Golden Lion** for a good number of years, certainly from 1811 to 1826, and the will of Thomas Nicholas, 'farmer and innkeeper', was proved in 1854. The records are sketchy, but his widow Mary seems to have carried on the pub trade and in 1862 the Court Leet and Court Baron of the Barony of Kemaes sat at the Golden Lion, Little Newcastle. At some stage it closed as a pub and became solely a farm.

The **Swan** was kept by Evan Morgan in 1871, followed by his widow Phoebe in 1881. Sam Hooper was there from 1891 to 1903. John Eynon kept the pub in 1906 and Daniel Rees was landlord from 1907 to 1912, in which year he and his wife Elizabeth were fined a total of £1 for brewing

The interior of the Swan during its days as 'Black Bart's Tavern'

beer without a licence. They left soon afterwards, and Isaac and Jane Jones ran the pub and village post office from 1912 to 1918, also promising good stabling. Mrs. M. Evans was in charge in 1920. It subsequently became the Vaughan family pub for a number of years, the licensees including Phoebe, Arthur and William Vaughan who was still there in 1944. William Baskerville became the new landlord in 1948 but William Morris was there in the 1950s and early 1960s. For some years in the late '70s the pub laboured under the sign **Black Bart's Tavern,** the new name being in honour of the pirate captain Bartholomew Roberts who was born in the parish. Harry Mills and his wife Trudie decked the place out with all sorts of maritime artefacts in keeping with the new theme. It became the Swan again when Mrs. Berenice Pepper took over as licensee in the early 1970s, helped by her son Dick who is now the landlord in his own right, presiding over a traditional village local which is a popular meeting place for the local farming community.

The unpretentious Swan in Little Newcastle

In 1861, 68 of the poor and aged residents of the area were treated to a meal at the **Drovers' Arms** in the village of Puncheston by the Rev. C.H. Barham of Trecwn. As the name implies, the pub was a gathering place for the drovers who herded the livestock between farms, fairs and markets, and it could be a lively place during Puncheston Fair; in 1869 two policemen found themselves caught up in a drunken brawl which erupted in the pub on Fair night. Seth Reynolds was landlord between 1861 and his death in 1872 and his widow Hannah Reynolds carried on running the pub until 1891 with the aid of her son Thomas. Mark Howells took over as landlord in 1893 and was still there in 1914, but Douglas and Harriet Howells were in charge by 1921. William Vaughan took over in 1924 and the pub remained in the Vaughan family for many years, with Hartley Thomas, who was licensee in the 1950s and '60s, having married into the family. The Thomases escaped unharmed when a fire swept through the pub in 1957, destroying the roof. The Drovers' was rebuilt and a decade or so later the pub was modernised and extended by Harold Aldridge, transforming what had previously been a no-frills village local. A new restaurant was opened in 1973, chalets were built in the grounds and the pub became known as a lively venue for dinner dances and sing-songs 'with Joan on the organ'.

Since those heady days the Drovers' has led a somewhat roller-coaster existence, doing well under some licensees, less well under others, and even

The Drovers' Arms has been much extended to the rear

being closed on a few occasions, Happily this friendly local is currently on an upswing under current licensee Sandra Davis, with the emphasis on good food and the re-introduction of live music recalling the glory days of the seventies.

CHAPTER SIX

Nolton, Roch and Newgale

Nolton is farming village with a much-restored Norman church, while a mile away is Nolton Haven, a narrow inlet which ends in a sandy beach reputed to have been the haunt of smugglers in past centuries; tradition has it that there was a smugglers' tavern near the beach in the 18th century. Nolton Haven was also the centre of a thriving coal-mining enterprise, and between the late 18th and early 20th centuries several local collieries exploited the seams of anthracite running out under the sea. A number of relics of this industrial age are visible; in particular the 'counting house' alongside the old tramway which carried the coal down the valley to the beach where it would have been loaded onto coasters. Another early industry was quarrying.

Thomas Twigg kept the **Bush** somewhere in Nolton parish from 1811 to 1815 followed by Thomas Evans who remained the landlord until 1825 when the pub appears to have closed. It was succeeded by the **Mill** which opened for business in 1827 when the landlord was Thomas Raymond. Mary Raymond had taken over by the following year while David Lewis was in charge during the 1840s and '50s and Margaret Davies was grocer and innkeeper in 1861; not surprisingly the pub stood near to Nolton mill at Nolton Haven, but when it closed isn't known.

William Warlow ran a pub just above Nolton Haven in 1851. This was possibly the **Rising Sun** where James Perkins was landlord from 1861 to 1891. Another Warlow took over the pub in 1892, almost certainly local grocer Thomas Warlow. It appears that he closed the Rising Sun and transferred the licence to his grocery shop in Nolton Haven which must have stood close to the site of the former Mill Inn. He called his new pub the **Mariners' Inn**, and remained the licensee until about 1908 (although the licence was held briefly by local joiner Thomas Davies in 1901).

According to an early 20th century newspaper report: 'The Mariners' Inn is the only public house in Nolton, which is known in Pembrokeshire as a village of teetotallers'. Through much of his tenure Warlow had to withstand

The Mariners' Inn at Nolton Haven is in the centre of this early postcard view

persistent attempts to close the pub, usually spearheaded by the Rev. John Rees, vicar of Roch. In February 1905 the vicar presented the Roose annual licensing sessions with a petition signed by 141 residents and ratepayers against the renewal of the licence. The petitioners claimed that the inn was 'unnecessary and injurious' in a parish with a small population like Nolton and they pointed out that proper supervision was impossible with the nearest policeman living four miles away. However the objection appears to have failed due to a legal technicality, to the relief of the licensee and also to Harold James of Spring Garden Brewery, Haverfordwest, who by this time leased the property from the owner, Col. Harries of Hilton.

A recent view of the Mariners', looking down towards the sea

The determined vicar was back in court in 1908, this time pointing out that the pub was definitely not needed, since 'of the five colliers remaining at the works, three are teetotal'. Once again the licence was renewed, only for the weary licensee to give it up as a bad job the following year. The Mariners' remained closed for upwards of 12 months before Thomas Redcliffe of Hilton Cottages, Roch, applied for a licence to re-open the inn in 1910. The Rev. John Rees again marshalled the opposition, arriving in court armed with yet another petition. If the house were re-opened, he chuntered, it would bring 'old topers from a distance' in the knowledge that they could drink at all hours in such an isolated pub, without interference from the law. The magistrates finally bowed to pressure, referred the inn to the compensation committee and it was closed officially in 1910.

The Mariners' remained closed for half a century, the name still visible above the door, until the tourist boom of the 1960s prompted the re-opening and wholesale redevelopment of the building into a spacious, modern inn with an 18-bedroom extension. Alan Bateman was behind the reopening in 1965, and he was succeeded by Eifion and Dot Morgan – career licensees who had previously run the Eastgate in Pembroke, the Castle in Haverfordwest and the Broad Haven Hotel. They left after a few years to run the Little Haven Hotel, being succeeded in the early 1980s by Mr. and Mrs. Peter Skudder and then by Mr. Chris Quinlan who has been at the Mariners' for the past 20 years. The original building can still be identified within the new-look inn; it is now a dining room, its low ceilings and narrow doorways contrasting with the later developments. Of special interest to visitors is Albert, a stuffed albatross with a 14-foot wingspan. Albert's original home was the Duke of Edinburgh in Newgale, but a series of misfortunes at that pub was blamed on the albatross, so he had to go. Alan Bateman gave him a home at the Mariners' (his case occupies most of one wall) and Albert has repaid this kind gesture by not causing any ill fortune to befall his new lodgings.

When the coal seams were being worked, the miners at Nolton, Folkeston and Trefrane would have needed refreshments, so that as well as the pubs listed above there were ale-houses kept locally by David Howell in 1784, by Richard Llewellin from 1784 to 1795, by Joseph Phillips (Trefrane Hill) from 1806 to 1811 and by Job Noott (Folkeston Hill) in the 1840s; the names of these ale-houses are not known. Collier John Francis, who lived at Cliff Cottages, near Trefrane Colliery, kept an ale-house called the **Fox and Hounds** according to the *Pembrokeshire Herald* in 1854.

Moving north past Trefrane to the Haverfordwest – St David's road, the **New Inn** once stood near the Roch Gate crossroads. This inn was recorded in 1729 and was considered significant enough to be named on Thomas Kitchen's 1755 map of Pembrokeshire. Henry Owen was the licensee at the time, followed by John Williams in the 1780s. Thereafter the inn seems to have dwindled in importance, although the name survived for a number of years, being applied to couple of dwellings which stood where the lay-by is now. One of these was run as an ale-house in the 1840s by coal miner David Williams who kept the name New Inn, but how long it lasted is hard to say; none of the subsequent occupants of New Inn are described as innkeepers in the census returns.

A couple of ale-houses lurked among the lonely moorlands to the east of Roch Gate. The **Step Inn** was on the north side of Dudwell Mountain, but when it functioned as a pub is not recorded. There was another **New Inn** near the quarries on Cuffern Mountain, between Middle Slade and Rock Farm, which was kept by Sarah John in 1851. Local legend has it that there was once a shebeen-cum-brothel for the miners of Nolton and Newgale in this fairly remote area; it was at Windy Hollow and went by the nickname of Pig and Whistle.

Martha Hire, a widow from Pembroke Dock, was living at Windy Hill (as opposed to Hollow) in 1841, but a few years later she opened the **Victoria** on the main road and was still in charge in the 1860s when she was in her 80s. Her son-in-law, neighbouring farmer Richard Thomas, kept the pub from 1871 until about 1909 and John and Elizabeth Watts were in charge in 1914. It seems to have become a James Williams house in the early 1920s and Samuel John was tenant from 1923 to 1930, followed briefly by Alfred John. Thomas Vaughan was the tenant for much of the 1930s followed by the well-remembered Martha Vaughan who was there until 1954, keeping the pub during the years when it was a popular haunt of service personnel from nearby RAF Folly radar station.

Mrs. Martha Vaughan with Ivy and Mansel Williams outside the Vic

Mrs. Vaughan's nephew and niece, Mansel and Ivy Williams, then had a spell in charge followed by John Davies – 'John the Vic' – who was there from 1973 until the late 1980s, followed by Mrs. Beryl Payne. Angela and Barney Ricketts refurbished the pub when they took over in about

The Victoria in Roch

1990, making a number of internal alterations – although the old 'snug' had already disappeared. This was a screened-off area within the pub where people could drink without being observed; it even had a bell-push to summon the landlord when service was required. Julie and Mark Williams were tenants from 1995 to 1999 when Julie Thomas became licensee. In 2003 she and her husband Antony bought the Vic, made a few more alterations and improvements, and are still in charge of this friendly local with its stunning views across St. Bride's Bay.

Down the lane behind the Vic is Roch Bridge, where Anne Griffiths kept the **Farmers' Arms** in Brawdy parish from 1851 to 1861 followed by her son-in-law John Reynish between 1871 and 1881. Reynish's widow Mary was the landlady in 1891 and their daughter, Miss Sarah Reynish held the licence from 1901

The Farmers' Arms at Roch Bridge stopped serving in 1928

53

to 1916 in which year she was fined 20 shillings for 'being very drunk and cursing and swearing' in her own pub. In 1919 the local magistrates declared the Farmers' surplus to requirements, ignoring a declaration from the licensee that ' this house does the best trade in the district and I always keep the best beer – when I can get it.' The magistrates passed their recommendation on to the compensation committee which was unable to do anything about it because there was no money in the kitty at the time to recompense the owners and licensee. The reprieve lasted nine years, for much of which time the landlord was W. Reynish, presumably Sarah's brother William. However a second recommendation for closure met with more success in 1928 when the pub was being occupied by David Symmons, his wife and two sons. On hearing that only one room of the tiny cottage ale-house was being used for serving a trickle of customers, that there was stabling for just two horses and that the licensee himself had no objection to the pub being closed, the magistrates duly delivered the *coup de grâce*. £90 was paid out in compensation, most of it to the owner, John Edwards of Wood Green, London.

Of the **Horse and Jockey** little is known, except that it too was in Brawdy parish and Elizabeth Walters was the licensee from 1825 to 1828.

Back on the Newgale road, Thomas Raymond, collier and innkeeper, opened the **Colliers' Arms** in the 1840s, serving the miners who worked at Southwood pit (he was probably the chap who had previously run the Mill Inn at Nolton). When the pub closed isn't known, but the name persisted until the 1890s. It was on the left-hand side of the hill going towards Newgale, perhaps where Southwood Bungalow now stands.

Down on the coast is the windswept expanse of Newgale Beach, backed by an equally long bank of pebbles. William Sinnett kept an alehouse at Newgale Bridge from 1795 to 1805, and it was this establishment which the two gentlemen compiling the *Cambrian Guide* – an early 'Rough Guide to Wales' – must have visited in 1800.

> We purported to breakfast at Newgin [*sic*] Bridge where we understood we should meet with everything comfortable; but to our disappointment we found a most miserable, dirty pot-house, destitute of even the common comforts of life. We were literally obliged to stoop in order to gain access to the kitchen which contained a small bed and a few chairs. Through this an elderly woman conducted us to what she distinguished by the name of a parlour. In this room the furniture consisted of two beds, a dirty table and a few chairs. With disgust we left this miserable hovel and contented ourselves with a basin of milk. We declined eating the bread, or rather oatmeal cake, which was of the coarsest kind.

The expanse of sand was ideally suited to horse racing, and Newgale Races were held every August, becoming an important part of the county's social and sporting calendar. Previewing the 1810 event, the *Carmarthen Journal* noted that there would be three prizes for the winning owners – a silver cup, a saddle, and a bridle and whip. 'After which a gown is to be run for by girls, men to jump in sacks for a new shovel and other rural amusements'.

After the racing and rustic fun came the evening's entertainment. According to a press report in 1808:

> The sports on the sands being concluded, the gentlemen retired to partake of a sumptuous dinner at Sinnett's Hotel and the ladies hastened to the Marine Villa on the Hill, to whom a general invitation had been given by its amiable inhabitant, Miss Stokes. Soon after dinner the gentlemen were summoned to the Villa when dancing commenced on the lawn to the charming music of a Pandean band stationed in the conservatory.

Nothing much changed over the next two decades. In August 1829 the *Carmarthen Journal* noted:

> The stewards, attended by a numerous host of friends adjourned to Sinnett's Marine Hotel, in the long room of which they sat down to a sumptuous repast furnished in Mrs. Sinnett's best style, followed by a costly dessert.

Which presents a puzzle; there is no mention in the licensing records of any establishment run by Mr. Sinnett after 1806, and certainly these flattering accounts of a 'marine hotel' do not square with the earlier report of a 'miserable hovel'. Was the newspaper correspondent pulling people's legs? Certainly the first reaction of Haverfordwest journalist and historian, W.H. Davies, when faced with the same problem in 1924 was to dismiss the reports as 'a joke'. He investigated further and managed to find someone who could remember the original inn at Newgale – a thatched cottage on the seaward side of the beach road which stood pine-end-on to the sea. The landlord, William Sinnett, had died at Newgale Bridge in 1833 at the age of 92.

In 1851 Thomas Bevans from Spittal was described as 'publican and schoolmaster, **Bridge Inn**'; probably the inn which superseded Sinnett's original cottage pub. By 1861 he was working as a carpenter, while his wife Elizabeth ran the pub and brewed the beer; they were both in their 70s by this time. Lodging with them was a Miss Jane Sinnett who died a few years later at the age of 83.

An early view of the Bridge Inn at Newgale, now the Duke of Edinburgh. Opinions differ as to whether this shows the old pub which was demolished by the sea, or the newer one built to replace it, with most of the evidence seeming to favour the latter view

James Bevans was licensee in 1871 and John Allen was landlord from 1875 to 1881 followed at some stage by his widow Martha. The inn acted as a 'halfway house' between Haverfordwest and St. David's, the horse-drawn waggons and coaches all stopping here to give the horses a rest before tackling the steep hills on either side of the valley. This meant that in 1882 the inn received a royal visit when Levi Harries' landau and four carrying the Duke of Edinburgh stopped off *en route* to St. David's. It is said that the Duke was so taken with the little pub and the welcome he received that he made a gift of ten guineas to the landlady. The chair in which the Duke sat became a treasured item and the name of the pub was subsequently changed to **Duke of Edinburgh** after Mrs. Allen had written to the Palace for the relevant permission.

In October 1896, one of the worst storms ever to hit the Welsh coast struck with devastating effect. Many ships were lost, including a Portuguese barque which was driven onto rocks off Skomer with the loss of 15 men drowned, and a Norwegian vessel which came to grief on Stackpole Head. In the Duke of Edinburgh, sheltering behind its

The Bridge Inn once had its own petrol pump to serve visiting motorists

*The Duke of Edinburgh has changed a lot over the years.
This is how it looks today*

storm beach of pebbles, were Mrs. Allen, her son Dickie Allen and her young grand-daughter. While the tide was out they were in no danger, and it was only as high tide approached that they became aware of the full fury of the hurricane. Huge waves began to crash over the pebble bank, one of which demolished the roof of an outbuilding, and the area around the pub began to flood with seawater to a depth of three or four feet. With the help of some brave neighbours, Mrs. Allen and her family managed to escape through the pounding surf to higher ground. As they made their escape she heard a roaring sound, looked back and saw a huge wave break over the pub; when the spray had cleared she saw that the roof and two of the walls had been demolished and several pieces of furniture – including the Duke's chair – were being dashed to pieces on the shore.

When the storm finally abated there was little left of the old pub. It was rebuilt, but on the other side of the road and a few precious yards further from the sea. For some reason Mrs. Allen decided to revert to the old name, and it reopened as the **Bridge Inn**. Eleanor Mary Walters took over in 1915 and Thomas Richard Walters is recorded as running the Bridge at Newgale in the 1920s and '30s. Thomas Nicholas Walters was licensee from 1937 to 1960 in which year the pub passed to Margaret Walters, known to all as 'Auntie Mag'. As recently as 1956 the only lighting in the pub was provided by Tilley lamps.

Lionel Jones took over in 1961 and set about modernising the premises, doubling it in size and changing the name back to **Duke of Edinburgh**. Having made various changes, Mr. Jones soon departed to be succeeded by

Reg Sutton. Mac and Irene MacDougal were there in the 1970s, followed by William Lambert in the 1980s and then David and Margaret Westmore. Two local couples, Richard and Kath Law and Keith and Pauline France took over their 'local' in 1994 and ran it for a few years. About ten years ago the Duke became part of the portfolio of pubs owned by Mr. Jason Slater, since when it has been successfully managed by Christian Lugg and Lisa Clifton who recently oversaw an extensive refurbishment of the bar and lounge.

Even in its new position the pub is still vulnerable to the worst of the Atlantic gales, especially if they coincide with a spring tide. In December 1910 a tremendous storm saw the waves burst open the door of the pub and sweep the bank of pebbles right across the road. It took five months to repair and reopen the road. In 1950 the pub was again badly flooded, while another ferocious gale in 1989 swept away the front porch.

CHAPTER SEVEN

Solva

Its fjord-like inlet makes Solva the safest harbour on this part of the coast and it has been a port since at least the 14th century. By 1811 more than two dozen locally-owned vessels traded from the harbour, and the row of sturdy lime-kilns shows that the production of lime to improve the fields was an important part of the trade. The area around Solva was also noted for its woollen mills, one of which is still in operation at Middle Mill.

The village itself is divided into two. The lower section at the head of the fjord, once well hidden from the eyes of pirates and other raiders, is now an attractive mixture of cottages, craft-shops, galleries and restaurants, some occupying old warehouses. The upper part enjoys fine views over the harbour entrance and was where the sea captains, the ship owners and the merchants had their houses. Both halves of the village have always been well served for pubs – far better than anywhere else on this stretch of coast – but it also had a strong temperance following and 30 people signed the pledge in Solva at a meeting in 1846, while a 'tea meeting' held by the Band of Hope in 1855 was well supported.

The village seems to have had a relaxed attitude to Sunday drinking in the days when Pembrokeshire was officially 'dry' on a Sunday. Mr. Paul Raggett has written about the time that his father retired from business in Cardiff and moved to Solva in the late 1930s. Being accustomed to enjoying a Sunday pint in one of the Cardiff clubs, he was unhappy at not being able to do the same in Solva, and voiced his complaint to a man mending lobster pots on the harbour. 'I'm sure if you walk down the side entrance of the Ship Inn the landlord will take pity on you', said the man. Sure enough, Mr. Raggett was ushered into the back room of the Ship for an illicit pint. It was only after he had lived in the village for some weeks that Mr. Raggett realised that the helpful lobster fisherman was actually the village policeman on his day off!

One of the earliest known pubs in Upper Solva was the **Swan** which was run by Martha Howell in 1795, by John Howell from 1805 until about

1809, and then by Martha Howell again until 1826. Sarah Propert was the ale-house keeper from 1827 to 1830, followed by saddle-maker Levi Prosser in 1835 and Daniel Arnold from 1844 to 1861. A tailor named Thomas Wilcox was in charge from 1867 to 1871, having previously run a pub in Croesgoch. It appears to have become the Swan grocery shop, near Chapel Lane.

The **Union** in Upper Solva was open between 1835 and 1852 with John Lewis as licensee. It closed in the mid-1850s and, like the Swan, became a grocery shop; it stood near the entrance to Portland Square. William Roch ran the **Blue Anchor** from 1808 to 1818 but its location isn't known. Elizabeth Richards opened the **Dolphin** in 1819 and was still there in 1841. F.W. Warburton's history of Solva places the Dolphin at Pen-yr-Aber and it is believed to have been the end house, now known as Bryn-y-mor.

Elizabeth Lewis was the landlady of the **Sloop** in 1822, and shoe-maker Edward Wagner ran a pub of this name from 1835 to 1841 after which it disappears from the records. It stood next to the original **Royal George** in Upper Solva, on a terrace overlooking the road leading from Haverfordwest to St. David's. There is a local tradition that the Royal George was Solva's oldest inn and that it was named when King George IV called for refreshment there, although that seems unlikely; perhaps the sign was a reference to a ship called the *Royal George* said to have been built in the village in 1802. In any case, there is no indication of the name Royal George in any of the records until a baker called Margaret Williams is recorded as licensee from 1835 to 1844. Margaret Prosser was behind the bar in 1851. Her husband was Captain Thomas Prosser who held the licence on and off for nearly 30 years; a master mariner, in later years he also ran a school of navigation

This early postcard view of Upper Solva shows the steep hill leading to the Royal George.
(Picture courtesy of Mr. Ken Daniels)

The former Royal George in Upper Solva,
with its successor to the right

for boys from Solva and district. When he was at sea, it was Margaret who ran the pub, as she did following his death in about 1880. The Prossers' widowed daughter Mrs. Mary Alice Lee kept the pub from 1889 to 1895 and her second husband Captain John Thomas was landlord from 1901 to 1906. William Beynon was there from 1907 to 1919 and he also ran a small drapery business nearby.

The inn was owned by the Harries family of Trevacoon until the break-up of the estate in 1919. At that time it was described as being a small house with two bedrooms, no stabling and 'up a blind alley and approached by a very steep hill', and it was this awkward situation and lack of facilities which led to numerous calls for the pub to be closed in the early part of the 20th century; however as the only licensed house in Upper Solva it managed to survive. William Griffiths was landlord in 1922 and the licence passed from Mrs.

The new Royal George was formerly the Bay Hotel

Lettice Lewis to Mrs. Emily Morris in 1927. She was licensee for five years, followed by Frank Jenkins who in turn handed over to County Councillor Roy Fletcher in 1942. In 1948 Mr. Fletcher successfully applied to have the licence of the Royal George transferred to a nearby, much larger house overlooking the bay which was once the home of one of Solva's well-to-do sea captains and merchants, Captain Rowe, and had its own sail loft. The new business was called the **Bay Hotel**, and that was the end of the original Royal George which became a private house, now called George Cottage.

Mr. Fletcher stayed at the Bay Hotel until 1952 when Emlyn Griffiths took over. He was succeeded by Mrs. Winifred Griffiths and, in the early 1960s, by Ann Thomas. Jean and Paul Raggett took over in 1969 and, becoming fed up with receiving letters meant for other Bay Hotels, decided to revive the **Royal George** name – in this case as a salute to the famous ship that sank at Spithead. Roderick Evans was in charge in the early 1980s, and although the Royal George closed in 1993 it was refitted and reopened the following year by David and Ann Fletcher, with Joe and Wendy Lodge as managers. Recent licensees have included 'Johnno' Voyce and current incumbent Barry Hankinson.

Down the hill and at the head of the fiord in Lower Solva is the **Harbour Inn**. This is a relatively new inn and was opened as the Harbour House Hotel by Margaret Canby-Lewis in the early 1980s in what had been her family home. It had completed the gradual change into a pub by the time 'Johnno' Voyce was licensee in the late 1990s, and after he moved up the hill to the Royal George it became an S.A. Brain and Co. house.

The Harbour Inn – Solva's newest pub

Solva harbour in the days of the coasting trade

The **Hope and Anchor** was an old Solva hostelry where Thomas Edwards was licensee from 1782 to 1818. It is hard to say whether this was the same Hope and Anchor as the one where milliner and dressmaker Ann Bowen held the licence from 1840 to 1844. It is even harder to say where it stood, although The Pharmacy is believed to have later occupied the site.

Thomas Edwards of the Hope and Anchor was one of the two ale-house keepers recorded in Solva in 1784, the other being William Bevan. His inn was called the **Ship** and a dozen years prior to this date he had taken in a lodger named Henry Whiteside, a young carpenter who had been given the task of designing and building a lighthouse on the exposed rocky reef known as 'The Smalls' off the Pembrokeshire coast. The remarkable structure which he conceived and built – described by one commentator as 'a shed on legs' – was an unexpected triumph and was not replaced by a more conventional stone tower until the 1850s. Whiteside, meanwhile, had settled in Solva, marrying William Bevan's daughter Martha.

Mariner Richard Williams subsequently took over the licence of the Ship and also skippered the *Unity*, the first communications boat used to link Solva with the Smalls lighthouse. Captain Williams was the landlord of the Ship from about 1805 to 1840 and for some reason, in about 1815, he moved the pub and its sign from one side of the road to the other, where it still stands. In 1831 he billed the Blue party for £13 for refreshments provided to people travelling to vote in the elections in Haverfordwest, and in 1846 the pub played host to 100 gentlemen who sat down to the annual dinner provided by the proprietors of the Folkeston Colliery, Nolton. Richard Williams' son, Captain

The Mariners is on the left and the Ship on the right in this early view

John Williams, gradually assumed responsibility for the business, taking over completely when his father died at an advanced age in the 1850s. William Lloyd had taken over by 1867 and tailor and publican William Davies was there from 1871 to 1875.

Alfred Madocks was licensee from about 1878 to 1882; at this time the property included a malt house and kiln, coach house, stables and four bedrooms. Henry Davies was landlord from 1891 until his death in 1899 and his widow Mrs. Florence Davies was still at the helm of the Ship in 1914 when it was listed as an hotel with 'good accommodation for cyclists and tourists'. The pub was also well placed for the GWR omnibus which stopped outside to pick up and put down passengers on the Haverfordwest station run.

Army veteran William Thomas took over towards the end of the war and remained in charge until 1930. He had a boat which he called *DORA* - an amusing reference to the Defence of the Realm Act which placed so many wartime restrictions on licensees. He was followed in that year by Edgar Philip Davies. Another ex-serviceman who had lost three brothers in the war and who still suffered bouts of malaria, Mr. Davies had previously run a boot and shoe shop in the village. It was reported in 1932 that the pub comprised four downstairs rooms and five bedrooms with a stable for two horses and urinals in the back yard, and that Mr. Davies had done much to improve the pub and its trade. Concerted efforts were made by the authorities to have the Ship closed in the early 1930s under the redundancy and compensation provisions, the local magistrates feeling that there were more than enough pubs in the village. Twice in as many years they recommended that the pub be closed; twice their recommendations were ignored by the county licensing committee which recognised that Solva was becoming popular with visitors and needed places offering refreshment and accommodation.

The Raggett family took over in the late 1930s, Mr. Raggett obviously being so impressed by the pub where he enjoyed his illicit Sunday drink that he became the landlord. Mrs. Florence Raggett remained the landlady until 1964 when she was succeeded by her son Paul Raggett and his wife Jean

The Ship Inn in Lower Solva as it looked in 2009

An artist's sketch of the characterful interior of The Ship

who were there for five years before giving up the tenancy of this James Williams house to move to the Bay Hotel. Clem and Nano Morgan were the licence holders in the 1970s and early 1980s, but the pub changed hands following Mrs. Morgan's death in 1983, the new landlord being Glyn Davies from Hubberston. It has changed hands a number of times since, the licensees including Paul and Sarah Edwards in the 1990s and Ashley and Sally Hart, who later ran the Grove in St. David's. An interesting old building, with lots of exposed timber, the Ship boasts a fine collection of Toby jugs and old photographs and memorabilia from the early days of Solva regatta.

The Mariners in its present guise as an apartment block

As was so often the case, when the Ship moved across the road, the original premises became the **Old Ship**. This was run by John Harries, who apparently decided in 1818 that he was fed up with the confusion and renamed it the **Mariners**. Harries remained landlord of the Mariners until his death in 1837 when an advert appeared in the local press advertising the 'modern-built house and spirit-shop known as the Mariners Inn in the improving seaport town of Solva'. It included a brewhouse, malthouse, stables and coach house. Carpenter and wheelwright John Davies, formerly of the nearby Square and Compass, took over and held the licence in the 1840s. Richard Davies was the licensee from 1850 to 1880 while Thomas Davies was landlord from 1891 until his death in 1902 when George Beynon Davies took over. The Mariners was listed as an hotel in 1906 when William Beynon was the landlord, but the licence changed hands several time over the next few years, the last landlord being William Evans who left in December 1910. When the licence came up for renewal a month or so later there were objections from the temperance lobby who claimed that there were only 30 men of pub-going age in Lower Solva and three pubs to serve them. Despite hearing that the Mariners' was 'doing £450 a year' the pub was duly closed under the redundancy ruling. It later became the Mariners Stores, the largest shop in Solva, before being converted into apartments.

The **Square and Compass** was at 1, New Street according to the 1861 census, five doors from the Mariners. Carpenter John Davies was the landlord from 1810 to 1835 before taking over the Mariners, and William John was landlord from 1840 until his death in 1857. His widow Lucy ran this beer-shop from 1858 to 1861 but seems to have retired and closed the business by

1871. (F.W. Warburton wrote in his history of Solva that this pub was on the corner of River Street). Mr. Warburton's history of Solva, published in 1944, also includes a reference to the **Travellers' Rest**, apparently opposite the Methodist Chapel. Perhaps this was the place run by David Roberts who is recorded as a beer-seller hereabouts in 1858.

It is said that there was an ale-house on the site of the **Cambrian** as far back as the early 1600s, but the present pub seems to have opened in 1828; it was once part of a terrace of two cottages and a stable, growing over the years to take over the whole row. Local auctioneer John Howell was the first landlord in 1828 and he was still there in 1852, during which time the pub became the meeting place of the True Ivorites benefit society. Mr. Howell was also heavily involved in the local lime trade, and the Cambrian was surrounded by a cluster of lime kilns. Jane Howell had followed John by 1858, but by 1861, at the age of 77, she was content to allow her daughter Mrs. Caroline Pritchard to do most of the work. Mrs. Pritchard ran the pub in her own right from 1867 until her death in 1895, while from 1896 to 1915 her daughter Mrs. Jane Propert was in charge. Following Mrs. Propert's death the licence passed to a Miss Howells.

CAMBRIAN HOTEL, SOLVA

Mrs PROPERT desires to announce that she has taken over the business so successfully carried on by her late mother.

EVERY ACCOMMODATION & COMFORT for VISITORS.

The Cellar will be found replete with CHOICE WINES, THE BEST SPIRITS INCLUDING: MARTELL'S BRANDIES, QUEEN'S OWN AND EXCELSIOR WHISKIES, BASS'S BEER (BOTTLED OR DRAUGHT), AND GUINNESS'S STOUT.

FAMILIES SUPPLIED AT THE LOWEST POSSIBLE PRICES

Mrs. Propert announces that she is taking over the Cambrian

Joseph Henry Trowsdale was innkeeper from 1920 to 1926. He had a solid Solva pedigree, his mother being the former Martha Whiteside Williams, a great grand-daughter of the lighthouse-building Henry Whiteside. Wally King took over, but the pub was sold to W.H. George, Haverfordwest, in 1933 by Mrs. Julia King. Tenants came and went fairly quickly for a couple of years, but Mary Pearce and latterly Miss Nellie Pearce kept the pub for some 16 years between them; the pub had acquired its own petrol pump by this time. Doug Turner took over in 1951 and was still there in 1958, while Frank Johns was in charge of what was by then an Ansells pub in the 1970s. The 'Cambo' changed hands in 1982 with Pietro Cerri becoming owner and licensee, and during his 20 years in charge it gained an increasing reputation for good food, a reputation since built on by Dave and Sandra Brown and current proprietor Adrian Moule who carried out a major refit in 2007 to create a new bar and lounge.

Being opposite the bottom of a very steep hill has meant a few hairy moments for the Cambrian, one licensee escaping injury by leaping over the bar when a runaway van ploughed into the front of the pub.

Mrs. Propert and family outside the hotel.
(Picture courtesy of the *Cambrian*)

The Cambrian, showing the garage on the left in what it thought to have been an old stable with granary above.
(Picture courtesy of the *Cambrian*)

The pub boasts a wonderful collection of old photographs of Solva, while two local traditions are still kept up, at least in symbolic fashion – the annual rook shoot and 'Rook Pie Dinner' in May and the 'Fox Pie Dinner' in December. The first of these origi-nated with the desire of local farmers to keep

A recent view of the Cambrian

the local rook population under control, and after a day peppering the trees with shotgun pellets the shooters would return to the Cambrian for a slap-up meal, allegedly featuring the celebrated rook pie, at which the best marksman would receive a special award. Similarly the 'Fox Pie Dinner' seems to have its origins in the annual meet of the hounds at the pub, after which the tradesmen of Solva would invite their counterparts from St. David's to a celebratory meal. No-one seems to know whether 'rook pie' or 'fox pie' were ever actually served at the Cambrian, but these days the events are popular village social gatherings, the suppers being attended by certain time-honoured formalities.

According to a pamphlet written in the late 1850s by one-time Solva printer John Williams (father of the aforesaid Martha Whiteside Williams), the

Penybont was a small, straw-thatched cottage inn opposite Solva Mill, at the foot of the hill, on the left-hand side of the road entering Solva from Haverfordwest. It was apparently in operation in the 1770s and the land-lady 'was a Mrs Jervis, the widow of a captain in the Royal Navy'. If so it had closed by 1780.

A mile or so inland, Martha Morse was the licensee of the **Llanunwas Arms** in the

The Llanunwas Arms would have kept many a weaver supplied with beer

milling village of Middle Mill from 1871 to 1881; she had also lived at the house in 1861, but with no indication that it was then licensed. George Prickett was the landlord from 1901 to 1906. In 1912, licensee William Griffiths was fined ten shillings for being drunk on his own licensed premises. Constable Bassett told the magistrates that the 62-year-old landlord was too drunk to stand. Griffiths quit soon afterwards, but the pub was forced to close in 1914 under the redundancy ruling. Owner and licensee Gilbert Davies Harries had the blow softened by a compensation payout of £350. The building still bears a slate plaque with the name 'Llanunwas Arms'.

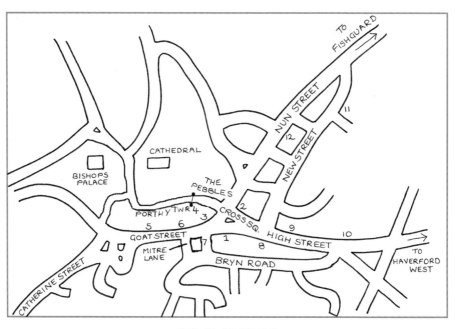

ST. DAVID'S

1	Black Lion	7	Mitre
2	Cross House Hotel	8	Mariners'
3	Fishguard Arms	9	Commercial
4	Tower Inn	10	Grove
5	Farmers' Arms	11	City
6	Carpenters' Arms	12	Prospect

CHAPTER EIGHT

St. David's

The smallest city in Britain has been a place of pilgrimage since the Middle Ages, when two treks to St. David's equalled one to Rome. David, the Welsh patron saint, had established a monastery here in the sixth century which flourished despite initial opposition from the local pagans who preferred their own Celtic deities.

Following the Norman conquest, David was canonised and a cathedral was built on the site of his monastery. This was enlarged and embellished over the centuries to create the present magnificent building – the resting-place of the bones of St. David and St. Justinian. The early monks were great brewers – Fountains Abbey in north Yorkshire could turn out a quarter of a million pints of beer every year – and in the Middle Ages surplus beer was often used to make mortar for building. According to Nona Rees:

> There was a local tradition in St. David's that all the mortar used in building the cathedral was wetted with *breci* or unfermented beer instead of water.

There is a certain irony in the fact that St. David – a confirmed teetotaller – should have as his shrine a cathedral built out of beer.

Alongside the cathedral in the valley of the River Alun are the impressive ruins of the 14th-century Bishop's Palace. According to St. David's historian Dr. George Middleton, a tavern called the **Ship** once stood between the cathedral and the Bishop's Palace. Wrote Dr. Middleton:

> The small building alongside the stream between the two bridges has been many things in its time. It had been a slaughter-house in Bishop Gower's time (1328-1347) and later it became a pub called the Ship.

The building subsequently became a lodging house for minor members of the cathedral staff and later still a cathedral workshop.

The city had three ale-houses in 1784, kept by John James, Essex Summons and George Arnold, and over the next couple of decades this figure fluctuated between three and seven. Hardly anyone had a good word to say about the early inns of this tiny and remote rural community. 'Wretched', 'miserable' and 'the worst I ever met with' were typical comments from travellers, while as late as 1871 Francis Kilvert was warned by a coach driver that the city inns were dirty and uncomfortable.

As the 19th century progressed the number and quality of the hostelries slowly rose, mainly to accommodate the demands of the growing number of tourists visiting this picturesque area with its wealth of historic monuments. Small hotels gradually replaced seedy inns so that by 1903 there were still seven licensed houses in the parish. Some of them must have been quite lively at times because, as Dr. Middleton has recalled:

> At one time a favourite occupation of the local children was to stand outside the open windows – after stop-tap – of the local hostelries and listen to the arguments of a man and wife somewhat under the influence. This served to perpetuate a good flow of abusive language to the next generation... .

The hub of St. David's has long been the triangular market square, known as Cross Square for the imposing preaching cross at its centre. All roads converge here and there was a smattering of hostelries around this focal point – although far fewer than might perhaps be expected. One of these inns was the **Black Lion**, sometimes given its Welsh name **Y Llew Du.** There are references to this inn as far back as 1749 when it was leased out by the landowning Harries family of Priskilly, and it was a meeting place for Dissenters before the first chapel was built locally in 1763. Essex Summons or Symmonds was landlord in the 1780s and may still have been there when Sir Richard Colt Hoare paid a visit in 1793. He wrote that St. David's

> Consisted of a few straggling, wretched houses and one long, wide, irregular street commanding a distant view of the sea. In this street is situated the inn, Black Lion, if it deserves that appellation, for it is by far the worst I ever met with... .

The *Cambrian Directory* of 1800 recommended the Black Lion as being the best inn for travellers in St. David's, probably because it was the only one. As the diarist Millicent Bant wrote in 1806, St. David's possessed

> one wretched inn which consists of a Kitchen (what is called a parlour), one horrible Bedchamber and a sitting room upstairs, whitewashed walls and broken windows.

72

William Rees was landlord of this dismal enterprise in 1805 followed by Martha Rees between 1807 and 1815. A carpenter named Thomas Propert took over but lasted little more than a year and the inn closed in 1817; possibly Probert then carried on his carpentry business from the building, which was set back a little from the road, with a courtyard in front. The site was redeveloped later in the century by the building of shops fronting the square, which in turn were converted into the present Lloyds Bank building.

Across the square, on the northern side, the house called 'Menai' was originally known as 'Cross House' and once housed a private school. In 1887 George Owen Williams opened the **Cross House Hotel** here, having previously cut his teeth on the City Inn. This 'snug hostelry' – as the Rev. W. Coolidge, Alpine mountaineer and tutor at Oxford, described it – was for a dozen years or so patronised by well-to-do visitors to the city, but closed in 1897 following the death of Mr. Williams' wife, Mary. It was renamed and became a private house soon afterwards. Although a much older building, the **Old Cross Hotel** next door is a relatively new enterprise, the property having been for many years a private house and the home of Alderman Adrian Owen Williams, sometime county council chairman and son of the aforementioned George and Mary.

On the southern corner of Cross Square and The Pobbles – the narrow lane down towards the cathedral – stood the short-lived **Fishguard Arms** where Thomas Jenkins was landlord from 1835 to 1840. At the bottom of The Pobbles is Porth-y-Twr – the Tower Gate – one of the four gateways to the Cathedral Close. Near here stood a pub which began life as the **Step In** where Henry Richard was landlord in 1795. He changed the name to **Tower Inn** in about 1815 and was still the landlord at the time of his death in 1830. The inn seems to have closed following his death; whether the later Tower Inn run by Anna Rees in 1871 was in the same building isn't known. Henry Rees was there in 1875, Anna Maria Johns was in charge in 1880, and from 1881 to 1899 the pub was run by John Thomas and his wife Emma; she took over the licence that year when her husband died.

The former Tower Inn near the Tower Gate

In 1901 Anna Sime applied to take over the running of the inn, but her application was put on hold until structural alterations were carried out. In 1906 the licence passed from W. Morgan 'to another Mr. Morgan' and in 1909 the local magistrates decided not to renew the licence under the redundancy ruling. The owner of the pub at the time was Frederick Sime, the local registrar of births, marriages and deaths, and the licensee was a Mrs. Campbell. Compensation was set at £500, of which £30 went to Mrs. Campbell. According to David James in *St. David's and Dewisland – A Social History*, the Tower Inn was the building just below the St David's Bookshop, the bookshop itself having at one time been a beer-store for the pub.

One of the main streets radiating from Cross Square is High Street, the road to Haverfordwest. Thomas Hughes, a retired mariner, was licensee of the **Mariners'** beer-shop from 1835 to 1852 which stood in the High Street opposite the New Street junction, more or less on the site of the present City Hall. The business had closed by 1858.

The Commercial Inn stopped serving many years ago

Thomas Williams was one of the sons of enterprising local farmer, merchant and shopkeeper Henry Williams. In 1809 Thomas married Martha Phillips, daughter of the parish clerk, and by 1811 they were running the **Commercial Inn** at 15 High Street, across the road from the Mariners'. It was an eminently respectable watering hole, as befitted such well-connected licensees, and became the meeting place for the Manorial Court of the City and Suburbs. Thomas remained in charge until his death in 1835, while his widow Martha continued as landlady until her death in 1852, having bought the property from the Priskilly estate. The couple's energetic and ambitious son William Williams then succeeded to the business, in which he was already playing an active role. In *St. David's and Dewisland – A Social History,* David James describes William Williams thus:

> He became farmer, property owner, shipowner, hotelier, agent for agricultural stuffs, agent for Lloyds, member of the school board, chairman of committees and precentor of Tabernacle. The second half of the century belonged to him.

Many of William Williams' enterprises were based at Porthclais where he involved himself in the lime, coal and corn trade and built up a fleet of coastal trading vessels; he also held the tenancy of Ramsey Island for a time. His ambitions as an innkeeper eventually outgrew the Commercial, and in September 1869 he advertised that he was leaving and moving along the street to a larger property, at the same time thanking people for 'the patronage so liberally bestowed on him for the past 30 years'. In 1871 it was described as 'Old Commercial' and was William Miles' grocery store.

Grove House, the premises William Williams moved to, had been built as a substantial town house, later becoming a private school, and the licensee named his new enterprise the **Grove Hotel**. It had (and still has) a fine walled garden, while nearby was an old cock-pit known as the 'Cocin Round'. Williams and his wife Martha remained licensees of this pub-cum-hotel for many years, helping usher in the tourist era to St. David's. Their horse-drawn omnibus 'The Duke' collected passengers from Haverfordwest station, and a regular stream of visitors stayed at the Grove, some having come to admire the cathedral, some for the shooting and fishing and some for the sea bathing at Whitesands. Not all were impressed by the inn, however, as James Baker, writing in 1888, revealed. 'We pulled up at a white, clean-looking house and ahead of us we saw a straggling line of cottages that formed the entrance to this remote city', he wrote in the *English Illustrated Magazine*. 'Our inn we found to be terribly dirty and strongly scented of accumulated dust, mildew

The Grove Hotel before recent extensions

A coach party outside the Grove.
(Picture courtesy of The Grove Hotel)

and stuffiness'. Perhaps the landlady was too busy to air the rooms; according to one account, in her younger days it wasn't unusual for Martha Williams to be up at 4am to cross to Ramsey Island to make 80lb of butter, returning to the Grove in time to cook breakfast for the guests!

William Williams died in 1899 and his widow announced that she was giving up the business in 1903. Edward Mathias was in charge in 1906 and some time before 1911 the Grove was purchased by Richard Barkway from Mr. Mathias for £2,450. In 1914 Barkway appeared before Pembroke Dock bankruptcy court. His financial failure was attributed to 'heavy payment of interest, heavy trade expenses, law costs and want of trade'. His successor, James Richards, made a much better fist of things and the Richards family continued to run the Grove until 1961. Humphrey Hague took over, followed

The Grove Hotel in 2010

by Cliff Price from Neath and later by Ronnie Davies of Solva. The aptly-named Groves family had charge in the early 1980s, and they were succeeded by Mrs. D. Pengelly and then by Ashley Hart, formerly of the Royal George in Solva. Much extended and improved over the years with the addition of conservatories and an accommodation wing, the Grove is now very much an hotel rather than a pub. For the past few years it has been owned by S.A. Brain and Co.

According to Henry Evans, who compiled the *Twr y Felin Guide* in 1915, a pub with the sign of the **Ship** once stood at the upper end of High Street 'and can still be remembered by old inhabitants'. It apparently had a little square in front of it, in the centre of which was a pump which drew water from a well. The well was later built over, 'and is now in the cellar of the City Stores in High Street', according to Mr. Evans.

Nun Street leaves Cross Square in the direction of Fishguard and had a couple of licensed premises at different times. On the left-hand side was the **Blue Bell** or **Blew Bell** where John James was licensee from 1781 until it closed in about 1811. There is a reference dated 1870 to a house and garden called the Old Blue Bell in Nun Street, occupied by Mrs. E. Griffiths; shortly after that date the inn appears to have been demolished and Cathedral Villas built on the site.

Across the road was a more recent Nun Street hostelry, the **Prospect**. John Davies and his wife Mary ran this small hotel from 1867 to 1880 and Thomas Davies, who had previously been a shopkeeper in the same street, was landlord from 1881 to 1884. Between 1891 and 1906 the landlord was William Howard Jones and twice a week a coach from the inn travelled to Letterston to meet the train. He was followed in 1914 by Mrs. Elizabeth G. Jones. Initially Mrs. Jones leased the Prospect from the Trevacoon estate, but when that was broken up in 1919 she bought the freehold. At the time the inn had five bedrooms, a bar, a dining room and a sitting room for guests, while the yard had a coach house and stabling for seven horses. In 1923 a petition opposing the renewal of the licence was presented to local magistrates on the grounds that a milk business was also carried on

The former Prospect Inn

from the premises and 'there was always a possibility of people going in under the guise of having milk and having beer'. While admitting that the house was well run, the police added their weight to the objection by declaring that the pub was not required. This was good enough for the bench and the Prospect closed soon afterwards. Licensee by the time was Hubert Jones and the owner was his mother, Mrs. Elizabeth Jones; they shared compensation of £425. This attractive building – which appears to date from around 1840 – is still called the Prospect.

Running parallel to Nun Street is New Street. Cooper John Stephens ran the **Bellevue** inn in New Street in 1861, close to Seion Baptist Chapel. Henry Child had become landlord by March 1866, when he was assaulted by a knife-wielding customer. According to *Potter's Electric News*, Lewis Lewis was fighting drunk and made several attempts to stab the landlord before being grappled to the ground by other customers. Lewis was sentenced to two months' hard labour at the house of correction and the pub seems to have closed shortly after this unpleasant incident.

In November 1876 the *Dewisland Guardian* reported that 'a new and attractive hotel, the **City**, will be opened shortly'. It is said that retired mariner Captain John Rees built the City as a station hotel for the proposed St. David's railway – a line that was never built. In *The Footsteps of our Fathers* Peter Davies noted: 'For many years the hotel stood in splendid isolation opposite the station that was not there'. Capt. Rees held the licence for a couple of years, but following his death in 1879 the City was purchased by George Owen Williams. He left a few years later to open the Cross House hotel on

The City Inn is believed to have been built for a railway branch line which never materialised

Cross Square, to be succeeded by a Scotsman named John Sime. Although Sime left to run the Swan in Haverfordwest in 1889, he retained a number of connections with the city; his 'Eclipse' omnibus ran between the county town and Cross Square every day and his son Frederick married George Owen Williams' daughter Esther and became a prominent figure in St. David's.

John Martin ran the hotel in 1891 and George Martin was in charge in 1901. He was helped by his sister Margaret Arnold and her husband George, and from 1906 until at least 1920 the Arnolds ran the City Inn as a family and commercial hotel, advertising 'splendid shooting over 1,000 acres'. In 1923 the Arnolds retired and sold the business to Polly Clayton and she was there until about 1934. Mr. and Mrs. Gwyn Davies were in charge from 1936 to 1950; Mr. Davies had a butchery business on Cross Square, so it was his wife who ran the inn. Tommy Narbett, formerly of the Farmers', took over and held the licence from 1950 to 1965 followed by Elizabeth Narbett. Talfryn Jenkins was there in the 1970s followed by Ronald Dawe and Mervyn Price in the 1980s. No longer standing in isolation following the building of new housing, the City Inn remains a popular pub-cum-hotel, the rise of motor transport over the years more than compensating for the railway which never materialised.

Goat Street was once called 'Ship Street', and Francis Green has speculated that either this was because it led to the harbour or because it once possessed an ale-house of that name. (However, it was sometimes spelled 'Sheep Street', from which the step to Goat Street is not a long one). Third door down from Tabernacle Chapel was the **Carpenters' Arms**, 'a favourite haunt of the beer drinkers and the scene of any brawls that were afoot' according to John Miles Thomas in *Looking Back*. Carpenter and joiner Thomas Hughes was the long-serving landlord between 1840 and 1884 and he was succeeded between 1891 and 1895 by his son William. Mrs. Florence Martin was the landlady from 1901 to 1906 but John James took over in 1911, it being reported that he was succeeding his sister who owned the property but who had been committed to Carmarthen Asylum. John Didwith was there in 1914 but the Carpenters' was forced to close in 1917 under the redundancy ruling, its lack of stabling counting against it. Of the £500 compensation agreed by the magistrates just £20 went to the licensee at the time, John Morris. The property burned down some 30 years later and after standing as a burnt-out ruin for several years was eventually rebuilt as a private house.

For many years the city's only out-and-out pub, the **Farmers' Arms** in Goat Street is said to have been created out of two adjoining cottages, one of which was a confectioner's. It appears in the 1835 and 1840 trade directories when the landlord's name was given as Thomas Harry; presumably this was the Thomas Harries who kept the pub from 1851 to 1875. He was followed by Jane Harries in 1880 and Mrs. Elizabeth Harries in 1884. Mrs. Anne Mathias was landlady from 1891 to 1895, Henry Morris was there in 1901 and James Richards was the landlord in 1906.

By 1914 the landlord was Thomas Morgan, a tenant of Narberth wine merchants James Williams. At this time the pub consisted of four rooms on the ground floor – taproom, bar parlour, kitchen and a small room used as a cellar – with four bedrooms upstairs and stabling for three horses at the rear. An attempt was made by the anti-drink lobby to close the pub in 1922, but for once the police did not concur, Superintendent Evans remarking:

> The main frequenters of the house are working men; there is a fair trade done and it is well conducted. I am not prepared to say that the house is not required.

The magistrates were told by the solicitor for James Williams that the other licensed premises in the city were all hotels – the Grove, the City and the Prospect – and that these catered for well-heeled visitors rather than the working man who 'in his working clothes and his humble way preferred to go to a house amongst his fellow workers', and it was for this class that the Farmers' Arms catered. The pub survived and Thomas Morgan remained licensee until 1935, while for the next ten years the licensee was Mrs. C. Morgan. Tommy and Elizabeth Narbett were licensees from 1945 to 1951 when they moved to the City Inn, and Gronw Rees was landlord from 1951 to 1969. David Richards – 'Dai the Farmers' – was landlord from 1969 to 1986 (and is still a pub regular) after which Mr. and Mrs. Jim Braby took over. They made a number of structural alterations, opening up the interior of the pub and exposing the stonework, as well as creating an attractive beer garden out of a patch of wasteland. Fortunately these changes did little to diminish the character of the pub, which is still the 'lifeboatmen's local', with the crew having its own 'Coxswain's Bar' full of life-

Tommy and Elizabeth Narbett outside The Farmers'
(Picture courtesy of The Farmers')

The Farmers' as it looked in 2009

boat memorabilia. For the past ten years the Farmers' has been owned by Mr. and Mrs. Matthew Blakeston, who also have the recently-opened **Bishops** just up the road in St. David's and the Sloop in Porthgain.

Mitre Lane, connecting Goat Street with Bryn Road (formerly Back Lane), takes its name from the **Mitre** inn which stood near the top corner, opening its doors for the first time in 1828. John James was the licensee then, and he was still in charge in 1844, also acting as the local schoolmaster. His widow Elizabeth James was landlady by 1851; rather surprisingly they did not live at the inn, instead occupying a house on Tower Hill. Everything

Bishops is the newest pub in St. David's

changed in the middle of the 1850s; the original Mitre closed and by 1861 it was being described as the 'Old Mitre, Back Lane'. Meanwhile the name and licence were transferred to a property in Goat Street opposite the Farmers' Arms. Mariner John Davies and his wife Jane kept this new Mitre Inn for a few years, but it closed in the 1860s. In the booklet *Looking Back*, John Miles Thomas records that Mrs. Morgan of Bryn y Garn (now Warpool Court) bought the ruins of the 'old' Mitre for stone for the walled gardens.

> There was a story current that some gold coin had been hidden in the chimney of the Mitre and Mrs. Morgan was a frequent visitor to the ruin when it was being pulled down. No gold was ever discovered, however.

The **Miners' Arms** was in Pig's Foot Lane, a narrow lane, still unmetalled, off Catherine Street; possibly the copper workings at nearby Treginnis inspired the name. Tailor William Griffiths ran this small beer-house from the early 1840s to 1858, and it was a sideline for shoemaker David Morris from 1861 to 1875; it seems to have closed soon after this date.

Two former St. David's pubs cannot be pinpointed. The **Rope and Anchor** began life in about 1800 with William Williams as landlord. Anne Williams had taken over by 1808, but the business closed a year or so later. The **New Inn** was kept by Jane Griffiths from 1795 to 1822. John Morris took over, but it seems that when he left three years later, the new licensee, Ann Summons or Simmonds, renamed it the **St. David's Arms**. She was still there in 1830 – the last time the pub is recorded.

Porthclais has always been the port for St. David's and was where the pilgrims would have landed in early times. It was a busy harbour in the 19th century, importing household goods from Bristol and timber from Canada as well as receiving regular cargoes of coal and lime for the kilns, and it later became the site of the city gas-works. The little harbour seems to have had a couple of alehouses in its time; as John Miles Thomas, who was born in 1889, recalled:

> There was a house with a small court in front of it and a garden behind it at the right hand side of the harbour, looking seaward. It appears the tide was encroaching on the house. I remember the family moving from there and the house was never again occupied. I believe this house was once a 'pub' where beer was sold.

The sign of this ale-house isn't known, but the other ale-house in Porthclais was called the **Mariners'** where a seaman called George Lile was the publican in 1871, with Amy Bowen employed as barmaid. 'Betty Lyle (*sic*) and her husband Georgie sold beer at Pentop, overlooking Porthclais harbour at that time, I remember,' wrote Mr. Miles Thomas.

CHAPTER NINE

East of St. David's

LLANRHIAN, MATHRY, TREFIN, CROESGOCH etc.

The road out of St. David's to the north-east soon splits into two – the main road to Fishguard via Croesgoch, and the coast road through Llanrhian and Trefin. A couple of miles along the main road is Carn Hedryn, still known to locals as 'Boncath'. Here stood the **Boncath Arms**, once a popular pub which served a scattered farming community as well as a regular passing trade of travellers, pig-drovers and cattle-dealers. Said to date from about 1850, it was kept then and for nearly 40 years by a tailor called John Thomas and his wife Ann. In 1888 the licence was transferred to David Thomas, presumably

The former Boncath Arms, where a customer was once tarred and feathered

a son. However, when he applied to Mathry magistrates a couple of years later for permission to transfer the licence to a local farmer named Tom Lewis, the bench unexpectedly refused to renew the licence. An appeal against this shock decision was even supported by the local police who preferred to see a properly run licensed house

in the area rather than have the local farm-lads sneaking off to drink and play cards in an out-of-the-way shebeen. But an impressive array of local chapel ministers lined up to criticise the pub, clutching the inevitable petition signed by all the 'leading residents' of the area. They argued that the Boncath Arms was close to the village school and church 'and was likely to counteract the good influences of these institutions'. According to one witness at the appeal:

Eighteen years ago there was a most disgraceful scene enacted at this public house. A man named Jenkins was there and had taken too much drink. The inmates of the house stripped him and covered him with tar and then put on him the feathers from a pillow belonging to the house.

Amazingly the appeal court took into account this drunken prank – which took place nearly two decades previously – and upheld the closure of this otherwise blameless pub.

The Morning Star has not been a pub for many a year

On the coast road, about a mile out of the city, was the **Morning Star** at Rhodiad, about which little is known. William Morris was there in 1875, butcher Thomas John held the licence in 1881 and Richard Evans kept the pub from 1891 to 1916. When it closed isn't recorded.

The coastline between St. David's and Strumble Head is spectacular, the towering cliffs being broken at intervals by small beaches and narrow coves. Several of these coves were sheltered enough to act as harbours for vessels involved in the coasting trade, especially the import of lime and coal and the export of bricks, stone and slate, and as always there would have been an ale-house on hand to supply refreshments to the labourers and deckhands. Beach Cottage at Abereiddi was built in the 18th century and was reputed to have been an inn used by smugglers. Possibly this also housed the **Abereithy Arms** which was opened in 1826 by Benjamin Roberts and ran for a few years serving the early quarrymen.

The most important harbour along this stretch of coast was Porthgain, although up to the middle of the 19th century, the inlet boasted little more than a tiny quay, a limekiln, a handful of cottages and small quarry. This changed in about 1850 with the arrival of a trio of entrepreneurs from London who acquired the rights to Porthgain quarry and also to the nearby slate quarries at Abereiddi and Trwynllwyd. The business was centred on Porthgain, where a water-mill was built to power the saws and planes used to 'finish' the slates. The harbour was improved, and rows of cottages were built to house the slate-workers, many of whom had moved down from north Wales. Although the slate business at Porthgain suffered several setbacks, the harbour continued to prosper and expand due to the opening of the nearby granite quarry at Penclegyr and the building of a brickworks capable of producing over 50,000 bricks per week. When this trade began to falter, Porthgain discovered a new lifeline – supplying crushed granite for road building. This trade continued until the depression years of the 1920s and the works were abandoned in the 1930s. Nowadays the harbour is a busy tourist destination and is especially popular with artists; there are two galleries in former slate-workers' cottages.

Another cottage in Porthgain houses the ever-popular **Sloop**, on the wall of which is a sign proclaiming that it was opened in 1743. Although the building certainly pre-dates the harbour, this date seems more than a little far-fetched since the first mention of an ale-house in Porthgain is at least a century later. Agricultural labourer Benjamin George from Fishguard and his wife Jemima had seven children by 1851, and in order to help feed his large family he turned his cottage at Porthgain into an ale-house to provide refreshments for the thirsty slate-workers who were flooding into the rapidly-changing village. Ben George remained the landlord of the Sloop almost up to his death, aged 80, in 1896. Fisherman Edward Powell was the landlord from 1895 to 1936 and Margaret Powell was there in the 1940s. Mrs. Margaret Walters was licensee from 1950 to 1964 when Sid and Mattie Phillips from Solva took over. They were followed in the 1980s and early '90s by Bertie and Margaret Phillips. Since 1994 the owner has been Mr. Matthew Blakiston, who also has a couple

A view of Porthgain in its industrial hey-day, with the Sloop to the left of the main stack

A great place to sit on a sunny day – the Sloop in Porthgain

of pubs in St. David's, and the Sloop has been sympathetically extended to cater for a growing clientele who include holidaymakers, coast path walkers, local fishermen – and cricketers from all over Pembrokeshire who invariably call here after a match in Llanrhian. Numerous old photographs of the harbour in its hey-day can be seen in the pub.

Moving along the coast, the next settlement is the large village of Trefin. Although not quite on the coast itself, the village has a strong seafaring tradition and was the home of many a 'Cape Horner'. Thomas David and Thomas Richard kept ale-houses here in 1782, but only Dorothy Richard appears as a licensee two years later and no pub at all is recorded in the village in 1795. Intermittent attempts were made in the village to combat the evils of drink, and in January 1842 a meeting was held at which 100 people signed the pledge. Exactly 60 years later, in January 1902, a Temperance Society was formed in the village, and at the inaugural meeting in the Calvinistic Methodist chapel nearly 50 people stepped forward to sign the pledge.

An early rhyme relates:

There are three ale-houses in Trefin,
The Ship, the Swan and the Fiddler's Green.

The **Ship** dates from at least 1805 when Sarah Francis was landlady. She had been widowed when her husband, Captain Thomas Francis was lost at sea off Anglesey in January 1802. Two of her sons, James and William, were also drowned off the coast of Ireland in March 1810; there is a memorial to them in Llandeloy Churchyard. Sarah continued to run the Ship until at least 1828, helped by her two other of her children, Thomas and Elizabeth. Perhaps because of the fate of his father and brothers Thomas never went to sea and instead moved to become a shipwright and innkeeper in Lower Fishguard.

86

Elizabeth married Thomas Rowland of Trefin and they kept the Ship in 1841, Thomas still being in charge in 1861 when he was a 64-year-old widower. The pub then began its long association with the Maddocks family, with John Maddocks becoming the licensee in the 1870s followed by the long-serving Mrs Anne Maddocks who remained the landlady until at least the 1920s. David Griffiths was there from 1935 to 1956, after which there

Mrs. Anne Maddocks and family members outside the Ship in Trefin.
(Picture courtesy of the Ship)

The Ship is the only survivor of the three pubs in the village rhyme ...

was a familiar name over the door again, with Glyndwr and Annie Maddocks running the Ship in the 1960s and '70s; locals still talk of the great sing-songs around the piano which were a feature of this period. Alan Rosser and

Peter Martin both had spells in charge, before Brian and Jackie Maddocks kept up the family tradition by steering the Ship for a number of years. (It had long been owned by the family, and still is). Meriel Murphy has been the licensee of this friendly and unspoiled village local for the past dozen years.

Of the other two pubs in the rhyme little is known; they were presumably the 18th-century ale-houses kept by the aforementioned Thomas David and Thomas Richard. The **Swan** at North End is still known by that name, having later become the Swan shop for a time, while the **Fiddler's Green** occupied a former sea captain's house that sits atop a grassy bank on the junction of Ffordd y Felin and Heol Crwys. A fourth pub, too

The Swan (top) and the Fiddler's Green (below) both closed long ago

recent to be mentioned in the rhyme, was the **Sailor's Companion** which is recorded in a sale document of about 1850. Sarah Rees was an innkeeper in the village in 1841 and presumably kept the Sailor's Companion, but no further information about this pub has come to light.

Abercastle was a busy little port in its day, importing limestone from West Williamston to be burnt in the four village kilns, and also coal and culm to fire the kilns. There was water-powered corn mill at the head of the inlet which also depended on the coasting trade for transport, and old warehouses in various stages of repair and restoration can still be seen near the quay wall. The coasting trade is now nothing more than a distant memory and, like so many villages along this coast, Abercastle now has more than its share of holiday homes.

Surprisingly for such a tiny village it boasted three pubs for many years, and three ale-house keepers appear in the 1795 records under Abercastle – James Lewis, Anne Saies and John Williams, the latter having run a pub in the village since at least 1782. Anne Saies' ale-house was the **Ship and Castle** which was taken over in about 1811 by William Rees who was still there, with his wife Mary and a maidservant called Elizabeth Sayes, in 1841. By 1851, 88-year-old William was being described as a 'retired maltster', the Ship and Castle having been taken over by John Phillips and his wife Hannah who were still there in 1871.

Much confusion arose when another William Rees opened a pub in the village in 1815; in the quarter sessions records they are distinguished as

This picture of Abercastle is thought to date from about 1920. The roofless building on the right was once the Blacksmiths' Arms, while the other roofless cottage just beyond is believed to have been the Ship and Castle

'William Rees the First' and 'William Rees the Second'. William the Second kept the **Fishing Boat** or **Fisherman's Arms** from 1815 to 1828 followed by Dorothy Rees in 1841. Close to Abercastle Mill, this ale-house was still going between 1861 and 1871 when farm labourer Levi Jenkins was the licensee; when it closed isn't known.

The **Blacksmiths' Arms** seems to have been opened in the 1850s by blacksmith Benny Watts who was still working at his forge in 1895. George F. Thomas was licensee in the early 1900s, his chief trade coming from men engaged in carting lime and culm. David Bowen was the landlord in 1905, but he left in October 1907 after which the pub was closed for a few months before Cecil Beynon Lloyd applied to take over. This temporary hiatus was the lever which the local temperance brigade needed to press for a complete closure of this otherwise blameless pub, and the Rev. Richard Jones appeared before the licensing magistrates brandishing a petition calling for the licence to be suppressed. Suitably awed, the magistrates invoked the redundancy ruling and closed the pub, with £70 compensation being paid to the owners, thought to be R.P. Lewis, wine merchants of Fishguard.

There was no pub at Abermawr, but there was a shebeen where a lady was well known for the quality of her home brew. To get around the letter of the law she would give customers the beer for nothing, but then charge them for having to polish the 'skew' (bench) on which they had been sitting!

Not far inland is a string of villages where the menfolk historically combined farming and seafaring as a means of earning a living on this exposed sweep of country. There were plenty of pubs scattered about, and plenty more unlicensed shebeens as well, since this was an isolated area and difficult to police. Tradition has it that the Black Lion between Llanrhian and Trefin was one such unlicensed ale-house. The little village of Llanrhian has not had a pub for many a year, but back in the 1820s it boasted the **Swan**, run by one of three licensees in the area called William Rees.

Just up the road, the **Artramont Arms** stands on the crossroads in Croesgoch. For the reason behind this rather unusual name we have to go back to the days of Cromwell. Richard le Hunte was a colonel in the New Model Army and the captain of Cromwell's bodyguard during the ruthless campaign to 'subdue' Ireland. As a result of this loyal service, le Hunte was rewarded with properties in Wexford and Tipperary confiscated from the dispossessed Irish Catholics. He became MP for Cashel and married a Pembrokeshire heiress, Mary Lloyd, whose inheritance included the manor of Llanrhian. Branches of the family continued to prosper down the centuries on both sides of the Irish Sea, and when a pub was opened on the Llanrhian estate it took the name of the le Hunte family seat in Ireland – Artramont House, just north of Wexford.

The Artramont was both pub and post office when this photograph was taken in the early 20th century

The Croesgoch pub seems to have been opened in the 1860s by draper James Wilcox; he was certainly the landlord in the 1870s, hosting regular dinners for the tenants of the le Hunte estate, and by 1881 he was also the local postmaster. The landlady from 1891 to 1906 was his widow Mrs. Margaret Wilcox, who also ran the post office. Gwylym Owen was landlord in 1914, while from 1919 to 1933 John Williams was the owner and licensee, also running a hackney car business and a small shop selling bicycle parts. With its five bedrooms and stabling for eight horses, the Artramont did brisk trade at the regular fairs and live-stock marts in the village.

Retired master mariner George Reynolds and his wife Martha were there from 1933 to 1935, during which time they sued the Fishguard dentist who held a surgery at the pub for one hour every Wednesday lunch-time. They claimed he owed them money for the use of the room and for 'cleaning up the bloodstains on the floor afterwards'. His response was that none of the previous licensees had ever charged him, especially as

The Artramont has been reshaped a couple of times recently following close encounters with delivery vans

they derived a useful income from the copious amounts of alcohol the patients consumed while waiting to be treated!

William Walters of Goodwick was licensee from 1936 to 1962. He was followed by Patricia Walters and then, in 1964, by Charles Davies. Ernest Angell ran the Artramont in the early 1980s, followed by Gareth Attley who ran disco nights on a Thursday but soon left to be replaced by John Vaughan, formerly landlord of the Three Salmons in Carmarthen. Ray and Margaret Nadollek were there in the late 1990s and early in the new century, while current licensees are Dave and Jan Evans. Recent licensees have had to contend with vehicles – mainly delivery vans – having close encounters with the front of the building, and the pub porch has had to be rebuilt on a couple of occasions.

The former Croesgoch Inn

A hundred yards away towards Fishguard was the **Croesgoch Inn**. (The two pubs were known locally as Tafarn Isaf and Tafarn Uchaf). Like the Artramont, it seems to have opened around the time Porthgain was developing, and the landlord in 1861 was Thomas Wilcox who was also the local census enumerator for that year. He moved to take over the Swan in Solva and Thomas Phillips, grocer and innkeeper, kept the pub from 1871 to 1881. James Evans was there in the 1890s, handing on to David Salmon in 1899. The pub passed from Daniel Harries to John Evans in 1906, and he remained licensee until 1929, also working as a butcher and hackney car proprietor. When Evans moved to the Farmers' in Mathry, Frank Jenkins took over, but the pub was referred for compensation and closed in May 1932. At some stage since then it appears to have been subdivided into two properties, now called Edge Grove.

James Rees was the landlord of the roadside **Square and Compass** from 1815 to 1861 when he was 75; surprisingly, given the name, he was a carpenter rather than a mason. The pub was regarded as a 'halfway house' between Fishguard and St. David's and was a regular stopping off point for coaches and carriages. (It is possible that a new pub was built up the road from the old one at some stage, because the name 'Old Square' appears in the 1841 census and there is still a roadside property in the village called 'Old Square').

James Rees' son-in-law and daughter – master mariner John Richards and Mary – kept the pub from 1862 to 1881 and John Charles was there from 1895 to 1901. Thomas Richards was the licensee from 1906 to 1920, followed shortly afterwards by Wintle Thomas. The pub closed when he left in 1922 but was reopened the following year by William Page, an employee at the Porthgain works, who held the licence until 1956. He was followed by Margaret Page while Jack and Eileen Williams were there in the 1960s. Mrs. Gwyneth Brown was granted a protection order in 1969 and also obtained permission to carry out alterations, and it was Derek Brown who enlarged the Square and Compass considerably, buying the cottage next door and incorporating it into the pub. James Redman succeeded the Browns, and Keith Johnston ran the pub in the early 1980s, making a number of internal alterations which opened up the original four-room pub into one open-plan space; his widow Eluned took over following his early death in 1983. John Hopkins was the next to run the Square, followed by Gerald Salmon who has been licensee for the past 18 years, during which time he has added a restaurant extension to the original pub, so that it is now a substantial and attractive roadside property.

A little further along on the same side of the road was the **Step In** which is mentioned in the 1840s; this was almost certainly a wayside alehouse at some stage, but as seems to be the case with so many of these 'Step Ins', concrete information is very hard to come by.

The Square and Compass began as the building in the centre, extended to include the cottage on the right, and then the restaurant extension was added on the left

A hilltop village surrounding a church, Mathry was an Iron Age settlement and an early Celtic Christian site before becoming a locally important market centre in the Middle Ages. A sixth-century Ogham stone stands in the porch of the church which was rebuilt in 1867. The hub of a prosperous agricultural area, Mathry had its own Michaelmas hiring fair as well as a market, and there was a magistrates' court in the village until fairly recently. It also had the **Blacksmiths' Arms** which was first mentioned in 1825 when John Thomas held the licence. When it closed is not known.

The Farmers' Arms, Mathry, in 2002

In the 1860s, George Walters was a farmer of over 100 acres by day, and pub landlord by night, although his wife Mary seems to have done most of the bar work. Their pub was the **Farmers' Arms** in the centre of the village, and they held the licence until the 1880s. In 1890, William Williams purchased the pub and freehold land from the church authorities and was still behind the bar in 1914. Benjamin Griffiths was licensee from 1920 to 1926, John Evans was in charge from 1929 to 1935, followed by Mrs. Mary Evans who ran the Farmers' until the war. David Evans then ran the pub for a time, being followed in turn by Ethel Walters, Anna Stephens and Nancy Williams. Sheila Lewis held the licence in the early 1980s followed by Gladys Reynolds and, more recently, Eric John. Now covered in creeper and a popular social centre for the area, the Farmers' has been run for the past 11 years – aptly enough – by Bryan Farmer.

94

CHAPTER TEN

Goodwick

Sparsely populated and windswept, the rocky peninsula of Pencaer is noted for its stunning coastal scenery and for hosting the unsuccessful 1797 French invasion. This was an abortive landing by a motley French force called the *Legion Noire* consisting of 600 troops and 800 released convicts. The invasion force had intended to sail up the Bristol Channel towards Bristol, but adverse weather conditions meant that the two frigates carrying the troops anchored instead off Carreg Wastad Point. Having landed the men and their supplies, the frigates sailed away, leaving the French force to ransack nearby farms and cottages for provisions. It is said that a ship carrying wine had recently been wrecked on the coast, so every house was well stocked with liquor – a fact which helped speed the invaders' downfall. Military discipline quickly broke down and the French surrendered to a rapidly assembled defence force under the command of Lord Cawdor. A memorial stone by the coast path marks the site of the French landing.

With few villages and little in the way of industry, Pencaer seems never to have supported a legal pub. However, it had a reputation for harbouring any number of shebeens which no doubt dispensed the contraband whisky and brandy smuggled ashore along this lonely coastline. One of these was probably the **Step In** at Henner Cross, marked on a 'Fishguard Invasion' map of 1797, while **Pass By** was described as an 'illicit pub' by Syd Walters in his account of the French landing. It stood at a fork in the road above Goodwick, where the lanes lead either to Henner Cross or Llanwnda. Many years later, in 1899, James Francis was fined a stiff £20 for running a well-appointed shebeen in Llanwnda.

The **Stop and Call** must have been an early cottage ale-house on the steep hill leading down to Goodwick Sands. According to Walters: 'Its proper location was in a cottage near Penfeidre', which would have made it a welcome place to stop and call after the long pull up the hill. He added that the cottage was still standing in the 1920s when it was badly damaged by fire. By then it had long stopped being an ale-house, but the name lives on as a local place-name.

Goodwick itself began life as a fishing village, with a lime kiln, a mill and a small quay which sheltered a handful of herring boats. Trading sloops and ketches would regularly beach on the sands and a few warehouses were built in connection with this trade. There was a smattering of pot-houses in what must have been a thriving little village, and one of the earliest recorded was the **Ship at Anchor** kept by Philip Williams between 1811 and 1815 and subsequently by Elinor Williams; perhaps Philip was away at sea, because he seems to have returned to take over the helm of the Ship in 1822 and was still there in 1830. Another early but short-lived ale-house was the **Peace and Plenty**, kept by Benjamin Lewis in the early 1820s.

Goodwick benefited from the growing popularity of sea bathing in Victorian times and had made a name for itself as a watering place long before the arrival of the railway in 1899. A guidebook of 1875 observed that Goodwick was 'the most delightful bathing place in the principality owing to the purity of the water and the salubrity of the air'. Marine villas were springing up overlooking the bay, and it was noted rather smugly in 1893:

> During the season many visitors take up their abode here, but they are guests of the quiet and sober kind and have nothing in common with the noisy crowds who come down from the manufacturing towns of the Midlands and during the summer months throng the better-known watering places on the Welsh coast.

So sober were the visitors, in fact, that a temperance hotel opened opposite the chapel in 1899, primarily to cater for passengers on the newly-opened rail link.

Goodwick in its days as a fashionable watering place

The whole area underwent a massive transformation a few years later with the creation of a purpose-built ferry terminal which not only saw the Irish ferry services switched from Neyland to Goodwick, but also, for a few glorious years, turned the former fishing village into a transatlantic liner port with the great Cunarders *Mauretania* and *Lusitania* making regular calls to land passengers and mail. The population of Goodwick increased dramatically, and in September 1906, the *County Echo* reported:

> Never before in its history – not even at the French invasion – have such large numbers of people been seen at Goodwick. Trade is exceptionally brisk in every section of business – especially pubs.

The influx of visitors, plus the great numbers of newly-arrived railway and harbour staff, sparked attempts to open two new pubs in Goodwick in 1908. One of these was to have been at Dyffryn, while the other near Goodwick Bridge was to have taken over the licence of the Ship and Anchor in Fishguard. The plans for the new hostelries met with strong opposition from an uncomfortable alliance of local temperance supporters and Goodwick licensees worried about loss of trade, and permission for both pubs was refused.

However Goodwick did acquire one smart new licensed hostelry. As part of its development plans, the Fishguard and Rosslare Harbour Company purchased a small hotel called Wyncliffe, together with seven acres, for £4,500, and planning permission was given in 1900 for the building of the splendid **Fishguard Bay Hotel** complete with tennis courts, tropical gardens and a telephone in each of its 40 bedrooms. Still open, it doesn't really qualify for inclusion in a book about pubs, having always been an out-and-out hotel.

However Goodwick still has two pubs, standing shoulder to shoulder. William Morgans opened the **Rose and Crown** in 1827, to be followed by Ann Morgans between 1828 and 1851. She was helped in her latter years by her daughter Mary and her carpenter husband, Ebenezer Davies, and the couple subsequently ran the pub from 1861 to 1884. From 1891 to 1895 the licensee was John Davies, and about that time it became the property of the Fishguard Harbour Company. Jane Evans was in charge by 1901.

From 1906 to 1915 David James kept the pub, his tenure ending when he was arrested in August of that year to face the charge 'that he did feloniously kill and slay one Catherine Jane James'. This was later reduced to manslaughter, which James denied, the victim of the alleged crime being his wife. Carmarthen Winter Assizes was told that a servant girl at the pub had discovered the landlord's wife bruised and bleeding and had helped her to bed where she died a couple of days later from her injuries. James' apparent

Clever signwriting on the Rose and Crown

indifference to his wife's condition weighed against him, but the prosecution case was entirely circumstantial and there was some evidence that Mrs. James liked a drop to drink and had been known to fall and hurt herself in the past. The jury did not even bother to retire in order to bring in a verdict of 'Not guilty'.

In James' enforced absence, John Eynon took over the pub and ran it during the 1920s, while Mrs. Sarah Rosie Eynon was in charge from 1936 to 1939. She had the licensed trade in her blood, having been born at the Seaman's Arms in Haverfordwest and grown up at the Bellevue in that town, the daughter of James and Sarah Ambrey. She was succeeded by John Cawdron who had previously kept the nearby Glendower Hotel. John Jones was the landlord in 1948, followed by Dick Pearson in the 1960s, Joe Coombes in the 1970s, Ken Grace in the 1980s and, more recently, Rob and Meg Salmon. Current licensee is Dave Cattell, and like his predecessors he has had experience of the pub's ghosts, notably the sound of children crying upstairs. Another ghost manifests itself in an unusual way, and is thought to be the spirit of a deceased pub regular who was a lifelong smoker; in an otherwise smoke-free bar, a small cloud of tobacco smoke keeps appearing in the corner where he used to sit... .

The **Sailors' Arms** next door was opened in 1826 by John Volk. By 1828 Martha Volk was in charge and Hugh Griffiths was landlord in 1830. Ann Morgans was there between 1841 and 1861; by a confusing coincidence, for nearly two decades Goodwick's two neighbouring pubs both had landladies called Ann Morgans, both of them widowed and both with a daughter called Mary. Everything changed with the arrival of new landlord Henry Griffiths in the early 1860s, not least the name of the pub which became the **Hope and Anchor**. For the next 30 years Mr. Griffiths combined being a publican with his business as monumental mason, but was given notice to quit in 1896 by his landlord. With the railway in the offing, Mr. Griffiths took the opportunity to open the Glendower Hotel. John Jones was at

The Hope and Anchor began life as the Sailors' Arms

the Hope in 1901 and between 1906 and 1910 the landlord was James Rowe Davies. From 1912 until well into the 1930s John Griffiths managed to hang on to his licence despite regular fines for serving out of hours. Elizabeth Griffiths took over in 1940, followed by Alexander Gracie. Edna Lees was there in the early 1960s before moving to the Pendre in Fishguard, and recent licensees have included Dai James and Terry MacDonald. The current owner is Sean Roche, well-known on the local footballing scene, and the pub has been serving as the unofficial clubhouse of Goodwick United AFC while a new sports complex is under construction on the nearby recreation field.

For many years the **Glendower** across the road was a small family hotel, later becoming a private members' club (this was a common way of getting around the Sunday drinking ban). It is now once more an hotel, but with a popular public bar, and the licensee for the past 20 years has been Bernard Jackman.

*The Glendower opened to coincide with
the arrival of the railway*

Of the **Sailor's Home**, little is known. Margaret Owens kept the pub in 1875 and Mrs. Mary Owen was there in 1891. It is thought to have occupied a building which was pulled down when a new harbour road entrance was created.

CHAPTER ELEVEN

Fishguard

THE SQUARE, HIGH STREET & WEST STREET

The town of Fishguard stands on a headland between the harbours of Goodwick and Lower Town, its narrow streets converging on the market square. As a port and market town, Fishguard has always been well supplied with inns and ale-houses and there were 16 ale-house keepers in the town in 1795, one of them a Captain Thomas Laugharne. In 1803 a traveller named Benjamin Heath Malkin spent a night at Laugharne's establishment and was singularly unimpressed, both with the inn and the town. He wrote in his journal:

> The town of Fiscard is so filthy, so ill-built and so uncivilised as almost to be interesting on those very accounts. The streets are barely passable for any sort of vehicle; the solid rock, worn into frequent holes for the reception of mud, is almost equally offensive to the foot of man or horse. ... It is the only town I ever met from which dung-hills are not excluded.

After being served a rudimentary meal at the inn by the old sea captain, Malkin wrote condescendingly:

> It is but justice to him to say that the deficiencies of his establishment are voluntary and that he means to be civil after the uncouth mode of his fraternity.

Malkin concluded by urging other travellers through Wales to avoid the town altogether and head straight for St. David's. His advice was not taken by the Rev. J. Evans who visited Fishguard the following year and wrote:

> The town is small, consisting principally of cottages, the roofs as well as walls whitewashed, which cleanliness is contrasted by the rugged, dirty streets with a dung-heap at almost every door. A small house, without a wine or spirit licence, is dignified with the name of 'The Inn'.

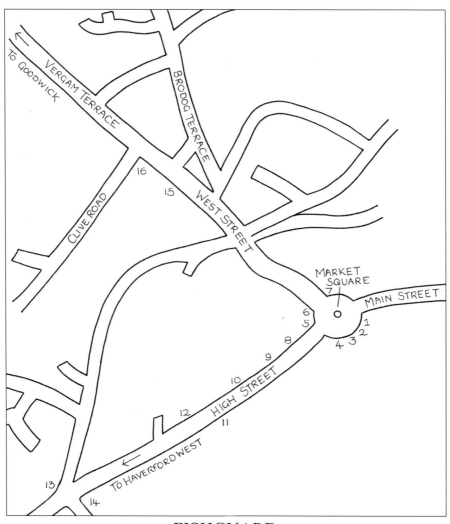

FISHGUARD
THE SQUARE, HIGH STREET & WEST STREET

1	Angel/King's Head	10	Ship and Anchor
2	Dolphin	11	Fishguard and Bristol
3	Farmers' Arms		Traders' Tavern
4	Castle	12	Weary Traveller
5	Black Lion	13	Masons' Arms/Pendre
6	Commercial/Abergwaun	14	Red Lion (2)
7	Royal Oak	15	Sailor's Return
8	Old Coach House/Swan	16	Welcome to Town
9	Bennett's/Red Lion		

By 1810 there were 25 inns and ale-house in Fishguard (including Lower Town) and the figure continued to grow during the 19th century as the town prospered from the sea trade and fishing. At one time it was part of the Kemaes licensing division which issued 85 licences in 1886, and 76 at the start of 1905 – about two-thirds of them in the parish of Fishguard. The town was also a hotbed of illicit drinking. When a well-stocked unlicensed beer-house on The Slade was raided in 1896, the local press noted that this was the 15th such shebeen to be busted in the space of ten years.

In 1909, after the opening of the ferry port, Fishguard and Goodwick became a separate licensing division and in 1925 the twin towns supported 32 licensed premises, while the whole of the rest of Kemaes could only muster 23. This large number of drinking houses, and the associated drunkenness, meant that the town was often a temperance battle-front. A temperance hall (now Theatr Gwaun) had been built in the 1880s and in 1903 there was a concerted campaign to reduce the number of pubs in the Kemaes licensing division, where there was one pub to every 130 people. In Fishguard town itself the average was even worse (or better) with one pub for every 90 residents compared with a national average at the time of one pub for every 326 people.

As the Great War came to an end, so the Fishguard and District Preachers Council went on the warpath, fiercely opposing the renewal of several Fishguard public-house licences. Among the pubs under attack were the Sailors' Arms and the Ship in Lower Fishguard, the Fishguard Arms in Main Street, the Three Crowns in Hamilton Street and the Red Lion and the

*An early postcard view of Fishguard Square with the Farmers' Arms
on the left, the former Castle Inn alongside and
High Street disappearing into the distance*

Bristol Trader in High Street. Some of these pubs survived and two are still going strong today; others were forced to close under the redundancy ruling as the local magistrates felt honour-bound to tackle the rising tide of drunkenness which seems to have increased considerably following the development of the ferry port. Partly as a result of the magistrates' efforts the number of prosecutions for drunkenness in Fishguard and Goodwick fell from 96 in 1914 to 25 in 1926 – although the sharp drop in the strength of beer during this period no doubt played a part.

Since Market Square has long been the centre of activity in the town, it seems appropriate to start with a look at the various hostelries which have stood around the square. One thing to bear in mind is that the square wasn't always the open space we see today; until at least the 1840s there were houses, including a bakery, occupying the centre of the main square, with narrow streets around the perimeter. The market place itself was originally confined to the triangle of land outside the church (rebuilt in the 1850s) where the square funnels into Main Street. As Malkin noted:

> The churchyard affords in some sort a market place. There are hooks
> all along its wall on which meat is exposed. There is no market house
> – the churchyard wall and the door of the public house opposite seem
> the principal stations of traffic.

The public house referred to was presumably the **Angel** – an appropriate name for a pub directly opposite the church. Thomas Richards, a Burgess of the town of Pembroke, kept this pub between 1811 and 1830, in which year a notice in the *Carmarthen Journal* advertised that the Angel was to be let on Lady Day. It stated that this 'well-known and old-established inn' had been 'lately fitted up and repaired at considerable expense' and that a storehouse, granary, malthouse and several fields were to be included in the deal. David Thomas was the landlord from 1840 to 1852, by which time it was a gathering

Re-opening of the Old Establishment,
The FARMERS' ARMS, FISHGUARD.

THIS Old Established House has been re-opened under the management of Mr and Mrs Geo. Moore.

Its convenient situation in the MARKET SQUARE, Fishguard, will recommend it to Visitors.

The Stabling accommodation is extensive and complete. The accommodation for visitors will be found trustworthy.—CHARGES MODERATE.

An advert announcing the re-opening of the Farmers' Arms after a dry period

place of the local Odd Fellows. It had closed by 1860 but seems to have been reopened briefly in the early 1870s as the **King's Head**, the licensee being Albert Furlong. The Angel/King's Head occupied the building which now houses Caffi Abingdon.

Looking from the square, to the immediate right of the Angel was the **Dolphin**. Joel Thomas, a local auctioneer, was the licensee here from 1835 to 1841 but it closed in the mid-1840s and is thought to have been demolished to allow the Town Hall and Market House to be built on the spot.

Moving round the square in a clockwise direction, the currently defunct **Farmers' Arms** would once have stood alongside the Dolphin. The pub had a big malting yard to the rear, running alongside the market hall, and maltster Thomas Jenkins was the landlord from 1822 to 1852. His widow Sarah, who was there from 1858 to 1867, also carried on the malting business. David Vaughan was in charge of pub and maltings from 1871 to 1874, as was the widowed Mary Vaughan in 1881. The pub was closed during the early 1890s, reopening in 1896 under the management of George Moore after its acquisition by the James Brewery of Haverfordwest. The brewery's early tenants included Annie Rees, who there in 1901, and William Griffiths. When he died

The Farmers' had been given the 'exposed stonework' treatment by the time this photograph was taken in 2004

in 1906 his brother John took over, having previously run the Ship in Lower Town. A regular turnover of tenants followed, including Alf Williams, Evan James (formerly of the Ivy Bush) and Henry Davies who was there from 1911 to 1914. The next few years saw yet more comings and goings at the Farmers' before John Underwood, formerly a stoker on the harbour, became landlord during the 1920s. Postwar licensees included Arthur Mayhew and David Thomas who opened a new lounge bar in the 1960s. He was followed by Brian Brooks, Ray Lewis and the long-serving Ron Pitt who was there for 23 years. Since his retirement a few years ago the Farmers' has changed hands a number of times and sadly was closed and boarded up as this book was being prepared for publication.

Next door to the Farmers' was the **Castle** where Peter Davies was the licensee from 1819 to 1839. It was a place of some note; in the 1820s and '30s the county's landowners met there to do business, and in 1832 the Rev. Samuel Fenton called a meeting of local worthies to be held at the inn – the intention being to form a Board of Health in Fishguard. In March 1839 a notice appeared in the local press:

> H.L. Williams respectfully acquaints Commercial Gentlemen, his Friends and the Public generally that he has succeeded Mr. Peter Davies in the management of the above Establishment where he hopes by every attention to their comfort to secure a share of their Patronage. Well-aired beds, choice Wines and Spirits, good Stabling and lock-up Coach house.

Henry Lewis Williams also ran a livery stable, but his stay at the Castle was brief, because he cannot be found in the 1841 census. Instead a 20-year-old innkeeper by the name of Jane Davis appears to be running the Castle, while Mary Francis was in charge in 1844. Five years later Peter Davies was back in command of the Castle, the *Pembrokeshire Herald* noting in 1849 that a housewarming party was to be held for him. This time his tenure was brief and accountant Thomas Davies and his wife Jane were in charge from 1851 to 1854, while John Davies ran the Castle Commercial Hotel from 1858 to 1861. It closed in the 1860s and eventually became the Castle Stores.

During his absence from the Castle, Peter Davies appears to have run a different pub on the Market Square called – somewhat confusingly – the **Old Castle**. This pub closed when he returned to the Castle in 1849.

Across the High Street junction on the west side of the square stood the **Black Lion**. Richard and Mary Barzey were the licensees from 1840 to 1851, but the pub seems to have closed by the time of Mary's death in 1854. No doubt the couple were some relation of Thomas Barzey who was landlord of the **Royal Exchange** from 1819 to 1840. A saddler and harness-maker by trade, Thomas Barzey was also the town's postmaster for much of this time and the Royal Exchange is thought to have stood somewhere on the square; it may even have occupied one of the properties in the centre.

Two doors along from the old Black Lion is the **Abergwaun**, formerly the **Commercial**. An inn of this name appeared in advertisements in the *Carmarthen Journal* of 1813 as the venue for auctions of various Fishguard properties, while the Commercial itself was put up for auction in 1827, when it was described as comprising two parlours, a shop at the front, a bar, seven bedrooms, brewing kitchen, dairy, malthouse and seven-stall stable. It was occupied at the time by Thomas Nicholas.

John Meyler was landlord in 1830, and when he died in 1834 his widow Ann Meyler carried on running the inn until her death in the winter of 1855. The licence passed to Miss Joanna Meyler but she soon departed and a housewarming party was held at the inn early the following year to welcome a young couple as licensees, Mr. and Mrs. Joseph Morris who were both aged about 20. Morris ran the inn until at least 1868, at some stage launching a new omnibus service from the Llwyngwair Arms in Newport to the railway station in Haverfordwest, calling at Fishguard Square. But he died young, and the landlady in 1871 was his widow Martha Morris, aged 33. Also there was Jane James, possibly a sister, and in 1874 the licensees were 'James and Morris'. Farmer and innkeeper John J. Morris was landlord from 1880 to 1884. One of the liveliest days of the year was the half-yearly rent collection when Sir James Cockburn's agent would receive rent from the tenantry.

Commercial Hotel,
The Square, FISHGUARD.

The Leading Family and Commercial Hotel.

Five Minutes from the Sea with Charming Sea View.

Coffee Room :: Private Sitting Room :: Baths (Hot and Cold) :: Billiard Room.

Motor Garage.

Recently improved and replete with every Comfort.

MISS REES, *Proprietress.*

FISHGUARD, Pembrokeshire.

Family and Commercial Hotel and Posting House to let.

The WELL-KNOWN HOTEL called the "COMMERCIAL," at Fishguard, which has been established since 1821, and has to the present time carried on a large and increasing Family, Commercial, and Posting Business. It is well and carefully furnished, with Commodious Billiard Room, and a table complete.

The posting department is in good going order, and very extensive; the Proprietor also holding the Government contract for carriage of Mails between Haverfordwest, Newport and Fishguard. The Proprietor is retiring from business, and is open to give over possession on the 29th day of September.

For further information apply to Wm. George James, Llysyronen, St. Nicholas, Pem.

Two press notices relating to the Commercial, above from 1893 and right from 1909

The inn was kept between 1891 and 1893 by John Davies when it was described as follows: 'Family and commercial hotel and posting house, well aired beds, with extensive sea view, good sea and fresh water fishing, snipe and other shooting'. In September 1893 the Commercial was to let, the proprietor retiring from business.

The Commercial on Fishguard Square with the Express mail coach outside.
(Picture courtesy of Mr. Roy Lewis)

'It is well and carefully furnished with Commodious Billiard Room and table complete' ran the advert. Rachel Davies was licensee in 1895, but a notice appeared in the press the following year to the effect that Miss M.J. Saunders had become the new manager.

In 1900 the Misses Margaret and Elizabeth Rees took over the inn, having previously run the Lamb in Llanboidy where their father John was huntsman to the Powells of Maesgwynne. When they finally gave up the inn in 1936, Mr. J.D. Thomas took over and was mine host during the war years, when guests who left a chink in the curtains at night were regularly in trouble with the ARP warden. John Robert Fox ran the Commercial in 1948,

A multiple-view card showing various aspects of the Abergwaun in the 1970s

The Abergwaun as it looked in 2004

but the name had changed to Abergwaun by 1952 – although it was still advertising 'commercial travellers and businessmen specially catered for'. David Reeves from Aberporth took over in 1959 but only lasted a couple of years before handing on to Brian Duckworth who was followed by Mr. and Mrs. Leonard Wildig who were also connected with the Cambrian in Hamilton Street. Subsequent licensees have included Mick Ogden, Richard Collier and Mick Schnelling. The Abergwaun became an S.A. Brain and Co. house in January 2005 when the Cardiff brewers took over the west Wales inns previously owned by Innkeeper Wales, since when the manager has been Helen Baskerville.

Moving clockwise around the square, the next pub is the historic **Royal Oak.** Hugh Meyler is recorded as being an ale-house keeper in Fishguard from 1795 onwards, and two years later he found himself at the centre of affairs when a rag-tag French invasion force landed at nearby Llanwnda and began to plunder the countryside. Meyler's house became a kind of 'command post' for the assortment of Pembrokeshire volunteers led by Lord Cawdor and Col. Thomas Knox which assembled in Fishguard to repel the French marauders. The ill-conceived invasion quickly fizzled out and it was in an upstairs room of the house that Knox and Lord Cawdor received two of the French officers to negotiate surrender terms. Although Meyler's ale-house is not named in the

*Its cement-wash roof was once a feature of the Royal Oak,
one of Pembrokeshire's best-known pubs*

early records, he is known to have been landlord of the Royal Oak from 1822 onwards, so it is generally assumed that this was the ale-house commandeered by Cawdor. As Commander E.H. Stuart Jones, historian of the French invasion, has written:

> Hugh Meyler was landlord of the Royal Oak for nearly sixty years, and died there on 20 March 1846, aged eighty-eight. For the last forty-five years he had been confined to the house.

Mary Hughes (née Meyler) was the landlady from 1850 to 1858, while Thomas Rees was landlord from 1861 to 1874 followed by William Rees. From 1881 to 1895 the landlord was Mark Howells and from 1896 to 1931 the pub was kept by David Richards. His daughter, Mary Thomas, was licensee in the 1930s and '40s, and in 1940 she was fined ten shillings for not observing the black-out restrictions. Doris Hoffmann had charge in the late 1950s and early 1960s, Peter Williams was there in the 1980s and local café proprietor Tony Conti – famed for his ice creams – also had a period in charge of the Oak. In 2001 the pub was sold by David and Mary Whelan

A recent view of the Royal Oak

110

to S.A. Brain, the Cardiff brewers, and their first tenants were Paul and Debbie Johnson who also ran the Old Coach House in High Street. It was music-loving licensee Dai Crowther who cemented the Oak's current position as the focus of the town's folk festival and the headquarters of a thriving folk club; the pub also houses a collection of artefacts associated with the French landing.

One of the busiest roads leading away from the square is High Street, for many years the start of the turnpike road to Haverfordwest. With just a couple of exceptions, the pubs in this street tended to be on the right-hand side of the street as one heads out of town. One of these was kept by John Harris in 1861. It was the first house in High Street but was short-lived and the name hasn't come down to us.

The first notable pub on the right was the **Swan** kept by Sarah Davies from 1805 to 1807 and by Sarah Williams from 1813 until her death, aged 83, in 1845. Landlord from 1846 to 1852 was Captain John Evans who played a leading role in the rescue of the crew of the *Sir Peregrine* which went ashore near Fishguard Fort during the 'Great Storm of 1846' when many ships were lost. The Swan Hotel Field behind the pub was often used for agricultural sales and was the original site of Fishguard Show which began in 1857. By that time another mariner named Benjamin Davies was keeping the Swan and it was home to the Loyal Gwain Lodge of Odd Fellows which had opened a lodge room here in the 1850s. Davies remained licensee until well into the 1870s, but by 1882, when 120 Odd Fellows sat down to dinner at the inn, Samuel James held the licence. Carpenter Dan Francis was in charge in 1889 and landlord from 1891 to 1907 was William Evans. John Williams held the licence from 1912 to 1914 followed by David and Mary John. It then became the Miles family pub for some years, with Mrs. Hannah Miles holding the licence from 1917 to 1923 followed by John Miles, Arthur Laugharne Miles and Mrs. Eleanor Miles. Albert Howells was there in the early '60s, followed by Jack Richards – 'Jack the Swan'.

Somewhere behind the murals, flags and floral displays is the Old Coach House

The Swan had a fairly small bar at this time, but when Paul and Debbie Johnson took over as licensees in 1987 they made a number of alterations, extending the bar area, creating a restaurant and changing the name to **Old Coach House**. By the time Alan Phillips and Paul Mason had taken over in 2003 the inn had become famed for its food, and also for the remarkable large-scale murals by local artists Leon Olin and Sylvia Gainsford depicting episodes from the French invasion which covered the front of the building.

Across the road at one time was the **Jolly Sailor**. Sarah Vaughan launched this short-lived ale-house in 1827 and was still there in 1835, but the pub had closed by 1840.

Back on the right-hand side is the building where a schoolmaster named James Davies opened the **Red Lion** in 1826 and ran it for a couple of years. However he soon discovered that the wine and spirit business was more to his taste and for the next 25 years conducted a successful wine merchant's business from the premises. In the late 1840s his daughter Elizabeth married a rising star of her father's business, a young man called George Bennett, and it was he who ran the company for over 40 years, expanding it all the while. Following the death of George in November 1888, Bennett's Old Irish Whisky and Foreign Wine Stores was run by his son William C. Bennett and nephew Thomas G. Bennett, both of whom had been involved in the business for some years. According to an account in 1893:

> The firm's premises are centrally situated in the High Street, to which thoroughfare they have a lengthy frontage. Immediately within the principal entrance is the office and general business department which is flanked on the left by three huge spirit vats, each capable of holding 400 gallons. The stores occupy a position on the left of the main entrance and cover a considerable area of ground, They are equipped with every requisite for maturing a large and valuable stock. Messrs. Bennett and Co. import their wine direct from Portugal, Spain, France and other wine-growing countries of the continent, receiving their consignments direct from vessels in the harbour at Fishguard.

When William Bennett died aged 48 in 1902, his cousin Thomas G. Bennett carried on the trade. Born in Saundersfoot, Thomas G. had worked as a draper in Dinas Cross and as a commercial traveller before marrying his cousin Hannah, George Bennett's daughter. This cemented his place in the family firm and he ran the business until his retirement, aged 80, in 1930. During this time George Bennett and Co. acquired a number of

The Lion in High Street welcomed charabanc parties

112

licensed premises along the north Pembrokeshire coast, while an on-licence was obtained for part of the High Street premises which became known as the **Lion** – an echo of its original name. It was extensively altered in 1932 and two years later the company was advertising that Bennett's Lion Hotel had facilities 'for receiving and accommodating both ladies and gentlemen' and that charabanc parties of up to 100 were catered for. Following T.G. Bennett's retirement his son Thomas had taken over, but two years later he moved to Cardiff, handing over the reins to his sister Mrs. W.R. Howell.

Bennett's in its days as a wine bar

By the 1960s the attractive premises had become a wine bar known as **Bennett's**, the business being run by Thomas George Bennett Howell and William Bennett Howell – the fifth generation. No longer in the family, the pub has since become **Bennett's Navy Tavern** and Peter and Christine Lloyd have been mine hosts for the past 17 years.

Bennett's Navy Tavern, pictured in 2004

A couple of doors along was the **Three Tuns**. The landlady from 1823 to 1825 was Elizabeth Eynon, James Jenkins was in charge in 1828 and the last licensee appears to have been Benjamin Williams, a saddler, who was there in 1835. A little further along were the **Cross** run by James Eynon between 1835 and 1867 and the short-lived **Groesgoch** where Thomas Phillips was landlord from 1867 to 1871.

No missing the Ship and Anchor, pictured in its latter days as a free house

Perhaps one of these became the present-day **Ship and Anchor** where Henry Garnon was landlord between 1891 and 1920. Ann Garnon was in charge by 1930, Olwen Brown was there from 1934 to 1940 and subsequent licensees have included Olive Moon, David Bryan, Brian Henry, local cricketer Geraint Phillips and the long-serving Arthur Aylward who was in charge from 1980 to 2005. He sold the pub to Celtic Inns, since when it has been run by various managers.

On the other side of the road, just above the police station, was the **Fishguard and Bristol Traders' Tavern** – often referred to as simply the 'Bristol Trader'. William Woodcock was the landlord in 1867 and James Gwynne kept the pub from 1871 to 1891, coupling this with his day job as the local rate collector. William Griffiths had charge in

The Bristol Trader closed in 1919 and no hint remains of its former function

1901 but left at Michaelmas 1902, after which the Swansea Old Brewery seems to have had great difficulty finding a steady tenant with George Williams, Benjamin Morgan, Lewis Llewellyn, Adolf Hoffman, Michael Holmes, John Symmons, Joseph Mills and Richard Wigley all having come and gone by 1916. No doubt this ridiculous turnover of licensees helped persuade the local magistrates to close the pub in 1919 under the redundancy ruling, with compensation of £287 being distributed. It later became the home of writer D.J. Williams (*The Old Farmhouse*) and is now a private house called The Old Pumphouse.

Back on the north side of the street, there were a couple of pubs in the terrace just before the vicarage. The **Weary Traveller** was kept by Mary Evans from 1844 to 1851 while next door was a pub kept by Elinor Morris at the time of the 1851 census. The evidence suggests that this was the **Fishguard and Haverfordwest Arms** which the trade directories indicate was kept from 1844 to 1852 by a weaver named John Morris. Perhaps the reason his name did not appear on the 1851 census was because he had been carted off to the lunatic asylum in 1849 after attempting to commit suicide with a corkscrew!

The **Masons' Arms** stood close to the toll-gate across the Haverfordwest turnpike road. The building itself seems to date from the 1790s and was at one time part of the Tregroes estate, being occupied by 'John Davies, Yeoman'. It had become a pub by 1851, the landlord between then and 1876 being stonemason Thomas Lewis who was no doubt responsible for the name. In 1876 the freehold of the property was put up for auction following the death of the owner, Elizabeth Harries of Lochmeyler. Included in the sale were a stable and coach house and a nearby field where livestock sales were held. Amos Evans was there in 1880 and he was the one who changed the name to **Pendre**, remaining landlord until at least 1891; there were still Evanses at the pub in 1898. Martha Young, innkeeper and farmer, was licensee in 1901. Mrs. Martha Evans kept the pub in 1906 and her son-in-law John Davies was the landlord from 1907 to 1923. Miss Winifred Mourley was licensee from 1931 to 1938, becoming Mrs.

The Pendre can be seen at the bottom left of this early aerial view, with the tollgate cottage alongside. The Red Lion is in the top right-hand corner

115

Winifred Harries on her marriage to Ailwyn Harries in 1945. In 1955 they sold the pub for £2,500 to Mrs. Agnes Mary Morgan who in turn sold it for £4,500 to Edna Lees of the Hope and Anchor in Goodwick in 1963. When she died three years later her husband William took over. Mike and Pam Starkey had a dozen or more years in charge and the present licensees of this popular local are Charlotte and Jason Morrell.

Diagonally opposite the Pendre and set back from the road was the **Red Lion** on the junction with Feidr Gongol. A carrier named David Tudor was landlord from 1858 to 1891. In 1896 the freehold of the inn changed hands at auction, the pub and two cottages being sold as one lot for £200. Taliesyn and Harriet Williams were there from 1901, Mrs. Williams being the licensee between 1913 and 1938. During this time she survived a call to have the place closed in 1920 on the usual grounds of redundancy. Morfydd Williams was in charge by the 1960s but the Red Lion closed in the early 1970s and is now a private house.

The Pendre in the days when Winifred Mourley was licensee.
(Picture courtesy of Mr. Philip Davies)

A recent photograph of the Pendre

The former Red Lion, still looking the part despite being closed for nearly 40 years

Returning to Market Square, and again moving clockwise round the square, the next road radiating away leads past the top of Penslade and on via West Street and Vergam Terrace to Goodwick, a route which took on increased importance when the Irish ferry port opened. The **Mariners** (sometimes **Three Mariners**) seems to have been located between the Square and the top of Slade Road, an area much redeveloped over the years. There is a mention of the pub in 1813 and Owen Williams was landlord from 1824 to 1827, followed by Elizabeth Williams. John Thomas was landlord of the Mariners from 1840 to 1852, followed by his sister Elinor Evans in 1861. The pub looks to have closed by 1867 and to have disappeared altogether by 1871.

The last of the West Street pubs to close was the **Sailor's Return**. Elinor Williams kept this pub from the early 1860s to 1874, followed by Miss Mary Williams in 1881. When he wasn't at sea, mariner John Lewis was landlord on and off from about 1891 to 1898, in which year he was charged with drunkenness and beating his wife Mary – very possibly the aforementioned Miss Williams. She was granted a separation order and became the innkeeper outright, remaining in charge until 1917. Mrs. Anna Mary Owen took over and was still there in 1923; during the war she fell foul of the Emergency Wheat and Rice (Restriction) Order, her alleged crime being to waste four and a half

Children pose for the photographer outside the Sailor's Return

The Sailor's Return in its new guise as the town's rugby clubhouse

ounces of bread. (She denied the charge, which was dismissed). She was followed by Benjamin Jones in 1926. Fishguard-born, Ben Jones was a keep-fit fanatic and became light-heavyweight boxing champion of Wales in 1912, going on to defend his title four times before the war ended his boxing career. He then became one of Fishguard's best-known licensees, keeping the pub for a quarter of a century. William Davies took over as licensee when Jones retired in 1948. John and Mona Lewis then ran the Sailors' Return for a number of years, handing over to John and Pat Phillips who turned out to be the final licensees, the pub closing in 1993 and reopening the following year as the clubhouse of Fishguard Rugby Club – a role it still serves.

The **Welcome to Town** was further along, possibly on the corner of Clive Road, and the name suggests it was once the first house to be encountered on the way into town from Goodwick. Maria Williams looks to have been the licensee in 1861 and it was described as a 'house of good character' when Martha Williams held the licence from 1867 to 1871. William Collins was the landlord in 1874, after which there are no further references.

CHAPTER TWELVE

Fishguard

MAIN STREET, HAMILTON STREET & PARK STREET

Main Street leads away from the Market Square before winding down a steep hill to the bridge across the Gwaun at Lower Town. (Part of the street went by the unfortunate name of Ballock Street for a time, but this was wisely changed). Many of the houses here were built in the early 19th century when the shipping trade was at its height, the merchants and ship-owners erecting their fine houses looking out to sea while the men who actually crewed the ships lived in the humble cottages of Lower Town or Wallis.

Early in 1804 the Aberdovey-built sloop *Endeavour*, on passage from Bristol to Lancashire, became stranded on Goodwick Sands. An advertisement appeared in the *Cambrian* newspaper on 21 April 1804 stating that the *Endeavour* was to be sold by auction for the benefit of the underwriters, the sale to take place at the **Fort and Castle** inn. Few other references exist to this inn, but it is thought to have stood on the seaward side of Main Street, opposite the entrance to Hamilton Street.

It could have been this house which became the **Great Western** in 1847 when John Furlong left the New Inn near Rosebush and took a lease on the building

GREAT WESTERN HOTEL,

Family, Commercial, & Posting House,

FISHGUARD, PEMBROKESHIRE.

T. FURLONG AND FAMILY, *Proprietors.*

T. FURLONG AND FAMILY, late of the Nantyddwylan Arms Inn, midway between Haverfordwest and Cardigan, avail themselves of the present opportunity of informing the Gentry, Tourists, and Commercial Gentlemen visiting this delightful Watering Place, that they will find the above Hotel replete with every comfort, combined with unremitting attention.

POST HORSES, PHAETONS, & GIGS

SUPPLIED ON THE SHORTEST NOTICE, AND ON THE MOST REASONABLE TERMS.

Press notice announcing the opening of the Great Western.

(Image courtesy of Mrs. Sybil Edwards)

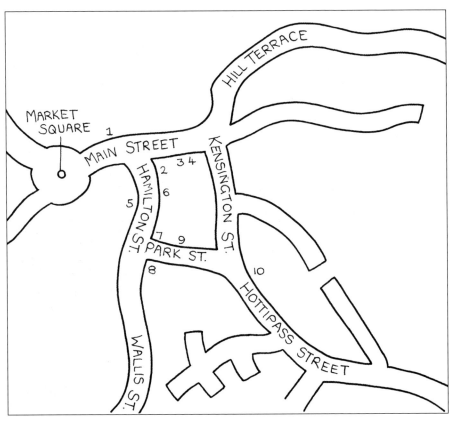

FISHGUARD
MAIN STREET, HAMILTON STREET, PARK STREET

1	Great Western	6	Ivy Bush
2	Three Crowns	7	Butchers' Arms/Cambrian
3	Fishguard Arms	8	Roch Castle
4	Cambrian/Globe	9	Prince of Wales
5	Plough	10	Golden Lion

Main Street, with the Great Western on the left and Albert Furlong's Temperance Hotel on the right.
(Picture courtesy of Mr. Philip Davies)

which he fitted up as a commercial inn and posting house. In 1856 the freehold was purchased from the Manorowen estate for £405 by a Mr. Morris of Letterston, father of Joseph Morris, the licensee of the Commercial Inn; three years later he sold the freehold to John Furlong for £340. Furlong remained in charge until at least 1871 and his widow Caroline Furlong ran the pub in 1874. In January 1876 the Great Western changed hands for £1,310, the *Welshman* newspaper speculating that the high price was connected with the increased importance of Fishguard and Goodwick as a 'watering place'. From 1880 to 1903, when he retired due to ill health, Robert Burge was in charge; during the early part of his tenure, when the nearest railway station was at Rosebush, two coaches left the inn every morning, crossing the Preselis to meet the trains. From 1906 to 1911 Mrs. Sarah Pryce was the landlady, offering 'baths hot and cold' and 'posting in all its branches'. W. John Owen took over in 1918, but it closed as a pub soon afterwards. Local solicitor Walter Williams converted the premises into offices, but for many years afterwards country people on a rare visit to town would wander in off the street and demand a pint of ale.

Diagonally opposite, just past the Hamilton Street junction, was Furlong's Temperance Hotel where Albert Furlong – son of John and formerly of the King's Head – also operated a thriving coach and carriage business from about 1880 until his death in 1905.

Great Western
Hotel
(FAMILY AND COMMERCIAL).

Centrally situated, with Splendid
View overlooking Harbour and Bay.

Every convenience and most comfortable for Family or single Visitors.

BATHS - HOT AND COLD.
PRIVATE SITTING ROOMS.

Stabling.   ::   Posting in all its Branches.

MOTOR ACCOMMODATION.

DAILY CATERING for VISITORS
LUNCHEONS. :: DINNERS. :: TEAS.

Hotel 'Bus from Station meets all Trains.

S. PRYCE, Proprietress.

*Advert for the Great Western
in 1909*

*The Great Western in Main Street
in its hey-day*

Further down on the right-hand side, is the **Fishguard Arms**. A pub of that name was mentioned in the *Carmarthen Journal* in 1822 and Ann Sambruck held the licence from 1827 to 1830, followed by Mary Griffiths in 1835. There is then such a long gap in the records that the present Fishguard Arms may not be the same place at all. Thomas Berry kept an unnamed pub hereabouts in 1840, but it wasn't until the 1860s that a butcher named William Lewis and his wife Mary can be firmly identified as the licensees of the present pub. Mary was landlady from 1875 to 1901, Benjamin Lewis was the landlord in 1906 followed by Thomas Williams between 1907 and 1920. The pub was recommended for closure under the redundancy ruling in 1918, but escaped the axe, apparently because the compensation committee had used up all its funds for the year and didn't have enough left in the kitty to recompense the landlord. W.F. Rees was behind the bar in 1923.

Boxing fan Henry Gibbons and his wife Martha ('Mattie') were there by the late 1930s and the walls began to be covered with signed photographs of boxing stars and also of local wrestling hero 'Bulldog' Bill Garnon. It was a marvellous place in the days when the widowed Mrs. Mattie Gibbons held sway in the 1960s and '70s. An inveterate gossip, Mrs. Gibbons discouraged women from visiting the pub as she enjoyed being the centre of attention herself. Crews from visiting Royal Navy ships would always head straight

A narrow sign for a narrow pub –
the Fishguard Arms

for the Fishguard Arms where Mrs. Gibbons would allow herself to be persuaded to play the piano for a sing-song. She was helped in the running of the pub by her daughter Glenda who later succeeded her, and subsequent licensees of this wonderfully unspoiled and traditional pub have included Eileen Gibson, Martin Hall and Gerald Parry.

Between the late 1850s and early 1860s the **Cambrian** stood just below the Fishguard Arms. John Eaton Griffiths was a tailor by day and a pub landlord by night, and at some stage in the 1860s he relocated his pub to Hamilton Street where it still survives. The former Cambrian then appears to have become the **Globe**. Pubs of that name had been kept in Fishguard by Ann Roberts from 1830 to 1835 and by Dinah Davies in the 1850s, but there seems nothing to indicate that these had any connection with the later establishment in Main Street which was run by three generations of the Phillips family. Plasterer David Phillips was landlord from 1867 to 1884 followed by Mrs. Charlotte Phillips who was landlady from 1891 to 1895. Their son Tom and his wife Sarah then took over, Sarah running the pub on her own for a number of years following her husband's death. In 1929 their son John Pardoe Phillips succeeded to the Globe and – being a painter and decorator – made a number of alterations, introducing 'modern

*The original Globe on the right had been doubled in size
by the inclusion of the property on the left when this picture
was taken in 2002. It has since closed*

comforts while preserving the beauty of the antique structure'. In 1932 he collapsed and died at the age of 44, ending his family's connection with the pub. Elizabeth Bowen and then Mary Ellen Young held the licence in the early '30s followed by Glen Moody, a heavyweight boxer and a member of a family of pugilists and publicans, several of whom feature in another book in this series, *The Pubs of Haverfordwest and Milford Haven.* Dilys Moody took over in 1940, mainly because her husband was away on active service. Mr. Llwyd James was there in the 1950s followed by Mrs. Sarah James in 1960, but Mrs. Doris Pratt had taken over by the following year.

The Globe was extended in 1974 with the incorporation of the house next door to create the Black Fox bar, the name deriving from various artefacts from a Dutch pilot cutter of that name which were incorporated into the new bar. Richard and Sonia Hall were licensees for a number of years, with bar duties usually being carried out by their business partner, a German national by the name of Heinz who was a very popular figure in the town. The Globe became one of the county's top live music venues under the next licensee Viv Judah (despite the ever-increasing bureaucratic restrictions imposed on pub music), but it closed as a pub when she retired four years ago. The original part then became a restaurant called the Coast, but that too is no longer open.

124

Not far along Main Street from the square is a junction from where roads lead out of town towards either Scleddau, the Gwaun Valley or over the moors to Maenclochog and Rosebush. This was the ancient gateway to the town from the south and east and the quarter was packed with ale-houses where hill farmers and drovers would gather on market days.

The Three Crowns was tucked into a corner

Tucked into a corner on the left, at the beginning of Hamilton Street, was the **Three Crowns.** A mariner named Benjamin Richards opened this pub in 1805 and ran it, on and off, until 1826. Thomas Hughes took over the licence in the late 1820s and was still pouring the pints in 1871 at the age of 67, also acting as grocer and 'dealer in sundries'. The ubiquitous Albert Furlong acquired the business in the 1870s and there are vague records of Josiah Davies and James Davies keeping the pub in the 1880s. James Lewis was landlord from 1891 to 1900, during which time it became a Swansea Old Brewery house. His widow Mary was in charge in 1901, but when she died two years later a campaign was launched by local temperance supporters for the pub to be closed. A meeting in the nearby Market Hall of various temperance and religious organisations ended with a delegation being appointed to travel to Eglwyswrw magistrates court to oppose the transfer of the licence to Mrs. Margaret Lamb. However their protests fell on deaf ears and Mrs. Lamb was still there in 1906. Eleanor Williams and Annie Gillett each held the licence at some stage, while from 1914 to 1924 Mrs. Hannah Williams was in charge of this little pub which had no bar, the beer being carried in jugs from the back room. The Three Crowns remained a target for the anti-drink campaigners and three times it was put forward for closure under the redundancy ruling, surviving in 1919 – when it was described as 'scrupulously clean, but structurally unfit' – and also in 1922. It was finally forced to close in 1924, the police pointing out that there were seven other licensed premises within 108 yards. It is now a private house called Ty Twt; recent alterations have disclosed that several of the original timbers used in the building came from a ship.

The former Ivy Bush has been divided into two houses

In the terrace known as Hamilton Place stood the **Ivy Bush**. A pub of that name was opened in 1826 by a builder and stonemason called George Lamb. There is then such a gap in the records that it cannot be stated with any certainty that when a widow named Mary Symmons or Simons ran a pub by the name of the Ivy Bush from 1851 to 1861, that it was the same place. William Owen kept the pub between 1867 and 1880 and Mrs. Ann Owen was the landlady from 1884 to 1891. The landlady from 1895 to 1907 was her daughter Miss Martha Ann Owen, followed in 1908 by Elizabeth Thomas. Mrs. Caroline James held the licence in 1910 when various structural alterations and improvements were carried out to what was a fairly large town pub. Josh Davies was landlord from 1912 to 1919, followed by Arthur and Elizabeth Bailey in the early 1920s. Mary Ann Thomas was there from 1926 to 1936 and Charles Thomas was landlord during and after the war. It subsequently became the Jones family pub, with Sarah Jones being in charge in the 1960s, eventually succeeded by her son Brian. The Ivy Bush closed in 1989 when the property was converted into two houses, with further development planned for the brew-house at the rear.

Opposite the Ivy Bush is the site of the long-lost **Plough** which was opened in 1826 by a farmer named Daniel Bowen. He was still there in 1835 but a map of 1839 referred to it as 'Old Plough'. Then in March 1843 an advert appeared in the local press as follows: 'Fishguard. To be let. A new and commodious, well-built house, formerly called the Plough Inn'.

Stephen Nicholas, publican and coach proprietor from Maenclochog, kept the **Butchers' Arms** from 1850 to 1861. It was a little further along the left-hand side of Hamilton Street, on the corner with Park Street. The pub changed hands in the 1860s and so did the name, John Eaton Griffiths arriving from the **Cambrian** in Main Street and bringing his signboard with him. A tailor by trade, Griffiths kept the pub until at least 1871, followed by his widow Sarah in 1881. Captain Levi Thomas was the long-serving landlord from 1884 to 1914 and he seems to have been a remarkable character. A guide-book of 1909 recorded:

Capt. Levi Thomas in the doorway of the Cambrian in about 1909.
(Picture courtesy of Mr. Philip Davies)

The Cambrian Inn is renowned throughout Wales for its quaint and pretty bar and collection of curios which the host never tires of showing to those who are interested in relics.

These curios included various relics of the French landing of 1797, a Japanese rifle, Zulu arrows and 'a clock still going after a three-day sojourn at the bottom of the sea in the year 1875'.

Joseph Davies was there from 1917 to 1920, being succeeded by George Chamberlain. A fire destroyed the premises in August 1934, two people dying after being trapped in an upstairs room; they were Mr. Chamberlain's wife and a 12-year-old grandson. The Cambrian was rebuilt and was operational the following year when Christina Inez Griffiths took over the licence. George Griffiths was licensee in the 1930s and '40s when the pub was known for having its own boxing gym at the back. The freehold was offered for sale by auction in 1948, but the property was withdrawn with the last bid on the table being £4,500. Cyril Cross, sometime licensee of the Abergwaun, took over in 1960 and immediately set about making a few alterations and improvements. Leonard Wildig took over the business in the late 1960s, the pub being run by his daughter Susan while resident chef Amon Moran presided over the newly-established 'Gourmet Room' with its portable dance floor. (Mr. Wildig also ran the Abergwaun). Phil Stead was at

*The Cambrian as it looks today, having been rebuilt in the 1930s
following a tragic fire*

the 'Cambo' in the late '80s and early '90s, followed by Edna May Howells and current licensee Graham Lloyd.

On the opposite corner – the corner of Park Street and Wallis Street – was the **Roch Castle**, often seen with the unfortunate mis-spelling 'Roach Castle'. Thomas Howells kept a pub hereabouts in the 1850s, while landlady from 1867 to 1891 was Mrs. Mary Fowler. The **Prince of Wales** was on the left-hand side of Park Street. Henry Bevan, a clogmaker from Llandeloy, was the landlord from 1844 to 1867, probably as a tenant of maltster John Smyth who had a large malting yard and stables nearby. Subsequent licensees included William Morgan, Thomas Absalom and John Thomas. By the early 1880s the pub and the maltings had been acquired by Robert Lewis to accommodate his growing business as wine merchant, maltster and hop and seed merchant. Lewis,

*This was once the Prince of Wales,
later a wine and spirit store*

128

from Begelly, had been an assistant at George Bennett's wine stores before going into trade in his own right and becoming a successful businessman with an interest in a number of local pubs. He died in 1895, after which his son Robert Parcell Lewis carried on the business, building up a small portfolio of tied houses which included the Royal Oak in Newport, the Square and Compass near Croesgoch and the Bridgend at Cilgwyn. By this time the Prince of Wales was no longer functioning as a pub but was the wine and spirit depot and bottling plant for the business. In 1930, Lewis disposed of all his tied houses and the Park Street premises to George's of Haverfordwest which had been looking to gain a foothold in north Pembrokeshire. Thereafter the Prince of Wales seems to have been known simply as 'The Stores'. It is now Walter Brearley House.

The **Grand Seignior** was also in Park Street. The unusual name refers to the former Sultans of Turkey and was once a popular coffee house sign in London, eventually spreading to inns and taverns. (The more common Turk's Head has the same origins). In 1849, Thomas Beddoe, formerly of the Grand Seignior, victualler, draper, grocer, ironmonger and general dealer, as well as sometime blacksmith in Llanychaer, appeared before the county court as an insolvent debtor. He had run the Grand Seignior in 1844 while James Harries seems to have been licensee in 1851.

Beyond the junction with Kensington Street is Hottipass Street, the name thought to be a corruption of 'haut pass' or 'high pass', indicating that this was the way to the mountains. There were a couple of pubs in the terrace, notably the **Golden Lion** where a baker named Mrs. Mary Adams from Cilgerran was the landlady from 1867 to 1899, latterly as a tenant of local wine merchant Robert Lewis. It had closed by 1901 and in 1905 a 30 shillings-a-week colliery fireman named Lewis Wilson of Porth in the Rhondda

tried unsuccessfully at the county court to recover possession of the Golden Lion, stated then to be unlicensed. It was reported that he had been working at the case for 20 years and had travelled 17,000 miles and spent £300 on his claim. He produced 81 certificates to back up his title to the property, which he apparently claimed as heir in law to his great grandfather.

It is believed that this house was once the Golden Lion; certainly the former coach arch (now occupied by two doors) on the left adds credence to this theory

William Williams had kept a Golden Lion in Fishguard from 1809 to 1823 and builder and stonemason Daniel Evans was landlord from 1825 to 1830. A noted builder of chapels, including Hermon and Tabernacle in Fishguard, he later moved to St. Dogmael's and will be encountered again in a later chapter. It could well be that this was the same Golden Lion as the one in Hottipass Street, but there is no chain of evidence to prove this. The **Letters** was another Hottipass hostelry; Mary Thomas held the licence in 1835 and was still living in Hottipass Street in 1871 when she was described as 'former innkeeper'.

Inevitably, given the paucity of records, there are several generally short-lived Fishguard inns and ale-houses which have defied all efforts to pin them down. Several date from the 1820s and 1830s, a period of house-building in the town when the scattered cottages of Malkin's day were being replaced by terraced streets, so there would have been plenty of thirsty labourers around to provide trade. These 'lost' pubs include the **Green Dragon** where James Jenkins was licensee in 1830; the **Fleece** where David Williams was the landlord from 1823 to 1826, followed by Mary Williams in 1827-28; the **Rope and Anchor** run by Elizabeth Thomas from 1824 to 1828; the **St. David's Arms** where William James was landlord in 1835; the **Ship Aground** run by Thomas Gould from 1824 to 1830 and by Mary Lloyd in 1835; a second **Ship Aground** recorded in 1826 with William Richards as licensee; and the **White Hart** which was another of the new ale-houses opened in Fishguard in 1826. A joiner named James Owen was the first licensee and he was still there in 1828.

Three Swans appear in the 1844 trade directory, one in Main Street, one in Lower Town and a third **Swan**, now untraceable, kept by Ann Davies. The **Blue Boar** was mentioned in an advertisement in the *Carmarthen Journal*, 1822, while the *Welshman* of November 1852 reported that the Court Leet and Court Baron for the Manor and Borough of Fishguard were held at the **Crown** inn, presumably in Fishguard. Perhaps this was the **Rose and Crown** which was run by David Thomas in the 1830s before he moved to the Angel. David Lewis was landlord of the **Alma** in 1875, while the **Ship and Anchor** run by Ann Thomas in 1867 does not appear to be the later pub of that name in High Street.

CHAPTER THIRTEEN

Lower Fishguard and the Gwaun Valley

At the mouth of the River Gwaun is Lower Town, once the port of Fishguard and now picturesque enough to have been used for the filming of 'Under Milk Wood'. Herring fishing was once the main occupation of the mariners of Lower Town, but there was also a lively trade in the export of wheat and corn. By 1792 there were 50 coasting vessels based at the port and in 1837 there were 28 shipowners and 42 master mariners living in Fishguard, although not too many of them chose to live in Lower Town which in its early days was a rather seedy collection of cottages and small houses clustered around the harbour. Indeed, early visitors queued up to be rude about the 'miserable port' with its 'lower orders comprising fishermen, mariners and smugglers'.

Lower Fishguard, showing the old Newport Road snaking up to the top right and the new road around the headland which replaced it in 1913

131

Shipbuilding, limeburning and milling were also carried on, while all traffic to Newport and Cardigan had to pass this way, over the narrow bridge and out past Parc-y-Morfa turnpike gate; originally it would have taken the steep and awkward Newport Road, but this was superseded in 1913 by a new road around the headland. All this local and passing trade meant that there were plenty of dingy taverns and pot-houses scattered among the cottages – seven in 1830. Trying to pin down the whereabouts of these taverns has been a headache; even the census returns – normally a reliable reference – are relatively useless since the early enumerators seem to have wandered around almost at random, lumping all the streets together as 'Lower Fishguard'. Therefore a certain amount of educated guesswork has had to be resorted to.

At least we can be fairly certain that the first ale-house to be encountered on descending the hill from Fishguard would have been the **Bridgend** where Daniel Jones was licensee from 1835 to 1840. In 1848 the Court Leet and Court Baron of the Town and Borough of Fishguard met to do business at the Bridgend Inn where the landlady was Elizabeth Rees. (The Courts Leet

Rees Bowen outside the Ship in Lower Town.
(Picture courtesy of the Ship)

and Courts Baron were something of a feudal throwback to the days when the Marcher Lords held sway over the Barony of Kemaes and were forums where freeholders and burgesses could air their grievances. Usually held in pubs right across the Barony, they later became largely ceremonial). Elizabeth Rees was still running the Bridgend in 1852 while Dinah Jones was the landlady from 1867 to 1871; it must have closed soon afterwards.

Turning left soon after crossing the bridge the narrow street quickly forks, the right-hand road going up towards Dinas and the left-hand fork leading to the quay. On the right is the **Ship**, the last survivor of the Lower Town boozers and a marvellously unspoiled pub which still retains much of its original character. Martha Jones ran the pub from 1817 into the 1840s, followed by Elizabeth Jones who was there until at least 1852. At some stage the pub seems to have closed and become a private house, but it was reopened in about 1867 after being purchased by enterprising businessman Thomas Davies of Railway House, Fishguard; the pub may also have been enlarged at this time to take in the cottage bakery which stood next door.

The Ship appears to comprise two – and perhaps even three – terraced cottages joined together

Thomas James was landlord from 1871 to 1879 followed in turn by James Jones and Jonah Phillips. William Griffiths was licensee in 1895 and John Griffiths kept the pub from 1901 to 1906 before moving up the hill to the Farmers' Arms; he was replaced by Rees Bowen, a Glamorgan man who had come to Fishguard to work on the new harbour at Goodwick. And it is thanks to Mr. Bowen that the pub is still open, because in 1919 the Ship was targeted by the temperance brigade who tried to have it closed on the grounds that it was 'not required'. Mr. Bowen – backed by his landlords, the Swansea Old Brewery – fought every inch of the way and eventually persuaded the redundancy committee not to scuttle the Ship; a rare victory for the licensed trade. The following year, however, Mr. Bowen was fined 40s. plus costs for 'selling rum at a price above that fixed by the Spirit Prices and Description Order, 1919'. He was still running the pub in 1935.

David Davies took over in 1948, while the best remembered licensees of recent years are Dilwyn and Morwen George who ran the Ship for a number of years and were the ones who bought it from the brewery, so that it is now a free house. They also took out the old bar counter and replaced it with the present long wooden counter (rescued from a shop) which is a feature of the pub. Since then, those who have stood behind this counter as licensees include John and Eleanor Channon, Tony and Sue Green, and current licensees Richard and Jan Davies. The pub's long and interesting history is reflected in the vast collection of photographs and memorabilia decorating the walls, much of it of a maritime flavour but some devoted to the filming of 'Under Milk Wood' in 1971 and to the day the film's narrator Richard Burton called in for a pint.

The terrace beyond the Ship once supported several pubs. This is thought to have been the Sailors' Arms

A couple of doors along was the later of Lower Town's two **Sailors' Arms**. This also appears to have opened in about 1867 after the property was bought by Thomas Davies of Railway House; perhaps the trading boom which followed the opening of the new pier in 1862 by the Fishguard Harbour Improvement Company had encouraged him to invest in the little port. Mary Harries kept the Sailors' Arms from 1871 to 1881 and Enoch Evans, her son-in-law, was the landlord between 1884 and 1916; when it closed isn't known, but it can't have been long after this date.

The next pub along in the row was probably the **Newport Arms** kept in 1851 by Mary Lewis and by Mary Ann Evans between 1858 and 1871; it seems to have closed soon afterwards, perhaps the two new pubs just down the road had taken away all the trade. Mariner Henry Symmons kept the **Plume of Feathers** somewhere along here between 1811 and 1835 and also in this area was the **Golden Lion** which was opened in 1826 by a widow named Elizabeth Griffith. She was still there in 1841 but seems to have changed the name of the pub to the **Mermaid** by 1844 – either that, or she had moved to a different place. Neither pub is heard of after that date.

Moving up the Old Newport Road, one of the houses on the right was the original **Dinas Arms.** From 1820 to 1826 John Llewellin was the landlord of this roadside ale-house and Ann Llewellin, widow, was in charge from 1841 to 1861. Originally the pub formed part of the Glyn-y-Mel estate but it was sold in 1866, the empire-building Thomas Davies once again acquiring an interest in the property. Anne George was the landlady from 1867 to 1881, retired coachman David Davies was landlord from 1884 to 1898, Jabez Evans was there in 1900 and Elizabeth Evans was in charge in 1901.

Cartoon from the days when the Ship and the Dinas Arms were friendly rivals

The Dinas Arms was closed to clear the way for
a road improvement that never happened

By this time the freehold had been acquired by Fishguard wine and spirit merchant Robert Lewis. He also owned properties at the bottom of the hill, forming the sharp end of the wedge created by the junction of Quay Street and the Newport Road, and at some stage he converted these properties into a new pub, moving the name and the licence down the hill to create a new Dinas Arms. Thomas Jenkins was the landlord in 1906 and Mrs. Mary Jenkins was landlady from 1911 to 1916. Mr. J. Owens was in charge by 1920 and Mrs. Mary J. Owens ran the pub from 1923 to 1945, during which time it became a George's house. Miss Elinor Davies was the licensee in 1958, after which it was run by the Macdonald family for a time and also by Howard Reynolds. The Dinas

Arms closed in the 1970s when plans were being mooted for a new bridge across the harbour, the link road to which would have meant the demolition of the pub. A public outcry caused the road scheme to be abandoned, but the Dinas never re-opened. Beyond Parc-y-Morfa turnpike gate, just out of town on the coast road was the **Morning Star** where Elizabeth Higgon was publican in 1841.

Back in Lower Town, the terrace opposite the Ship which leads from Bridge Street to the left of the newer Dinas and on towards the quay must have had its share of ale-houses, but pinpointing them seems impossible. They probably included the **Fishguard and Newport Arms** run by Margaret Jenkins in 1851 and the **Swan** which was run by Ann Evans from 1840 to 1844. William Davies was the landlord of the **Friendship** from 1822 through to 1840, followed by Mary Davies; she was still there in 1844 when she was well into her 70s. The landlord of the **Globe** in 1822 was David Jenkins and David Davies was in charge from 1825 to 1835. These two ale-houses also seem to have been in this area.

Quay Street itself is a long straggle of waterfront cottages reaching out to the quay. Several pubs stood along here, one of them being the **Sailors' Arms**, the earlier of two pubs of that name in Lower Town. Peter Thomas was landlord in 1835, having recently moved from the nearby **Jolly Sailor** where he had been landlord since 1817. Peter Vaughan succeeded him at the Jolly Sailor, but neither pub seems to have survived into the 1840s. (There was actually a third 'Sailors Arms' in Lower Town, but this one doesn't really count – it was a pink-washed cottage on the quay which was made up to look like the pub in Llaregub where 'it is always opening time' for the filming of 'Under Milk Wood').

Thomas Francis – son of Sarah Francis who ran the Ship in Trefin – was the landlord of the **Shipwrights' Arms** in Quay Street from 1840 until his death in 1855. As might be expected from the name he was a boat builder, and shipbuilding was obviously in the blood because his sons later ran a shipyard at Castle Pill, Milford Haven, and one of his grandsons, George Francis, moved the yard to Front Street, Pembroke Dock where it later became Hancock's shipyard. Following Thomas' death his widow, another Sarah Francis, ran the pub until at least 1861, shortly after which it must have closed. The **Ship and Castle** which was kept from 1805 to 1813 by James Evans, a Burgess of the town of Pembroke, may also have been near the shore here, together with the **Blue Anchor** where Anne Thomas was the landlady from 1822 to 1830.

From Lower Fishguard the Afon Gwaun can be followed upstream along the beautiful Gwaun Valley, a long wooded defile slicing through the Preseli Moors. Steep roads from the moors lead down to occasional bridging points over the river, such as at Llanychaer, and where there is a bridge there is usually an inn nearby. Thomas Thomas kept the **Penybont** in Llanychaer in 1824 and William Roach ran the **Sailors' Arms** at Llanychaer Bridge in 1826. The **Cross** at Llanychaer is mentioned in the 1851 census when Matthew Lamb was licensee. These all seem to have been precursors of the present-day **Bridge End** inn which was mentioned in 1859 as the venue for one of the annual dinners given by the Rev. C.H. Barham of Trecwn for the farmers on the estate. Licensees at the time were a Mr. and Mrs. James and the

widowed Phoebe James, then aged 78, was in charge in 1861. James Cornock, blacksmith and innkeeper, was the land-lord from 1871 to 1881. His son, another James Cornock, took over at some stage and was licensee from 1891 to 1915 when the third genera-tion took over in the shape of William Cornock who was still there in 1928. James and Olive Cornock were licen-sees from 1935 to 1939 when

A family celebration at the Bridge End in the days of James Cornock

The smithy at the Bridge End Inn, Llanychaer, was still in operation when this evocative photograph was taken a century ago.
(Picture courtesy of Mr. Philip Davies)

*A recent view of the Bridge End. The original front door is now
a window, and the smithy has become a restaurant*

Eva Cornock took over the running of the pub and Philip Cornock was
licensee in 1948. In 1957 Mrs. M. Murphy was licensee and Donald Williams
was in charge in 1960. Thomas 'Jackie' Jenkins took over the following year
and immediately made a number of structural changes, at the same time
applying for a supper licence. He was there until 1964 when Gareth Falcon
Evans took over, followed by Malcolm and Rose Bowen who ran the Bridge
End for about 20 years, making further alterations and improvements. Recent
licensees have included Julian Fry, Ann Billington, Tom Healey, Diane Lewis
and the present incumbent, Ann Williams; the pub is particularly noteworthy
for its restaurant which has been created out of the Cornocks' former smithy
and still retains many features from its previous life.

Further up the valley, the **Smiths' Arms** stood on the north side of the
Gwaun, next to a forge. David James was the blacksmith-cum-innkeeper from
1871 to 1891 and the widowed Mary James was the landlady from 1901 to
1907. The pub was reported as doing little trade in 1908 and appears to have
closed soon afterwards. It is now known as Gwaun Villa.

A little further along, the **Holly Bush** opened in 1845, probably being
built by contractor Seth Havard who inscribed the date and the name Llwyn
Celyn (Holly Bush) on the front of the building. He was licensee until the
1860s and for well over 20 years the Holly Bush was run by the widowed
Mary Havard. Landlord from 1901 to 1937 was David Evans and it was
during his time that the name was changed to **Dyffryn Arms**. His daughter,

Mrs. Mary Howells eventually took over the pub, being helped for many years by her daughter-in-law Mrs. Bessie Davies. Mrs. Davies subsequently became the licensee in 1972 and such has been her personality that the pub is now invariably known as 'Bessie's' and is very much a Pembrokeshire institution, featuring regularly in books and television programmes about the county and

Like the Bridge End, the former Smiths' Arms had its own forge attached to the building

The Dyffryn Arms was originally the Holly Bush and is now always called 'Bessie's'

Mrs. Bessie Davies serves a customer at the Dyffryn Arms in the 1990s.

(Picture courtesy of *Pembrokeshire Life*)

winning accolades for its unaltered interior. With its quarry-tiled floor, stone fireplace, serving hatch and mis-matched though comfortable furniture, 'Bessie's' has barely changed since the last war, and is a living example of how many of the pubs featured in this book would have looked before modernisation overtook them. As John Fenna, writing in *Pembrokeshire Life* put it:

> The limited range of drinks available are served through a small hatch in the wall opposite the window. The sliding glass doors back a deep shelf where Bessie will be found dispensing beer from a Tupperware jug, when she is not sitting by the fire. When Bessie is tired, the pub closes no matter how thirsty the customers and everyone leaves with good grace and good humour.

Above the valley, on the moorland road from Fishguard to Maenclochog, was the **Half-way House.** Agricultural labourer John Williams ran the pub as a sideline in the 1870s and early '80s; it was near Pen Bank. Also near here is the successful Gwaun Valley Brewery – a micro-brewery reviving the tradition of farmhouse brewing which was once so strong in the Gwaun.

CHAPTER FOURTEEN

Dinas

Dinas is made up of a number of settlements, mainly fringing the east-west highway but also clustered along the occasional side roads leading down to tiny harbours on the rugged north Pembrokeshire coast. The main harbour for Dinas was Cwm-yr-eglwys, with its storm-battered church, and two of the earliest pubs in the parish were to be found here. John Lewis ran a pub at Cwm-yr-eglwys from 1795 to 1813, apparently being succeeded by William Lewis who was there in 1817; this was probably the **Waterman's Arms** overlooking the beach, now and for many years a private house called The Bont. According to Rev. David Charles Jones (an early 20th century local historian): 'Thomas Williams, Waterman's Arms, was the last verger, bell-ringer and grave-digger in Cwm-yr-eglwys when the church was destroyed in 1859'. The other village pub was the **Dolphin** which opened in 1828 when the landlady was Mary Griffiths, and she was still in charge in 1841 at the age of 70.

There was a wealth of pubs in Dinas parish, partly because of the passing trade along the coast road and partly because the hard-working seafarers and farm labourers of the area enjoyed a pint and had little truck with temperance. In fact there was outrage in the summer of 1898 when two farmers in the Dinas area decided not to give their harvesters the usual home-brewed beer to quench their thirst in the fields, but instead offered them flagons of ginger beer. This did not go down at all well with the haymakers who threatened to boycott the two farms the following year. As one reaper declared: 'If all they are brewing is ginger beer, they can get the Rechabites from Newport to do their haymaking next harvest!' On other farms, where the 'customary beverage' was served, the *County Echo* was able to report that 'there has been nothing approaching a disgraceful scene anywhere, each man drinking like a Christian and no more'.

Like so many of the villages along this coast, Dinas produced more than its fair share of mariners, so that dotted around the various little settlements are houses which are surprisingly substantial, built on the earnings of deep

There have been no customers at the Clover Hill since 1926

sea sailing captains and ship-owners. Travellers from Fishguard towards Newport would have encountered numerous ale-houses, each of the settlements having its own watering hole often overseen by the wife of a deep sea sail-orman. These included an unnamed pub at Clyn which carpenter John Roach ran from 1841 to 1851. This may have been the **Clover Hill** where a draper named Thomas Stephens was landlord from 1867 until about 1910 when his son-in-law Ben Evans took over. Evans was employed at Fishguard Harbour, so it was his wife who was usually in charge of the tiny pub, which had no bar counter and no stabling and only a trickle of passing trade. As owners and licensees the Evanses must have been quite pleased to receive £200 in compensation when the local magistrates refused to renew the licence in 1926, decreeing that the pub was surplus to requirements.

In Bwlchmawr was the **Anchor**, sometimes described as **Rope and Anchor** in early references. James Rowlands was the landlord from 1819 to 1826 and Margaret Rowlands – described as 'mariner's widow' – was licensee from 1828 to 1867. Her son-in-law, retired mariner William Williams, held the licence from 1871 to 1881 but the building was unoccupied in 1891. It stood on the seaward side of the road in the middle of the terrace where the road narrows; not Anchor House, oddly enough, but the house alongside.

A few doors further along was the **Glanffynon**. This had previously been a sea captain's home, but had become a pub-cum-hotel by 1895 when it was kept by Mrs. Rosina Williams. The following year she was charged with keeping open after hours on a Friday evening; eyebrows were raised when it was revealed that the eight people enjoying a late drink had all gravitated to the pub straight from a meeting at nearby Tabor Chapel. Thomas Jenkins

Business card of the Glanffynon Hotel from about 1900.

(Picture courtesy of Christine Page)

was the next licensee, followed by George Williams who left at Michaelmas 1902 to go to the Bristol Trader in Fishguard. Advertising for a new tenant, Fishguard wine and spirit merchant Robert Lewis pointed out that a three-stall stable, small field and large garden went with the property. Mrs. Alice Jones from Aberdare was the new tenant, notifying the public that the premises had been refurbished to accommodate 'Visitors, Cyclists and Commercial Gentlemen'.

The Glan Hotel when Midland Bank ran a branch from part of the property.
(Picture courtesy of Christine Page)

Dewi Harries kept the Glan Hotel off and on between 1907 and the Second World War, making extensive alterations to the property in 1912 and apparently entrusting the running of the hotel to various managers. One of these was Garfield Harries who was operating a

The Glan Hotel in retirement

motor car service between the hotel and Goodwick station in 1915, while by 1927 the Glan was being run by William Griffiths. Midland Bank had an branch office in part of the building for a time, and a doctor held surgery once a week in another room. Dewi Harries' daughters Martha and Patty took over after the war, making a number of structural changes in 1950; Martha was fined for allowing poker dice to be played on the premises in 1957. Alan and Edna Walters took over in 1973, being succeeded by Elphin and Non Davies. The last licensee, Roger Wade, was in charge from 1987 to 1997 when the pub closed.

The Star was a small ale-house which closed in 1924

Across the road and a little further along was the **Star**, a small ale-house with a bar and parlour but no stabling. Thomas Roch or Roach was the landlord from 1817 to 1828 after which the records become sketchy for a time, although it appears that Mary John was licensee from 1851 to 1867. Carpenter David Harries then kept the pub for over 30 years, from 1871 to 1907, William Morris was landlord in 1914 while Mrs. William Morris was the landlady in 1923. She gave up the running of the pub in September that year due to ill health and the owners, George Bennett and Co. of Fishguard, failed to find a replacement tenant. As a consequence the pub was declared 'redundant' the following February and compensation was set at £150. The building was auctioned in 1925 as a dwelling house and fetched £110. It is still called Star House. David Rowlands kept the **Newport Arms** in Bwllchmawr in the early 1850s. It was near Tabor Chapel, but its exact whereabouts is unknown.

The former Rose Cottage. The house alongside was once a coffin-making workshop

Further along in the direction of Newport and on the left-hand side of the road was **Rose Cottage**, rather a twee name, although it started life as 'Rhos' cottage, rhos meaning 'moorland'. The landlord from 1861 to 1895 was joiner Joseph Thomas, and it appears that he was also the local coffin-maker, his workshop standing alongside the pub. From 1901 until the last war David Stevens was in charge, after which Joe Stevens and his sister Maggie Mary took over; Joe also ran a garage with its own petrol pump and repaired bicycles, while Maggie Mary sold sweets and lemonade. Joe died in the late 1960s and Rose Cottage became a restaurant but it is now a private house, the old coffin-making workshop having become a house as well.

In 1851 the nearby **Black Horse** was the home of Samuel Evans, a blacksmith, and in 1895 a woman named Ann Phillips burned to death here after her clothes caught fire. It was also the birthplace of Captain Stephen Gronow who skippered the great Cunard liners *Saxonia* and *Pannonia*, successfully bringing the latter vessel into New York harbour after she lost her rudder in a mid-Atlantic hurricane in 1922. Tradition – and the name – suggest that it was a pub at one time, but when that was cannot be determined.

Several other Dinas pubs have defied all attempts to track them down. Mary Davies was the licensee of the **Dinas Arms**, Dinas, in 1822, while the **Mariners'** was opened in 1827 by Thomas Harry; both must have been short-lived enterprises. And a notice appears in the Cilciffeth Estate papers dated 19 November 1863, which records a sale to be held at the **Victoria Inn**, Dinas Cross, of 14 acres of land 'adjoining the village of Jericho, parish of Dinas, through which the Manchester and Milford Haven Railway, which is in contemplation, will run'. (It didn't).

Still surviving, the **Ship Aground** at Dinas Cross is mentioned in 1851; according to one account it began life in a cottage and bakery across the road, at some stage moving to its present site. Eleanor Griffiths was the innkeeper in 1851, while a young widow of 23 called Eliza Rees was licensee in 1861. Elizabeth Francis was in charge by 1867 when she became Mrs. Henry

A meet of the hounds at the Ship Aground in the 1950s
when Mrs. Vaughan (left) was licensee.
(Picture courtesy of the Ship Aground)

145

Owens, and she continued as licensee for a further 40 years, for much of which time her husband was away at sea. She remained the tenant until 1910 when the freehold was purchased by Dewi Harries, who also owned the Glan Hotel; he immediately added an extension to what had been little more than a two-room cottage. David Thomas was behind the bar from 1912 to 1915, followed by Benjamin Spencer Davies who was forever in trouble with the authorities for petty offences such as driving a pony and trap at night without lights or buying rabbits from poachers. Thomas Griffith Edwards was the landlord for a number of years from 1920 onwards, and Mary Mendus took over as licensee in 1947. James Kenneth Vaughan replaced her in 1951 but died two years later to be succeeded by Jenny Vaughan; she struggled to make a living, eventually selling up in 1957. 'The pub lost money every year,' she lamented. The new owner was Wing Commander Harold Dickson who immediately refurbished the premises. Further improvements, including the addition of a 'sun lounge' were made by William Odlum during his brief tenure in the early 1960s, while Aubrey Clayton from Penarth took over in 1962, followed by Fred Hoyland. In the late 1960s and early '70s the licensees were Mr. and Mrs. William Hunt followed by John Preston, while in the late 1970s the landlord was Phil Smith – now better known as the stepfather of the pop singer Duffy. It was around this time that the pub enjoyed a spell

The Ship Aground has been extended many times over the years

in the limelight as part of 'Operation Seal Bay'. A smuggling gang was using a remote cove on the nearby coast to land vast quantities of drugs which were cached in secret chambers on the beach. It was a sophisticated operation, but was rumbled because the smugglers couldn't resist flashing their cash around the village, especially in the Ship Aground, producing wads of £20 notes to pay for food and drink. Tipped off by suspicious locals, the police mounted 'Operation Seal Bay' to nab the free-spending smugglers.

Barry Nicholls was landlord in the 1980s and current licensees Colin and Christine Hill have been at the Ship Aground for 22 years, during which time they have extended the property in most directions to cope with the growing trade, especially during the tourist season.

The **Sailor's Safety** at Pwllgwaelod occupied a marvellous position at the head of a sandy cove where coasting vessels, often delivering fertiliser, were still unloading at the beach in 1915. A pub guide published in the 1980s stated that this had been an inn 'since 1593', while an article in the *Western Mail* plumped for 'since 1686' – both remarkably precise claims, but there seems no evidence that the pub

The original Sailor's Safety, pictured in about 1900

was much more than 130 years old when it closed. Also, people of a romantic nature have conjectured that the name might refer to a lantern which was hung outside the pub to guide ships into Fishguard Bay or to warn smugglers that the revenue men were about. Sadly the truth is more prosaic, since the name belongs to the family of signs which includes Sailor's Return, Sailor's Home and Sailor's Rest – a place of refuge to which a mariner could return after the perils of an ocean voyage. It referred to the first licensee, John James, a master mariner who held the licence from 1867 to 1881. His widow Mary James, who was much younger than her husband, was in charge from 1891 to 1902 when the freehold of what was described as 'an isolated, old-fashioned licensed house' came up for auction. It failed to reach its reserve price and was withdrawn. Breeze Williams was the licensee from 1906 to 1908 and John Jones Williams was in charge in 1911. Elizabeth Beer took over the licence in 1914, but she was only there a year and from 1915 to 1923 the landlady was Mrs. Mary Morgan; she kept pigs which were forever escaping and wandering up into the village.

John Harries ran the Sailor's Safety in the mid-1920s and from 1928 until at least 1944 the landlord was an Irishman named Arthur Duigenan whose first job was to switch the focus of the pub from the old house – which became his living quarters – to a new building alongside in which he installed a beauti-

In the 1920s the high-roofed building in the middle of the photograph took over from the original Sailor's Safety on the right

Arthur Duigenan with family, friends and cockatoo outside the new Sailor's Safety

fully carved wooden bar, formerly a ship's dresser, which he imported from Calcutta. The new pub had a high pyramid-shaped roof because Mr. Duigenan became irritated by cigarette smoke and thought that the added height would help disperse it. Mrs. Doris 'Monté' Manson ran the pub in the 1950s, turning it into a popular venue for functions before moving to the Bristol Trader in Haverfordwest. Malcolm Allen took over, and subsequent licensees included J.E. Edwards, Royston Beddoe and Langley Forrest.

148

*The Old Sailors Restaurant now occupies the buildings that housed
the latter-day Sailor's Safety and adjoining beach café*

By the time Peter English was in charge in the early 1990s the Sailor's
Safety was only open on a seasonal basis, serving as a beach café as much as
a pub. Reporting on its demise in 1996, the *Western Mail* noted:

> For the last two years, after the bankruptcy of a former landlord, the
> pub has been closed and its windows overlooking Fishguard Bay
> boarded up.

What became of Abe, the ghost of a fisherman with no legs said to
occupy a dark corner of the inn, no-one seems to know. However he may still
be about, because former licensee Langley Forrest has since re-opened the
business as a pub-cum-licensed restaurant known as the **Old Sailors**, with
many of the old interior features still intact. The adjacent building which
housed the original pub is no more, having been rebuilt as a private house.

The **Freemasons' Arms** stands in the 1834 terrace known as Jericho
and nowadays occupies two adjoining properties in the row. Capt. Joseph
Propert Davies and his wife Mary were there in the 1870s and '80s; their
son, Capt. David Propert Davies, who was born at the pub, became Assistant
Harbour Master for the Port of Melbourne and Director of Navigation for the
Commonwealth of Australia. The widowed Mary Davies was in charge from
1891 to 1898 and Stephen Davies and his wife Martha took over in 1900. The
pub was closed for several months in 1905, but was spruced up ('papered and
painted throughout') by the Swansea Old Brewery, which found a tenant in

The Freemasons' Arms in the 1960s

Owen Davies. He was soon followed by Albert Stevens who handed over to Miss Rachel John from Eglwyswrw in 1908. T.G. Edwards was there from 1911 to 1914 and Benjamin and Bertha Davies, formerly of the Ship Aground, became the licensees in 1920. In 1927 a fire broke out in the outbuildings of the pub, but the house itself was saved thanks to the efforts of villagers who made a 'human chain' to pass buckets of water enabling the fire to be extinguished. Mrs. Bertha Davies died at the pub in 1933 and Sarah Ann Wigley was licensee in 1936 when the building was again damaged by fire. Bill and Freda Howarth had charge from 1948 through to the 1970s, by which time the Freemasons' was said to be 'completely unspoilt by gimmickry' and 'just as the real Welsh pub was years ago'. This began to change when Mrs. Isis Joan Brooks took over in 1971, because she immediately made some

A recent view of the Freemasons' Arms

structural alterations. Subsequent licensees have included Graham Hitchens, who had a dozen years in charge, and current licensee Norman Wilkinson whose name has been over the door for the past decade.

There was once a pub at Bwlch-y-groes, near the junction with the lane going down to Cwm-yr-eglwys. This was the **Cross**, which was run in the 1840s by Llewellyn Rees and his wife Elizabeth. She seems to have been 30 years younger than her husband who was still running the Cross in 1851 at the age of 87. By 1861 the licensee was Jane Morgans.

Further east, where the road once dipped to cross Cwm Fforest at Pont Felin-wern-dew, is Bridge farm and, like the highway, the farmhouse has been much changed in recent years. This was once the **Bridgend** inn where Newport-born shoemaker Benjamin Laugharne (or Larn) held the licence from 1861 until his death in 1875, when he was succeeded by his widow Maria who was still the innkeeper in

A century ago this was the Bridgend Inn

1881. Mrs. Mary Thomas kept the pub from 1891 to 1895 and David Gibby was the landlord from 1901 to 1914. The Bridgend closed under a redundancy ruling in November 1919, although the pub had been more or less empty for some time when the axe fell. A little further on, at Feidirgerrigog, was the **Lamb** where William Rees was landlord from 1867 to 1875.

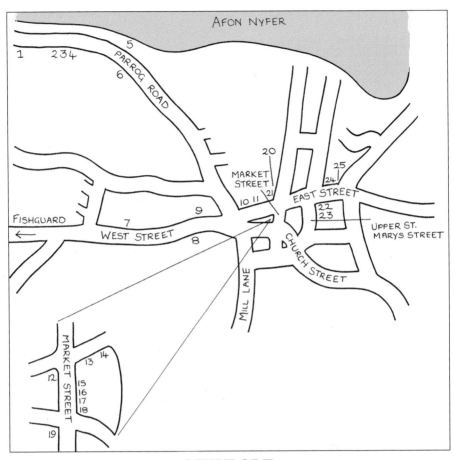

NEWPORT

1	Mariners' Arms	14	Britannia
2	Ship Afloat/Aground	15	Mariners' Arms
3	Parrog Arms	16	Farmers' Arms (2)
4	Sloop	17	Jolly Sailor
5	Crown and Anchor	18	Barley Mow
6	Queen's	19	Ship
7	Farmers' Arms	20	Angel
8	Plough	21	Queen's Head
9	Dolphin	22	Globe
10	Butchers' Arms/Royal Oak	23	Rose and Crown
11	Castle/Commercial	24	Golden Lion/Golden Dragon
12	Castle (2)	25	Prince of Wales/
13	Llwyngwair Arms		Masons' Arms

CHAPTER FIFTEEN

Newport and Nevern

The historic township of Newport is beautifully situated where the Preseli Hills meet the estuary of the River Nevern. The number of prehistoric sites in the vicinity shows that the area had been inhabited long before the Norman lord William Martin built a castle here in about 1195, below which the township grew up. The castle still stands, although much altered, and is now a private residence. By medieval times Newport had become an important settlement and the street layout remains largely unchanged from those days. There were regular fairs and markets and plenty of inns to cater for the country people who attended them; as a justice of the peace for Kemaes in the 1580s, the historian George Owen of Henllan once tried a man for murder following a brawl in a Newport inn. However, it was for its seafarers and shipbuilders that the township became best known. More than 50 sailing vessels were built alongside the estuary, and local merchants had shares in dozens of ships which traded along the Irish Sea and much further afield. An old storehouse on the Parrog has been preserved as the home of the town's yacht club.

Many of the town's early cottage pubs were run by old sea-dogs who had 'swallowed the anchor' or, in all too many cases, by the widows of men who had failed to return from sea. However, it was for its abstinence that Newport was famed a century ago and more. In 1876 a lodge of the Independent Order of Good Templars was founded in the township, 'to do something in a legal way to put down drunkenness – one of the greatest vices of the present day'. Temperance parades, lectures and concerts became commonplace, and several remorseful publicans chose to shut up shop as the various revivals swept the area. And while many innkeepers elsewhere in the county saw the '*bona fide* traveller' rule as a sneaky way of subverting the Sunday Closing Act, in Newport the converse was true. So strongly was the Sabbath observed in the township that even people who really _were_ *bona fide* travellers found it difficult to obtain as much as a cup of coffee on a Sunday. Boozy charabanc outings soon learned to steer well clear of Newport on the Sabbath.

As the local press noted in 1922:

Newport Pembs. is fast becoming one of the most important strongholds of temperance in the whole of Pembrokeshire. Energetic efforts on behalf of the cause of total abstinence have been made in recent years among children and adults and it can be confidently asserted that the district will soon be ripe for Local Option.

This 'Local Option' was an attempt, now largely forgotten, to introduced prohibition to Britain along the lines of the United States. Instead of a national ban on public houses, however, the idea was to give each community the right to decide whether it wanted a local ban – piecemeal prohibition. At public meetings held in places such as Fishguard, Dinas and Goodwick to debate the 'Local Option', opinion was firmly against a local prohibition order, but in Newport the reverse was the case, with hardly a hand raised in opposition to proposals for a blanket closure of all the town's hostelries. Fortunately, perhaps, the 'Local Option' legislation never made it through Parliament otherwise Newport might have had Pembrokeshire's only 'speakeasies'. However the redundancy ruling proved nearly as formidable a weapon for the anti-drink lobby with several of the town's pubs being axed in the 1920s, while closing time in Newport remained at 8pm well into the 1930s, although it was 9pm or even 10pm in adjacent parishes.

It was all very different in the 18th and early 19th century. Newport had eight licensed alehouses in 1780 and this had risen to ten by 1810. Not all of these were in the town itself, there being several pot-houses at the Parrog where the town's seafarers would gather to swap yarns. This was the harbour of Newport, where coasting vessels would discharge anthracite and limestone for the numerous limekilns as well as house coal, bricks, roofing slates and general goods, while taking away cargoes of corn which was stored in warehouses along the shore. Quay walls were built in the early 19th century on a fairly *ad hoc* basis by various entrepreneurs, one of whom, John Jenkins, also ran the optimistically-named **Prosperity** ale-house from 1809 to 1828; there is no sign of the pub in a trade directory of 1830 and its location is unknown.

A 19th century view of Newport Parrog

Some of the pubs along the Parrog have come and gone without any record of their names, such as the ones licensed to Thomas David in 1780, John Griffiths in 1807 and James Bowen in 1809. Many are known, however, starting to the west of the Parrog at Bettws where Benjamin Roach was the landlord of the **Mariners' Arms** from 1826 until at least 1871. In 1842 Mr. Roach was badly hurt falling off some rocks while helping Whit Monday excursionists board their boats for a trip around the bay. He was helped to run the pub by his wife Sarah, and she eventually succeeded him as licensee in the 1870s. Master mariner James Evans was the landlord from 1880 to May 1905 when he successfully applied to have the licence transferred to the **Bay View**, a small hotel which he opened nearby, overlooking the sea (obviously). But the new venture wasn't a success and the licence wasn't renewed in 1907. Today the Mariners' is the large house called Bettws.

Strolling along the Parrog from Bettws would have taken you past various quayside pot-houses full of grizzled Cape Horners reminiscing about life at sea. Seven pub names crop up here at different times, although in some cases it might represent a change of name rather than a new enterprise. First up was an old establishment called the **Ship Aground** where Margaret George was landlady in 1823 followed by her second husband John Havard, shipwright and victualler, who held the licence from 1825 onwards. It was also John Havard's second marriage; by his first wife he had four sons, all of them mariners or shipbuilders, and three daughters who all married seamen. John Havard died in 1839, but Margaret Havard kept the pub going until her death in 1852 at the age of 70. Sarah Williams had charge in 1861 and Thomas Lewis was the last landlord in 1867. It then became the **Ship Afloat** kept by former sea captain David Thomas from 1871 to 1875 and by David Evans in 1881; it is now Seagull Cottage.

The inns came thick and fast around the quay itself, the first being the **Parrog Arms** which was run by David Lewis and his wife Martha from 1871 to 1881. They were followed in 1891 by Thomas Evans and his wife Margaret who subsequently converted the premises into a temperance hotel. Nowadays it is a house called Morawelon. More or less next door was the **Sloop** where Sarah James was in charge from 1871 to 1881.

Out on the quay, the **Crown and Anchor** was a popular Parrog pub where the licensee from 1819 to 1825 was David Thomas. His widow Mary took over the business and ran it as a beer-house and bakery into the 1840s. Lime-burner and ship-owner William Matthias was the next occupant, being assisted in the running of the pub by his wife Sarah. He died in 1861, bequeathing 'the Crown and Anchor and the lime kiln attached thereto' to his son David, a mariner, who seems to have allowed the licence to lapse.

Close to the corn warehouses which once stood here was the **Hope and Anchor** where John Bowen held the licence from 1858 to 1861, while a

The Queen's Hotel on the Parrog (right) was handy for boatmen

couple of cottages along was the **Waterman's Arms**. Thomas Roach opened the Waterman's in 1828 and Charlotte Roach was landlady from 1840 to 1861.

The **Queen's** was a substantial Parrog hostelry of somewhat later date than most of the quayside pot-houses and is first recorded in 1880 when Richard Jenkins was in charge. Margaret Williams was licensee in the 1890s, her husband Capt. David Williams being master of the *Asiana* and the *Neptune*. David Nicholas was landlord from 1901 to 1906 and his wife or widow Margaret Nicholas held the licence from 1907 to 1909. After the pub had changed hands a couple of times in quick succession, Mrs. Annie Edwards provided a steadying influence, holding the licence from 1911 to 1922. David Thomas, a colliery engineer from Port Talbot, took over, but for some reason the Queen's seems to have closed in May 1924. It is now a private house called 'Morfan'.

Between the Parrog and the town of Newport itself is an area once known as 'Undertown'. Thomas Hughes kept the **Carpenters' Arms** here in the early 1840s and Elizabeth Parry was the licensee of the **Fishguard Arms** from 1858 to 1867.

Many of Newport's inns – and all the surviving ones – could be found on the main through road. Anyone entering Newport from the direction of Fishguard first has to pass along West Street, a thoroughfare reasonably stocked with ale-houses in its time. On the left was the **Farmers' Arm**s which Rees Daniel, a clogmaker by trade, ran from 1871 to 1875. William Lewis was there in 1880, Mary Lewis, a widow of 32, ran the pub in 1891 and David Lewis was in charge in 1895. Mary Anne Rayner was fined ten shillings for serving after hours in 1898 while Dan Davies held the licence in 1901; his wife or widow Mrs. Mary Davies was the landlady by 1906. James Phillips held the licence from 1907 to 1920 followed by Johnny Edmunds. He left in 1923 to run the Tunnel Hotel at Abergwynfi near Port Talbot, leaving Miss Rachael

Thomas in charge of the Farmers'. She became Rachael Llewellyn in 1924 but the sands of time were running out for the Farmers' which had been targeted for closure by the Newport Temperance Movement. The Farmers' was closed under the redundancy ruling in 1928, with £650 being paid out in compensation – mainly to Mr. Edmunds, who was still the owner. A substantial building, it is now a private house called Porthmeor.

The Farmers' Arms has not served beer for many a year

Nearer town and on the opposite side of the road is Welford House, once the **Plough**. In a seafaring town like Newport it is not surprising that the recorded licensees of the Plough were often women; the menfolk were probably at sea. Hannah George opened the Plough in 1827 and she was succeeded by Ann Rees in the 1840s, John Davies in the 1850s, Ann Reynolds and Martha Williams in the 1860s and cabinet-maker Daniel Davies in the 1870s. Master mariner Thomas James and his wife Margaret ran the Plough in 1880 and another master mariner, Captain John Evans, was the landlord from 1891 until his death in 1898. He was followed by his daughter Miss Blanche Evans, 'a small timid lady who was a devout member of Ebenezer', and in 1905 the licence was discontinued, the landlady having apparently been swayed towards the temperance movement during the great revival. She changed the name of the property to Welford House and continued to run it as a guest house.

David Shadrach was landlord of the **Ship and Crown** somewhere in Newport from 1819 to 1822. A master mariner, he seems to have gone back to sea for a few years, returning to run a beer-house in West Street from about 1835 to 1841 which was called the **Dolphin**. It was across the road from the Plough and nearer the centre of town. A couple of doors from the Dolphin was the **Butchers' Arms,** possibly the pub with that sign where the licensee from 1805 to 1827 was Thomas Llewhellin. Butcher, and beer retailer John Hughes was the landlord from 1840 to 1844, but was simply recorded as a butcher in a trade directory of 1852. It appears that following his death his

The Royal Oak is still going strong

widow Elizabeth reopened the pub and changed the name to the **Royal Oak**; she was still in charge in 1881, by which time she was 82. John Evans kept the pub from 1891 to 1911, during which time a conveyance left the premises at 7.40am each day to connect with the train at Crymych, returning at 3.15pm. Mrs. Letitia Harris was there from 1911 to 1914 while David Gibby was the landlord from 1914 to 1932. In 1920 the freehold changed hands for £1,000, the purchaser being Fishguard wine merchant Robert P. Lewis, and ten years later he sold the pub to George's of Haverfordwest. Magdalen Gibby was licensee during the 1930s and Mary Edwards was in charge in the 1950s and '60s. Subsequent licensees have included Brian Evans and John Hipperson, while John Denley and R.M. Junaideen took over in 1997 and increased the emphasis on food. Mr. Denley moved on to run the Salutation at Felindre Farchog, but the latter – a native of Sri Lanka and universally known as 'Dean' – is still licensee at the Royal Oak and as a consequence the much enlarged pub restaurant has become highly regarded for its Asian cuisine.

West Street becomes Lower Bridge Street before morphing into East Street as it heads out of town. The widowed Mary Davies kept the **Ship Aground** in Lower Bridge Street from about 1861 to 1875; her sea captain husband James had died in 1856. Their son was Captain William Davies and it appears that in about 1876 he built the substantial **Commercial Inn** on the site of the Ship Aground, perhaps hoping to attract the commission salesmen or 'commercial travellers' who were appearing in great numbers following the spread of the railways into west Wales. Captain Davies was an active member of the community, becoming a magistrate and mayor of the township.

He was also a prominent Forester and the Court Carningli lodge of the benefit society known as the Ancient Order of Foresters had a lodge room at the Commercial from 1877 onwards; its members would occasionally parade around the town wearing their uniform of Lincoln Green and brandishing little bows and arrows.

Locals pose for the photographer outside the Commercial Inn

Newport was growing as a tourist resort by this time, and Captain Davies advertised that there was good shooting and fishing to be had in the neighbourhood. The Commercial also boasted a 'conveyance' which ran daily from the inn via Eglwyswrw to meet the trains at Crymych station, a service which carried many a Newport mariner on the first stage of his journey to meet his ship in Cardiff, Liverpool or elsewhere. This coach service ran for 23 years, usually with John Peregrine as coachman, and it was his proud boast that in 23 years, summer and winter, he had never missed a train connection. Reporting on this remarkable achievement, the *County Echo* noted that the coach had never suffered an accident, 'although one horse did fall dead on the Cardigan road from sheer old age and decrepitude'. When Captain Davies retired from the Commercial in 1902 the coach service was taken over by David Thomas and used the Royal Oak as its Newport terminus.

Joshua Miles was landlord of the Commercial from 1907 to 1911 when he moved to Treorchy. Daniel Thomas, who was landlord from November 1911 to 1918, advertised motor cars for hire, one of which could carry 12 passengers. The Commercial also boasted the only billiards table in Newport. By 1920 the licensee was Mrs. Mary Thomas, but John Humphrey Evans bought the freehold in 1924 and was landlord until 1931. Elizabeth Rees was licensee in the early 1930s, and when she left in 1936 it became a William Hancock house. They installed Thomas Vaughan as tenant, and he was mayor of Newport in 1946-48. In May 1948 Thomas Vaughan handed over the reins to David Vaughan who remained in charge until 1956. William Charles took over, being quickly succeeded by Dorothy Charles. She became Dorothy Davies a year or two later and the licensee in 1960 was Brinley Davies, one of whose first moves was to change the name of the inn to the **Castle**. Peter

A recent view of the Castle Inn, once the Commercial

Lewis took over in 1962 and was still there in 1968, while Windsor Davies subsequently had a lengthy spell as licensee – to the extent that people began calling the pub the 'Windsor Castle'. Alison Edwards also enjoyed a decade in charge of this attractive and imposing town centre hostelry which is still very much at the heart of life in the township.

East Street was known in Victorian times as Cross Street and sometimes Grogland Street, perhaps from Crog Lane, 'crog' being the Welsh word for cross – although grog-land would have been just as good a name given the number of pubs hereabouts, including the **Angel Inn** which at one time stood on the right-hand side just past the Market Street junction. Anne Morgans kept an Angel in Newport from 1805 to 1807, probably not the place of the same name which Mrs. Sarah James (daughter of Thomas and Sarah Mathias of the Mason's Arms) opened 20 years later. She was still there in 1843 when she married local surgeon Thomas Bevan. The Bevans remained in charge for the next ten years, hosting the local lodge of Odd Fellows and sittings of the Mayor's Court.

Things were about to change, however. In May 1853 an advertisement appeared in the local press offering the lease of a newly-built inn in the township plus up to 40 acres of land. According to the advert:

> The **Llwyngwair Arms**, which has been recently erected on the site of the old Angel Inn, embraces excellent accommodation, with good stabling, coach house and other premises, and is situate in

160

The Llwyngwair Arms dates from the 1850s

the principal street of the town of Newport through which all those travelling between the important towns of Cardigan, Fishguard and Haverfordwest pass.

The name of the new inn reflected the fact that it was part of the estate of the Bowens of Llwyngwair mansion. Thomas and Sarah Bevan seem to have been given first crack at running the pub and were there until Michaelmas 1855 when they opened a new Angel only a few steps away in Long Street, and John Davies kept the Llwyngwair from 1856 to 1858. At Michaelmas in 1860 the lease of the Llwyngwair Arms again became available, along with stables and coach house, but only three and a half acres of meadow land. Elizabeth Harries was the new licensee, but it was her sister, Swansea-born Mrs. Mary Seaborne, who was the landlady from 1867 to 1891. By 1895 Mary's sister Elizabeth was back in charge, although by now she was a widow named Mrs. Elizabeth Thomas. She held the licence from 1901 to 1914 when she was 79 and claimed in an advertisement that the inn had been established in 1820 (roughly the date the Angel opened) and added that 'a copy of the original charter of the town and corporation is on view here'. Thomas Lewis was landlord from 1913 to 1920 (when the inn possessed a car which could be hired out by guests) followed by Benjamin Williams who was there until 1933. Miss Clara Williams ran the pub from 1934 to 1941, followed by Edith Griffiths who left in 1950.

It was at this time that the inn passed from the ownership of the Llwyngwair estate and into the hands of wine merchants James Williams. Tenants during the 1950s included Basil Chessington, Marjorie Briddon and Barbara Scarr, while Norah Haswell was in charge during the 1960s and T.W. Haswell was there in the early 1970s followed by (among others) John Stanton in the 1980s, John Denley (later of the Royal Oak) in 1992 and Dyfed Williams. The pub had been closed for several months when this book was going to press, although local people were hopeful that this was only a temporary state of affairs. Certainly it would be sad if this historic pub were to close, having served variously as the courtroom for the petty sessions of the hundred of Kemaes (1854), the local Inland Revenue office (1859), as the registered office of the Loyal Kemes Lodge of the Odd Fellows Friendly Society (1880) and as the meeting place of the Court Baron and Court Leet of Newport for more than a century.

Next door was the **Britannia** which was kept by mariner John Lewis and his wife Margaret Lewis from 1861 to 1880. Mary Evans held the licence in 1881 while Daniel Davies was landlord from 1891 to 1895. The Sessions Room was later built on the site. A 46-year-old widow named Mary Thomas ran the **Sailors' Home** in 1861; it was just along from the Britannia and later became a grocer's shop.

Across the road, the **Green Dragon** in East Street was owned by the Bowen family of Llwyngwair, and in 1790 a lease was granted to John

The Golden Lion takes its name from the coat of arms of the Bowens of Llwyngwair

Hughes, yeoman, who was still running the inn in 1812. Oddly there is no further mention in the alehouse records until 1826 when the tenant was William Owen, victualler, who changed the name to **Golden Lion** four years later. No doubt the new name was a reference to the golden lion in the Bowen family coat of arms. William Owen remained at the Golden Lion until his death in 1848, by which time it had become a meeting place of the Ivor Hall lodge of True Ivorites. He was succeeded as licensee by his son John Owen, but Eleanor Gilbert was there by 1861 with husband Tom. A farmer named George John was the long-serving landlord between 1871 and 1921, William Evans was the licensee from December 1921 to 1935, followed by Mary Jane Evans who remained in charge until 1954. David Fisher then held the licence for a couple of years, followed by Harold Griffiths whose name was over the door until about 1967 when Michael Ward took over. Glyn and Penny Rees then ran the Golden Lion for nearly 30 years, from 1971 to 2000, adding a hotel wing with 13 bedrooms at the rear of the inn. These rooms have recently been refurbished and the restaurant extended by Daron Paish, who has been licensee for the past ten years. None of these changes seem to have dislodged the pub ghost which manifests itself as a spooky 'presence' in the former servants' bedrooms in the attic.

Thomas Mathias was landlord of the neighbouring **Masons' Arms** from 1780 to 1833 followed by Sarah Mathias who remained in charge until her death, aged 88, in 1842. Benjamin James took over behind the bar and he was still there in the 1860s, presiding over meetings of the Taliesin Ivorite Club. It then became the **Prince of Wales**, noted for its horse-drawn coaches (notably the *Shah*) which connected with Crymych railway station from 1876 onwards. Richard Jackson was landlord from 1867 to 1875 but Thomas Gilbert and his wife Eleanor – previously of the Golden Lion – were running the Prince of Wales by 1881 and their son Llewellyn was in charge in 1891. The pub had closed by 1895 and Llys Meddyg now stands on the site.

Further along, the **Tafarn Spite** was on the left-hand side of the road out of town towards Eglwyswrw, just past the turning to Pen-y-bont. This was a name often applied to an inn which was opened to 'spite' a rival publican, although it could also have the meaning 'respite', indicating a place to rest and recuperate. In this case the name seems to have pre-dated the pub. In 1825, Elinor George 'a widow residing in a dwelling house called the Spite' was granted an alehouse licence; she was still the landlady in 1830. Evan Jones and his wife Elizabeth had taken over by 1835 and Elizabeth was still in charge in 1871 when she was a widow in her 70s. Presumably the pub died when she did.

While most traffic passed through Newport on the east-west highway, with plenty of taverns to catch the passing trade, a number of pubs also existed on the various streets which cross the highway at right angles. South

Market Street in the 1890s

of the main crossroads (originally called 'The Cross' but later 'The Square') is Market Street, formerly Upper High Street, once the focus of the town's livestock and hiring fairs. Most of its pubs seem to have been on the left going up the hill, the first being the **Mariners' Arms** where sailor's wife Eliza Davies was in charge in 1861 and Thomas Phillips was landlord in 1867. Four pubs stood along here in close proximity at one time, the next of which was the **Farmers' Arms**. Mary Thomas was the landlady between 1830 and 1844, while from 1846 to 1861 James Nicholas was at the Farmers'. The **Jolly Sailor** was next in line. A mariner called David Williams was the landlord in 1844 and his wife Anne Williams was there from 1851 to 1861. Dillwyn Miles (who called it the 'Jolly Tar') believed that it subsequently became a garage. All three of these pubs seem to have closed by 1871; presumably they were beer-houses that failed to survive the changes in the licensing laws at around that time.

Almost at the top of the street on the left was the rather more resilient **Barley Mow** from where a horse-drawn omnibus departed three times a week in the 1850s to connect with the new train service from Haverfordwest. William Shadrach appears to have been landlord in 1841 and salt merchant and butcher Joseph Williams was the licensee from 1851 until at least 1881. His married daughter, Mrs. Maria Owen was landlady from 1891 to 1911. She was the wife – and widow – of mariner John Owen, who spent much of his life sailing to the East Indies and the Pacific. A Miss Margaret Owen is given as licensee from 1911 to 1914 – probably their daughter. She married master

A busy scene outside the Barley Mow

mariner David Isaac in 1915, but the pub began to go downhill when Mrs. Isaac, not surprisingly, 'became ill following a report that her husband's ship had been torpedoed in the war'. By 1925 trade had dwindled to the extent that her sales for the entire year amounted to just four barrels of beer, 24 dozen bottles of beer and three and a half gallons of wine and spirits. In 1926 the Newport Temperance Movement opposed the renewal of the licence at the annual brewster sessions. Faced with a fearsome array of chapel ministers, deacons and Rechabites, the magistrates duly called time on the 'Mow'. They invoked the redundancy ruling, with compensation totalling £310 being shelled out.

On the other side of the road, nearer the bottom, was the town's first **Castle Inn**. Thomas Lloyd was licensee from 1805 to 1825, the landlady from 1826 to 1844 was Anne Lloyd and Miss Mary Lloyd was there from 1847 until her death, aged 55, in 1852. It was a notable house and the local Court Leet and Court Baron for the Barony of Kemaes was held here in 1850, as were occasional petty sessions for the Hundred of Kemaes. In 1852 the lease became available following the death of Miss Lloyd, the advertisement describing the pub as 'eligibly situated near the market place and in the best part of town'. It is not heard of again.

Upper Bridge Street crosses the top of Market Street and there were two pubs with similar names close to the junction. Mr. Miles has written that the Ship and the Ship and Castle were one and the same place, but they appear as separate entries in Upper Bridge Street in the 1861 census – just part of the immense confusion surrounding these two pub names in Newport. In 1828, William Williams took out an alehouse licence for the **Ship** in Newport, although this could have been anywhere and we have no firm ground to go on until carpenter David Evans and his wife Margaretta Evans held the licence of the pub on the corner of Upper Bridge Street and Castle Lane between 1861 and 1867; she was a baker and was widowed by 1871. She was still in charge in 1875 but by 1881 a widow named Margaret Thomas ran the Ship. William James was the landlord between 1891 and 1907 but no application was made for the licence to be renewed in 1910. It is now a private house called Gwynfi.

According to Mr. Miles, a meeting of bards was held in Newport 'under the sign of the **Ship and Castle**' on Whit Monday 1774. It was attended by Llechryd-born poet and schoolteacher Ioan Siencin, and was conceivably the first-ever 'Poems and Pints'. Landlord at the time was one John Davies. It must have closed as a pub soon afterwards, because there is no further trace of a Ship and Castle in the licensing records for Newport until the 1830s. (Dr. Reginald Davies has pointed out that the Vestry book for 1813-17 records that a building called the Ship and Castle was divided between four people, each of whom contributed to the Poor Rate, and was thus a substantial building). However it does appear to have re-opened as a pub, because Stephen Davies was landlord of the Ship and Castle from 1835 to 1840. Of course, the bardic meeting place may have been a different hostelry altogether – nor is there any guarantee that either place was the later Ship and Castle where Margaretta James was licensee in 1861 and which stood a couple of doors from the Ship.

Coedfryn, next to the old malt-house in nearby Church Street, was once a pub according to Mr. Miles; he thought it was called the Pig and Whistle but this seems unlikely. No such name appears in the records, and 'Pig and Whistle' was usually a nickname for a pub, rather than a genuine name. A baker named Ann Martin ran the **Commercial** in Church Street during the 1850s, which may be the pub Mr. Miles was referring to.

North of the main crossroads there were a couple of pubs in Lower High Street, now Long Street. On the corner was the **Queen's Head** where Frances Owen was the landlady and also the town postmistress from 1852 to 1867, running the pub with the help of her sister Sarah. They had both retired by 1871 and the pub was closed.

Next door down was the **Angel** which replaced an earlier pub of the same name in East Street demolished in about 1853. Thomas and Sarah Bevan had run the earlier Angel and opened the new one and Sarah was still the landlady in 1867. Mary Bowen was the publican in 1871. A mother and daughter, both called Esther Lloyd, kept the Angel from 1875 to 1881 and Hannah Griffiths, 76, widow and grocer, was there in 1891. It had become James Thomas' Angel Temperance Hotel by 1901 and is now a shop called Angel House.

*The Angel in Newport during its time
as a Temperance Hotel*

The former Angel is now Angel House

The Globe hasn't been a pub since 1929

The **Globe** was on the bottom corner of Upper St. Mary Street and was run by Margaret Morgans, baker and wife of a master mariner, from 1861 to 1881. Mrs. Esther Davies was the landlady between 1891 and 1906 when John Owen Davies took over. George Howells ran the pub from 1914 to 1925, in which year he advertised a motor service to Cardigan every Saturday, via Nevern, in 'a comfortable Daimler seven-seater'. However, the pub was on the market by the end of the year, the notice of sale recording 'eight rooms, out offices and garage'; the Daimler was also up for sale. Thereafter the Globe seems to have died a lingering death, finally giving up the ghost in about 1930.

Next door to the Globe was the **Rose and Crown**. In 1849 the pub was the scene of an inquest into the death of a Newport lady who had apparently swallowed arsenic in mistake for headache powder. Shoemaker David Thomas was landlord at the time and his widow Mary held the licence from 1861 to 1871. Their daughter Sarah Thomas held the licence from 1875 to 1881; possibly she was the Mrs. Sarah Harries who was the landlady from 1891 to 1901. David Davies was the landlord in 1906 followed in 1907 by Margaret Jane Davies. No application was made for the pub licence to be renewed in March 1910 and it is now a private house called Cilhendre.

The Rose and Crown once rubbed shoulders with the Globe

As ever, several Newport pubs have defied all efforts to place them. David Jenkins, who was created a Freeman of the town of Pembroke in 1811, was the landlord of the **Union** from 1809 to 1827. Llewellin Griffiths opened the **Swan** in 1826, but it appears to have been more of an ugly duckling and was closed by 1830. The **Black Horse** was opened in 1826 by a widow by the name of Margaret Williams but had only a brief existence, while another widow

The former Rising Sun on the Cilgwyn road

named Mary Rees opened the **Cross** in 1826 and was still there in 1828. The **Corporation** was kept by carpenter John Owen from 1824 to 1826, David Owen was landlord of the **Cambrian** in 1852 and John Mathias was landlord of the **Maltsters' Arms** in 1867.

Moving out of town, the **Rising Sun** was at Pleasant View on the road to Cilgwyn and is recorded as a pub in 1875. In 1881 it was being kept by two sisters – Eleanor Thomas and Margaret Richards – but Eleanor was in charge on her own by 1901. Former master mariner John Vaughan was landlord in 1907 followed by his widow Mary Vaughan in November 1908. No application was made to renew the licence in 1910.

Just beyond Cilgwyn was the **Bridge End**, a cottage ale-house attractively situated near the top of the Gwaun Valley. Thomas Davies, cooper and innkeeper, was the long-serving landlord from 1871 to 1915. The Bridge End subse-

The Bridge End at Cilgwyn is now a private house

quently became the property of Fishguard wine merchant Robert P. Lewis and in 1915 the pub was offered to let plus five-and-a-half acres of 'good pasture'. Lewis struggled to find a steady tenant and the licence changed hands on an almost annual basis over the next half-dozen years before John Rees took over and ran the pub from 1926 to 1933. By then it had become a W.H. George house, but in 1935 the local licensing justices noted that the Bridge End had been closed 'for some time'. They came to the conclusion that this rather remote pub had outlived its usefulness and consequently the licence was not renewed the following year. George's received £100 compensation and nowadays the property is a private house known as Pen-y-bont. (In 1953 an attempt was made to obtain a liquor licence for a café at Banc-y-rhyd in the upper reaches of the Gwaun Valley. This was refused; it was stated that 'during recent years, a licensed house, the Bridge End, was closed through lack of custom').

There are various references in the 1840s and '50s to a property called **Step Inn** on Newport Common, the home of James Thomas. And the *Welshman* newspaper for 27 June 1862 reported a violent disturbance which took place 'at the Step Inn on Newport Mountain, the home of James Thomas and his wife Mary'. Late at night the building was surrounded by a mob who set the place on fire. Fortunately for James and Mary they were spending the night at a nearby residence called Soar. On discovering this the gang turned their attention to Soar, broke into the building and gave James a merciless beating. Eight men later appeared before Kemaes magistrates in connection with the affray, but all were freed for lack of evidence. James Thomas is described as a 'labourer' in the court case, and there is nothing to indicate whether the Step Inn was still functioning as a beer-house at that date.

Now a quiet and picturesque village, Nevern was an important administrative centre in medieval times. It has a wealth of historic monuments, including the remains of a motte and bailey castle above the village and an ancient bridge. In the churchyard is a 'bleeding yew' which drips blood-red sap; legend has it that the tree will continue to bleed until the Welsh are once more in command of the nearby castle. There are a number of notable country houses nearby, one of which, Llwyngwair Manor, is now an hotel.

This widespread parish once boasted a number of pubs; Thomas Martell ran a pub called the **New Inn** somewhere here in the 1780s and there were seven other people in the parish licensed to keep ale-houses in 1784, which might account for local house-names such as Black Lion, Red Lion, Cross Inn and Temple Bar. In any event, if they were pubs they had closed by the turn of the 19th century. In February 1852, the *Pembrokeshire Herald* reported that Mary Williams of the **New Inn** public house in Nevern had received a counterfeit half-crown from a cattle dealer who had called in for a drink on his way home from market. She was the wife of licensee John Williams, but the whereabouts of this evidently short-lived pub isn't known.

John Lloyd was licensee of the much longer living **Bridgend** inn in 1806 and 1807, followed by Martha Lloyd, while Stephen Lloyd was the land-lord for many years from 1817 onwards. The lease of the inn, which appears to have been part of the Berry Hill estate and stood on the riverbank near the bridge, was advertised as becoming available at Michaelmas 1853. 'Coaches from Haverfordwest to Cardigan pass and repass the house twice daily', declared the advertisement, suggesting that the coach road in those days was the present B4582 rather than the longer A487 route via Eglwyswrw.

A blissful setting – The Trewern Arms at Nevern

Following the sale the name was changed to **Trewern Arms**, perhaps reflecting the identity of the new landowners. The pub was visited by tragedy in February 1859 when Lydia Hughes, daughter of landlord Stephen Lloyd, died while giving birth to a stillborn child; three days later Stephen Lloyd also died, aged 73. Elizabeth Lloyd, Stephen's widow, took over as licensee and remained in charge until her death in 1876 at the age of 87. Thomas Daniel was landlord from 1880 to 1891 and his widow, Sarah Daniel, was there from 1895 until her death in 1904. Their two spinster daughters Misses Eliza and Martha Daniel kept the pub from 1906 to 1923. Martha ran the pub on her own from 1924 to 1936 when John Williams took over and he was still there in 1948; during the war the local Home Guard had a supply post at the back of the pub. Esther Williams, formerly of the Salutation in Felindre Farchog, then ran the pub until early 1957, followed briefly by her sister Clara Williams.

In that summer, Wing Commander George Nelson-Edwards and his wife Pamela were holidaying in Pembrokeshire. They were a colourful couple, Pamela being the step-daughter of the Rector of Stiffkey who was notoriously unfrocked after becoming too closely involved in his mission to save fallen women in London's East End; she was also a former 'Windmill Girl' – one of the scantily clad troupe of dancers that performed nightly at London's Windmill Theatre. They were introduced to the Trewern Arms by a friend, the German artist Friedrich Könecamp, and fell in love with the pub and its 'blissful setting' alongside a salmon stream. The pub was about to come up for auction, but Nelson-Edwards pre-empted the sale by paying the landowning Lloyd family £3,500 for the pub, ten acres of land and half a mile of fishing rights. The furnishings still belonged to the outgoing tenants, however, and this auction took place in the road outside the pub, with the auctioneer standing in the porch and buyers sitting along the wall opposite. Fortunately, Mrs. Nelson-Edwards managed to buy nearly all the bar fittings at the auction (her husband was still serving in the RAF) and re-opened the Trewern soon afterwards.

Big changes soon followed to the little rural pub, as the Nelson-Edwards opened a successful pub restaurant and added a small extension which became a large extension in 1963, nearly doubling the size of the original building and including a large kitchen and function room, plus a wine cellar with racks for 1,000 bottles. Chef Francis Fane arrived from the Noel Arms in Chipping Camden to oversee the kitchen, and for four consecutive summer seasons The Dark Blues jazz band entertained diners from far and near every evening.

It was the imminent arrival of the breathalyser which prompted the Nelson-Edwards to give up the Trewern in the mid-1960s. They moved into Newport to open The Pantry bistro and later ran the Swan at Little Haven, having sold the Trewern for £23,000 to Mr. Vladimir Schults who took over in 1966. ('To our mortification', Mr Nelson-Edwards later wrote, 'we discovered that it was sold again three years later for £85,000'). Mr. and Mrs. S. Bruce Reed were there in the 1970s and Peter and Molly Saunders were in charge in the 1980s. Since 1991 the Trewern has been owned by Tony Jones of Saundersfoot, and for nearly all of this time the innkeepers have been Alwyn and Shirley Phillips. It is now a small hotel, popular with anglers and regularly featured in the top food and drink guides, but it has happily managed to remain a village local as well, especially the 'Brew House' bar in the oldest part of the building.

The **College Inn** at nearby Felindre Farchog is recorded in 1751, occupying the building where, tradition has it, George Owen of Henllan founded a school in the 16th century. Between 1780 and 1811, Evan George held an alehouse licence for the 'College in Nevern' following which Jane George kept the place going for a couple of years, after which it seems to have closed.

Felindre Farchog is in Bayvil parish, and William Reynolds is recorded as keeping a pub in Bayvil in 1780. This could have been the **Salutation**, which crops up intermittently in the licensing records in the early 1800s (but can be hard to distinguish from the Salutation at Tafarn-y-Bwlch). Certainly William Lewis ran the Salutation at Bayvil in 1822, followed by William Williams in 1825. Stonemason Ebenezer Lloyd and his wife Sarah kept the Salutation from 1851 to 1867 while from 1871 to 1913 their son, monumental mason John Lloyd ran the pub and Mrs. Elizabeth Lloyd was there from 1914 to 1934. Miss Esther Williams took over, becoming Esther Elizabeth Mullaney in 1944 when she married Major Robert Mullaney MC and Bar. Shortly after the wedding, the smooth-talking Major was posted abroad, and while he was overseas it emerged that he was already married with a wife and home elsewhere in Britain. Charged with bigamy, the Major pleaded guilty and was bound over for two years at Carmarthen Assizes. Shortly afterwards, Esther Williams moved to the Trewern Arms, to be succeeded at the Salutation by David Newcombe. George Morgan took over in 1952 and soon began upgrading the business to cater for the growing tourist trade, being granted a supper licence and altering the building to improve the catering facilities. Peter and Joan Voyce continued the transformation in the 1970s by adding a large accommodation wing and converting a nearby paddock into a large car-park. Former RAF officer Richard Harden and his wife Valerie were mine hosts in the 1990s, and John Denley – formerly of the Llwyngwair and Royal Oak in Newport – has carried on the good work for the past 11 years.

A recent view of the much-extended Salutation at Felindre Farchog

CHAPTER SIXTEEN

Moylegrove, Eglwyswrw and surrounding villages

Moylegrove, an attractive village on the ancient road between Nevern and St. Dogmael's, takes its name from Matilda, wife of Robert Martin, the Norman Lord of Kemaes. The first ale-house recorded in the parish is the **Chance,** known to have been kept by Margaret Rees in 1782 but not heard of again. A mile from the village is Ceibwr Bay, a sheltered cove where coasting vessels once discharged their cargoes of lime and culm; Thomas Lloyd kept an unnamed pub at Ceibwr from 1805 to 1807, evidently succeeded by William Davies who was there until 1813.

Morris Morris kept a pub at Moylegrove from 1805 to 1812 when he seems to have moved to Nevern and become posh – his name thereafter is spelled Maurice Maurice. The sign of his house in Moylegrove isn't known, but William and Rachel Lewis were the licensees of the **New Inn**, Moylegrove between 1819 and 1824.

David Griffiths kept the **Bridgend Tavern,** Moylegrove, in 1841 and Mary Griffiths, innkeeper's wife, was there in 1851. By 1861, when it was the venue for the Court Leet and Court Baron of the Lordship of Moylegrove, Mary was a widow aged 71. In 1871 there is a reference to John Thomas, aged 80, living at the **Moylegrove Inn,** Bridgend, which is presumably the same place.

Some time in the 1870s the village acquired its second **New Inn,** perhaps to replace the old Bridgend Tavern. Caleb Richards was there from 1881 to 1891 and the widowed Rachel Richards held the licence from 1901 to 1910. When she died in September 1910 it was tersely reported in the licensing minutes: 'House closed since by heir'; local legend has it that this decision was made under pressure from the neighbouring Tabernacle chapel. A small garage, complete with petrol pumps, was subsequently added to the former pub and the Richards family began a modest haulage company which eventually developed into the well-known coach company Richards Bros. of Moylegrove. Still in the Richards family, the former New Inn is now known as Bro Dawel.

The former New Inn at Moylegrove as it looks today

*A poster for a sale of stock at Cross Inn.
It was no longer a pub by this time.*
(Picture courtesy of Eglwyswrw Heritage Society)

Somewhere to the south of Moylegrove was the **Fountain Inn,** mentioned in the 1871 census when the innkeeper was a widow named Hannah Lodwig; it seems to have been a short-lived enterprise.

Most of the other inns in this chapter were located on or just off the ancient road over the Preselis from Cardigan to Haverfordwest. Three of these roadside inns were north of Eglwyswrw, the nearest to Cardigan being at the five-way crossroads known as Crossway. David Williams was landlord of the **Cross Inn** at Crossway in 1822, but Watkin Owen was in charge by the following year. David James, a box-maker by trade, ran the pub with his wife Mary in 1851. By 1861 it was being called **Croft House** with Mary James as licensee, and she was still there in 1867. James Williams was in charge from 1871 to 1875, while Stephen George ran Croft House from 1877 to 1880, shortly after which it seems to have closed.

Half a mile south was **Halfway House** where a widow named

Eleanor Rees ran an ale-house and farmed ten acres in 1851. She was still there in 1861, although by this time there is no mention of it still being a pub and it subsequently appears to have been a smithy. The property is still called Halfway House. And further south again, on a relatively busy rural junction, was another **Cross Inn** at Traws in the parish of Eglwyswrw. This was referred to as early as 1712 according to B.G. Charles, but seems to have stopped being an inn in the 18th century. Presumably this is now Cross Inn Farm.

Entering the village of Eglwyswrw from the north, the first hostelry the traveller would have encountered would have been the **Plough**. It was first mentioned in 1826 when William Griffiths was granted an ale-house certificate and he was still there in 1851, aged 79. John Evans was landlord from 1861 until 1882, also farming a 200-acre holding; the Plough served as the village post office for a time, local mail being deposited at the pub and then taken by pony and trap to the station at Narberth Road. According to the book *Eglwyswrw District – History and Memories of a Community* the Plough Hotel moved location at some point, its later position being on the roadside, slightly closer to the village square.

The original Plough Inn at Eglwyswrw

Jenkin Jenkins was licensee in 1886 and David Edwards was there from 1891 to 1895, followed by Eleanor Edwards in 1901 and Miss Hannah Owen in 1906. It was reported in 1913 that the pub was doing very little trade, especially with the

The Plough moved to this building, which later became the village post office.
The former Plough can be seen beyond it

competition from the Sergeant's Inn and the Butchers' Arms just up the road. As a result the Plough was an obvious candidate for redundancy and the axe fell the following year, with compensation of £250 being shared by the licensees Daniel and Hannah Davies and the owner Mrs. Mary Davies of Cardigan. The building later became the village post office – a reprise of the Plough's earlier role in community life – but that, too, has now closed.

A little further along at Bank Uchaf stands the building which once housed one of the county's most historic pubs, the **Sergeant's Inn**. Known locally as 'Ty Mawr', the building may have its origins as a Welsh longhouse, while the name appears to be connected with a nearby armoury, built at the end of the 16th century when there was a threat of invasion from Spain. The yeomanry would muster for training at Eglwyswrw, where their weapons were stored under the guardianship of a full-time soldier – presumably the 'Sergeant' in question.

The inn was kept by Rowland Watkins or Watkyns between 1782 and his death in 1808 when he was described as 'a man beloved by a numerous circle of friends for his uprightness and rectitude'. Another Rowland Watkins, probably a son, took over and was there well into the 1840s. Richard Fenton, writing in 1810, recorded that for many years the inn:

Had the honour of entertaining the gentlemen of the bar attending the Carmarthen circuit annually on their way from Haverfordwest to

The Sergeant's Inn at the turn of the 20th century.
The inn occupied the right-hand side of the long building.
(Picture courtesy of Eglwyswrw Heritage Society and Mrs. Doris Davies)

through Alice a tedious and fatiguing stage across the mountains, in the course of which no convenient baiting place occurs before, to meet with a decent public house, bearing so specious a name as that of Serjeant's Inn, must be highly gratifying.

According to Fenton, the itinerant judges and learned counsel would while away the evening at the Sergeant's Inn by staging mock tribunals 'in carrying on which mock process an infinite deal of wit, humour and festivity is excited'. Real tribunals were also held at the inn, the petty sessions for the Hundred of Kemaes being held here for many years, as was the Court Leet and Court Baron of the Lordship of Eglwyswrw.

Margaret Watkins, daughter of the previous Rowland Watkins, gradually took over from her father in the 1850s, while another Rowland Watkins – brother of Margaret – was landlord from 1861 until his death in 1886. There was a Rowland Harries in charge from 1891 to 1895, William Daniel was the landlord from 1901 to 1911 and his widow Mrs. Lydia Daniel held the licence from 1911 to 1933. Busiest time of the year at the Sergeant's – and both the other pubs in the village – was the annual Meugan Fair in November when Mrs. Daniel would spend the day preparing and serving meals for the drovers

The Sergeant's Inn in later years.
(Picture courtesy of Eglwyswrw Heritage Society)

and livestock dealers who came from all over the country and who sealed many of the transactions in the pub itself.

Between 1933 and 1945 Elizabeth James was licensee, followed in turn by Howard Thomas, John Davies and William Charles. Stan Whittle was behind the bar in the early 1960s, with Ron Andrews taking over in 1964. Subsequent licensees included Trevor Andrews, Henry Franks and Nikki Paton, the latter earning the Sergeant's a reputation for excellent food. With its red and black quarry-tiled floor, old settles and ancient wooden beams, this remained one of the most characterful inns in the county, but sadly that didn't prevent it from closing in about 1995. It is now a private house, with its historic features carefully preserved.

A butcher (naturally enough) named David Phillips held the licence of the **Butchers' Arms** at Bank Isaf, Eglwyswrw, from 1867 to 1875, after which it became the Thomas family pub for several generations. This was another centre of great activity during Meugan Fair, so much so that the licensees always cleared out all the furniture in advance, leaving standing room only for the thirsty fair-goers. Daniel Thomas ran the pub from 1880 to 1923 and his widow Lydia Thomas was licensee in 1924; she died at the pub in 1933 at the age of 91. Their son Thomas Thomas was landlord from 1926 to 1934. Vince Thomas took over, being helped by his mother Mrs. Ann Thomas (Aunty Ann) until her death in 1948.

The Butchers' Arms before it was extended.
(Picture courtesy of Eglwyswrw Heritage Society and Mrs. Doris Davies)

In the book *Eglwyswrw District* there is a story about a tramp and rogue named Albert Hitchings who regularly dropped in for a pint at the Butchers' when he was passing through the district:

> In those days the Butchers' Arms was run by Vince and Aunty Ann. Vince used to sell rabbits from one of the outbuildings. There is a legendary tale about Albert sneaking into the shed and stealing Vince's rabbits. He then had the daring to sell the pair of rabbits back to Vince and spend the proceeds on beer in Vince's pub.

Vince Thomas remained in charge until his death in 1974, the pub having been enlarged at some stage by the addition of a two-storey extension on the right-hand side. His daughter, Miss P.A. Thomas, then carried on the family tradition, running 'The Butch' for a further ten years. Since then it has changed hands on several occasions, the licensees including Mary Delaney and Jean Webb, and is still open for business.

There are other possible references to alehouses in Eglwyswrw. B.G. Charles has uncovered several 18th century references to **Tavern y Spite** while the 1851 census shows properties called White Lion and Black Lion near the Plough.

A recent view of the Butchers', showing the extension on the right

A mile outside the village on the Crymych Road was the apparently unremarkable **Bryngwyn Arms** run by tailor Daniel Williams from 1875 to 1891. Ann Williams was licensee between

The Bryngwyn Arms has been a private house for many years

A poster advertising one of the regular auctions at the Cwmgloyne.

(Picture courtesy of Ken Maycock and Nerys Hughes)

1901 and her death in 1908. Miss Mary Williams took over and held the licence until 1915, after which John Phillips was in charge until 1924 when no application was made to renew the licence. Now a private house, it is still called Bryngwyn.

The widowed Mary Rees kept the **Cwmgloyne Arms**, Crosswell, between the 1850s and 1871, although this fine, stone-built property is of earlier construction and appears to date from the late 18th century. In *A Book on Nevern* Mr. Dillwyn Miles writes of the local Nonconformist worshippers:

> Family devotion was held in most houses in the vicinity, including the Cwmgloyne Arms at Crosswell where, in the absence of any males, the widowed landlady, Mary Rees, led the prayers. John Owen, the author of the ballad Y Mochyn Du, who was a servant at the pub before he became a minister, observed he was glad when there was no man present so that he could enjoy his mistress's intonations.

William Williams was the licensee between 1881 and his death in 1915 and he also farmed the 20-acre smallholding that went with the pub. His son Thomas Williams took over and was both owner and licensee in 1923 when the pub was declared surplus to requirements by the local magistrates. It limped along until finally closing in April 1925. It is now known as Crosswell House and still retains many of the features of the old inn, including wooden beams and flagstone floors and an interesting collection of old posters advertising auction sales on the premises. One of these proclaims 'A Great Sale of Drapery' in December 1893 which comprised all kinds of clothing as well as hurricane lanterns, ladies' umbrellas and 'about a ton of cheese'. The old brewhouse can still be seen at the rear of the building, and the cart-houses and stable block (across the road) indicate

The former Cwmgloyne Arms at Crosswell still looks like the country inn it once was

that this was once a crossroads inn of some note in this remote moorland area.

The nearby **Royal Oak** may well have been an ale-house at one time, but that must have been in the distant past, while there is a local tradition that a cottage at Temple Gate was once the **Red Cow** ale-house (or shebeen). Better documented is the **Swan** near Pontyglasier which was up and running by 1842 and was kept by William Williams and his wife Mary from 1851 to 1861. The widowed Mary was licensee from 1867 to 1871 and Thomas Thomas, draper, grocer and innkeeper, was there from 1880 to 1906. According to *Eglwyswrw District:*

> The brewhouse was at the rear of the property and the brewing ingredients were transported to the site, The finished product was 'cwrw cartref' – home-brewed ale.

John Jones was landlord from 1907 to 1910 after which Phoebe Davies had a couple of years in charge. David George took over in 1913 but the pub was closed under the redundancy regulations in 1919 when owner John Thomas received compensation of £315 and licensee George pocketed £35. The business carried on as The Swan shop, and – to quote from *Eglwyswrw District* once more, kindly translated from the Welsh by its editor, Mrs. Beatrice Davies:

> John Thomas (Thomas y Swan) and his wife ran a shop on the premises until the middle of the last century. The Swan was a meeting place where the occasional salmon from the nearby River Nevern or a few rabbits crossed the counter in exchange for basic goods. A true social centre.

It is now a private house.

The Swan near Pontyglasier has long been in retirement as a pub

The Salutation Inn was usually called Tafarn-y-Bwlch

For travellers on the mountain road from Cardigan to Haverfordwest, the **Salutation Inn** at the foot of the Preselis was the last chance for rest and refreshment before the steep pull over the open hills to the New Inn. It was even mentioned as a landmark in *Paterson's Roads,* a guidebook for stagecoach passengers published in the early 19th century. Usually known as **Tafarn y Bwlch** – the 'tavern in the gap' – this farmhouse inn was mentioned in 1752 and the Friendly Society which was based there was the unlikely subject of a poem by a local bard a few years later. Records relating to this inn are particularly sketchy, but it seems to have been kept from 1780 to 1784 by Lettice Thomas and by Stephen Jenkins from 1809 to 1813. Thomas Griffiths, an insolvent debtor, was forced to sell the property in May 1838 together with 'the rights of Common and Turbary there belonging' – turbary being the right to cut peat on the mountain. It was said that the dwelling had been used as a public house 'for many years'. A slater named William Jones was there in 1841 and his widow Eleanor had charge in 1851. Simon Harries and his wife Mary were in residence from 1871 to 1881, farmer John Williams was there from 1891 to 1902 and William James kept the pub from 1906 to 1908 when no application was made for the licence to be renewed.

CHAPTER SEVENTEEN

St. Dogmael's

The community of St. Dogmael's stands right on the county boundary, and parts of it were bandied between Pembrokeshire and Cardiganshire in the 19th century for political purposes. In later years, when Cardiganshire was 'dry' on a Sunday and Pembrokeshire 'wet', the contentious county boundary meant you could get a drink on the Sabbath in parts of the village and not in others. Even on weekdays there was a difference, with houses in one licensing division closing at 9pm and those in the other division staying open to 10pm, prompting a late evening migration of drinkers from one part of the village to another. In 2003 the boundary was changed yet again, so that the village proper now lies within Pembrokeshire. The nearby hamlet of Bridge End, which links St. Dogmael's to Cardigan, presents an even bigger problem of identity, and it is a toss-up whether it should be included in this book or in some future volume on Ceredigion pubs. Since the census enumerators usually placed most, if not all, of Bridge End in Pembrokeshire, it seems appropriate to include it here.

Bridge End once boasted a high concentration of inns and pot-houses, partly because this was the ancient approach to Cardigan bridge and castle from the south, and partly because it developed into an important centre of trade and industry, with a busy quay backed by warehouses, timber yard, rope-walk, iron foundry and lime kilns. Farmers from a wide area would be constantly coming and going with cart-loads of butter in casks, oats and barley to sell either at market or direct to dealers and agents for shipment around the coast. Much of the prosperity of the area was due to the enterprise of the Davies family of mariners, merchants and ship-owners from along the coast at Newport. John Davies and his brother Thomas set up in business in St. Dogmael's as general merchants in 1785, gradually building up their enterprise until Bridge End was the hub of a highly successful trading, banking and property empire which flourished during the 19th century.

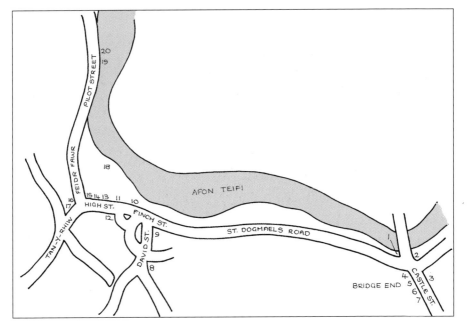

ST. DOGMAEL'S

1	Eagle	11	Sloop
2	Castle	12	Ship
3	White Lion/Liverpool Arms	13	Red Lion
4	Fishguard Arms	14	Mariners' Arms
5	Square and Compass	15	Sailor's Home
6	Shipwrights' Arms	16	Corner House
7	Farmers' Arms	17	Rose and Crown
8	Cardigan Bay	18	Tivy/Teifi Netpool
9	Treffynnon/Fountain	19	Royal Exchange
10	White Hart	20	Ferry

Castle Street in Bridge End – one of the booziest thoroughfares in Pembrokeshire

Crossing the bridge from Cardigan, the first pub to be encountered would have been the **Bridgend Arms** which was kept by Margaret Sanderbrook in 1844 and by a maltster named David Davies in the 1850s. It was probably on the quayside, while most of the Bridge End pubs were in Castle Street, the road leading south from the bridge, where the **Castle** still stands at No. 1 Castle Street. Richard Harris seems to have kept the pub in the early 1840s and architect and builder Daniel Evans was licensee from 1850 until his death in 1852. This was almost certainly the chapel-building Daniel Evans who at one time kept the Golden Lion in Fishguard. Architectural historian Julian Orbach has attributed a number of fine buildings to this talented architect/ innkeeper, including Tabor Baptist Chapel in Dinas and Bethania Baptist Chapel in Cardigan. Evans appears to have moved to St. Dogmael's to act as clerk of works at Cardigan Workhouse in the late 1830s and he also oversaw repairs to Cardigan jail. There is a suggestion that he was responsible for rebuilding the Castle Inn to his own design.

He was followed by his son John and then by John Evans' son-in-law John Jones who remained in charge until his death in 1864, after which Sarah

There have been relatively few changes at the Castle Inn

Hughes ran the Castle from 1867 to 1871. Jacob Watkin was the landlord from 1873 to 1884, being succeeded in turn by Thomas Jones, William Lloyd and Griffith James who was in charge from 1906 to 1914. George Mathias then had a long spell in charge which spanned both world wars, after which Ellen 'Nellie' Hopkins had an even longer stint as licensee, running the Castle for some 60 years until her death in 2002. Her son Bernard took over, and the Castle remains a classic example of an unspoilt family-run pub, little changed in half a century.

Two doors from the Castle Inn was the **Hope and Anchor**, run by George Lloyd from 1819 to 1840 and by James and Elizabeth Owen from 1841 to 1852. Thomas Harries was publican in the late 1850s, but the pub closed in about 1860.

On the corner of the muddy track that was later to become Station Road was the original **Shipwrights' Arms**, presumably the inn kept by Dinah Thomas in the 1841 census. According to local historian W.J. Lewis:

> On this lane stood the Shipwrights' Arms which was later moved over the road. When the inn's lease expired David Davies [of the Davies family of entrepreneurs] had numbers 6-10 Castle Street built in its place.

Further along, Mary Rowlands ran the **Liverpool Arms** at 12 Castle Street from 1858 to 1871 with the help of a servant named Mary Harris; no doubt the customers included the furnace hands and puddlers who worked at the nearby iron foundry. There was another Liverpool Arms just over the river at Bridge Parade and this may have prompted Mrs. Rowlands to change the name of her pub, because between 1875 and 1880 she is listed as running the **White Lion**. By the time of the 1881 census Mary Harris had become the licensee and she was still running the White Lion in the 1890s when she was in her 80s. In 1905 the pub was described as being very small, having just two public rooms with a store-room under the stairs and very little accommodation. The occupant by this time was Daniel Lloyd Jones and the following year he decided not to reapply for a licence.

It is impossible to be certain, but its seems that the next pub on the left was the **Newport Arms** which was run between 1817 and 1830 by John Mathias, master of the schooner *Victoria*, and later by Margaret Mathias who was there until 1864. According to local historian Glen Johnson, the pub then closed, being re-opened 20 years later at a different location in Castle Street. Miss Ellen Mathias is recorded as being licensee of the Newport Arms in 1884 and John Jones was licensee in 1891. By 1901 it was being described as the 'old' Newport Arms, suggesting it had closed; however the licence seems to have been kept up, although 'dormant', until 1906. In that year the Newport Arms was put out of its misery when the magistrates formally quashed the licence.

The other side of Castle Street had an even higher concentration of pubs. The first hostelry on the right after crossing the bridge would probably have been the **Eagle**. The early history of this pub is sketchy, but Captain John Mathias, master of the ketch *Heart of Oak*, kept this tavern from 1840 to 1853, followed by cabinet-maker John Havard. Following his death in the 1860s, his widow Phoebe became licensee. Thomas

The Eagle in the days of Zephania James.
(Picture courtesy of the Eagle)

Mathias was in charge from 1871 to 1883 followed by Abel Isaac who died here in 1886. John Lewis was in charge from 1891 to 1901 followed by Mrs. A. Lewis in 1906. In 1909 the police expressed some concern that the pub had four exit doors leading in different directions; they felt that this represented far too many ways of sneaking in and out undetected outside licensing hours. Evan Jones was in charge in 1912 followed by Zephania and Catherine James who were there until the 1930s and also ran a small tea-room. David Owens

Happily the Eagle Inn is open again after a fire

and William James were licensees in the 1940s and '50s, followed by George Hopkins. Islwyn and Doreen Mathias were in charge in the 1960s, since when the longest-serving licensees have been Brian and Elizabeth Dixon, during whose time the pub's tug-of-war team acquired a formidable reputation. Peter Warren took over in 2007, but the pub was damaged by fire in August 2008 and was closed for a time. Happily it is now open again, the landlord having taken the opportunity to refurbish the building and carry out a number of improvements.

The Eagle is on one corner of the junction of the road leading to St. Dogmael's; beyond the junction the pubs came thick and fast. At number 25 Castle Street was the **Fishguard Arms** run by David Jones from 1835 to 1844 and by baker Ann Jones from 1850 to 1875. In the days when the Davies family of merchants owned most of the properties around Bridge End, rents would be collected annually at the Fishguard Arms and the tenants suitably entertained at the inn. It was also pressed into service from time to time as a petty sessions house for the Hundred of Cilgerran. William Morris was licensee in 1880, David Morgan was in charge from 1884 to 1891 and Mrs. Elizabeth Morgan was there in 1895. Hubert Williams was landlord in 1901 and when he left the pub in 1904 he held an auction of his household furniture, plus 'six store pigs and a barrel of Hawthorn's Condiment'. John Davies was licensee from 1905 until the pub closed in 1925.

David Jones was landlord of the **Compass Arms** from 1805 to 1810. Perhaps this was the same place as the **Square and Compass** at 24 Castle Street, kept between 1840 and 1878 by Thomas and Martha Jones. John Williams was landlord from 1878 to 1887 and Thomas Morris was there in 1891. He was followed by Josiah Evans in 1895 and then by John and Hannah Thomas who also ran the Shipwrights' next door. It became part of the portfolio of pubs owned by the Swansea Old Brewery but closed in 1903, reopening in 1905 with Lydia Greenaway behind the bar (her husband Fred ran the Shipwrights', the two pubs having become virtually an item by this time). However Cardigan magistrates had it earmarked for closure and took away the licence the following year on the grounds that there were five other pubs within 100 yards.

Making it three pubs in a row, at number 23 was the later version of the **Shipwrights' Arms** which had apparently moved from across the road. William Jones was in charge from 1844 to 1850, followed by Catherine Jones. In 1860 she married mariner John Lewis, master of the *Amity*, and he became licensee until 1882, after which Catherine carried on until about 1900. She was followed by John and Hannah Thomas. Fred Greenaway was in charge in 1906 and Simon Jenkins was landlord in 1912, but the licence was revoked two years later.

Two doors further along at number 21 Castle Street was the **Farmers' Arms**. Evan Jenkins was in charge from 1840 to 1844 and a cooper named

William Phillips kept the pub from 1850 to 1875. John Roberts was landlord from 1880 to 1901, followed by Mrs. M. Roberts in 1906. John Davies held the licence from 1908 to 1914; possibly he also ran the Fishguard Arms. Edward Lewis was in charge of this apparently unremarkable pub from 1917 to 1926 when the Farmers' was referred to the compensation committee and duly closed.

There were several other pubs in or just off Castle Street at various times, including the **Joiners' Arms** run by Simon James from 1840 to 1844; the **Half Moon** where Margaret Griffiths was licensee from 1844 to 1850; the **Coopers' Arms**, known to have been open in 1835 and kept by Elizabeth Williams in 1840 and by Thomas Williams in 1848; and the oddly-named **Bryn-Bwa Arms,** an ale-house cum lodging house run by Sarah Mathias at 45 Castle Street from 1871 to 1875.

Elsewhere around the dockside and timber yard at Bridge End in the 1840s were the **Pelican** run by John Matthews and a second **Castle** kept by Evan Elias between 1844 and 1850. Also nearby was the **Tivy Side** run by Thomas Thomas in the 1840s, followed by Captain John Jones, master of the *Sarah Ann*, and then by Elizabeth Jenkins; it closed in the 1860s. The **Railway** was kept by Morris Davies from 1854 to 1858; it would be 30 years before the line from Whitland reached Cardigan, so the name possibly signified that a coach service ran from the pub to the nearest railhead. (Davies had at one time been coachman on the Cardigan to Carmarthen run).

St. Dogmael's itself is former fishing village on the bank of the River Teifi, not far from where it joins the sea. Named after a 5th century Welsh monk who probably founded a cell here, it developed when a Benedictine Abbey was established by the Normans in 1115. The monks weren't always as pious and abstemious as they might have been. In 1402 they were criticised for visiting taverns and were suspected of 'meeting women in the town'; one of them – Brother Howel Lange – was ordered to give up wine for a year as a punishment for his misdeeds. The monks must have been expert brewers and seem to have left the community with a legacy of brewing and selling beer – not always legally. In 1615, Hugh Johnes of Llanychaer, smith, and Thomas Price, were presented at the Great Sessions 'for keeping at St. Dogmells without a licence a common tippling house and for selling ale and beer'. Unfortunately Price happened to be Vicar of St. Dogmael's at the time. In 1850, a 'quack doctor' by the name of John Davies was arrested for operating an illegal still in the village, while at Cwmdegwell was a notorious shebeen, run in 1892 by Elizabeth Thomas. When police raided the place one day they found 60 gallons of beer in different stages of brewing. It was said that a neighbouring pub had been reduced from four brewings a month to one because of the illegal trade at the shebeen. The police were also very vigilant about enforcing the Sunday Closing Act in St. Dogmael's, adopting a 'stop and search' policy towards anyone suspected of buying a jug of beer from the back door of a pub. Noted the *Cardigan Observer* in 1885:

> It is difficult to traverse the street in company with anything in the shape of a jar, jug, bottle or even tea-pot without having to answer a number of pertinent questions put in the most polite way by PC Something-or-other.

The ruins of the abbey are now preserved, and the village is an attractive mixture of terraced fisherman's cottages and marine villas built to take advantage of the estuary views. The village fishermen were thirsty enough to ensure that St. Dogmael's was well supplied with taverns down the years. There were usually around half-a-dozen ale-houses in the village between the 1780s and 1813, but this dropped to three in the years of national depression which followed the Battle of Waterloo, before recovering in the 1820s and reaching a peak of about 15 in the 1850s. Among the early alehouses was the **Bear** run by David Nathan from 1819 to 1823. He changed the name to **Royal Oak** in 1824, but it seems to have been the kiss of death for the pub because it wasn't heard of again. The **Salutation** run by Thomas Davies lasted from 1817 to 1823 while the **Swan** had a much shorter lifespan, Elizabeth Davies running it for two years from 1822. Even less successful was the **Anchor** which lasted barely a year in 1827; James Rowlands was the landlord. Another early pub was the **King's Head** where William Bowen was landlord in 1805 and where Mary Bowen was landlady from 1810 to 1823 when – like a number of other village pubs – it disappeared from the records. The **King's Head** kept by George Lloyd (ex Hope and Anchor?) from 1844 to 1850 was probably a different place. Thomas Owens ran the **Rope and Anchor** between 1820 and 1823 and maltster David Owens ran the **Crown and Anchor** from 1835 to 1850; perhaps they were the same place, but it is impossible to say for certain.

Approaching St. Dogmael's proper from Bridge End, there was once a pub on the junction at the bottom of David Street. This was originally called the **Fountain** and Elizabeth

The Treffynon at the bottom of David Street no longer stands.

(Picture courtesy of Mr. Dai Griffiths)

James was licensee in the 1830s and '40s. She died in 1850 to be followed by butcher Daniel Morgan and his son Thomas who adopted the Welsh version of the name, changing the sign to **Treffynnon**. The Morgans were followed by Rees Jones in 1867 and Ann Jones from 1871 to 1881. Thomas Griffiths, who ran the pub in the 1880s, was often in trouble for keeping a rowdy house; no doubt the fact that the Cardiganshire-licensed Treffynnon was able to keep later hours than its Pembrokeshire neighbours had something to do with this. George Adams was the landlord from 1891 until his death in 1921 and John Isaac brewed and sold his own beer between 1923 and about 1930. Licensees came and went regularly in the 1930s, the licence lapsed in September 1943 and the pub has since been demolished.

Along David Street, at the junction with Longdown or London Street was the **Cardigan Bay.** James and Elizabeth Tucker were the publicans from 1861 to 1878 and Captain John Jones kept the pub from 1895 to 1906 when it was described as having just two rooms downstairs for customers and a rather smelly urinal in the back yard 'not properly drained and made of wood'. It was doing little trade at the time and closed soon afterwards.

Back on the main road through the village, Ann George, baker and publican, kept the **Angel** on Angel Bridge, near the mill, from 1835 until her death in 1870, after which it became a grocer's shop. Across the road the **White Hart** is still going strong. The pub was kept by master mariner William Evans from 1858 to 1871 and his widow, Mrs. Mary Evans, was landlady from 1875 to 1911. Their daughter Mrs. Eleanor Richards then took over the business, still brewing her own beer until well into the 1920s. In 1937 it was reported that

The White Hart stands opposite the ruined abbey

the White Hart did the best business of the surviving pubs in the village and that it had been in the same family for 80 years. Miss Sarah Ann Richards took over in 1942 but died in 1949 aged 69 to be succeeded by Phoebe Parry. The pub subsequently changed hands every couple of years, the licensees including Alexander Dashwood, Stanley Whittle, Ronald Hills and Mona Hills. Stan Ricketts was in charge between 1962 and 1968 followed for a number of years by William Chandler. Hugh Samways was there from 2001 to 2005 followed by Ann Duckworth and the current licensee Andrew Monaghan.

Further along on the right, just past Feidr Fach, was the **Sloop**, which still bears the name although it hasn't been a pub for nearly a century. This was the headquarters of at least two Friendly Societies – the Fishermen's Benefit Society, which is recorded as meeting here in 1869, and the Ancient Britons' Friendly Society. This latter lodge was apparently founded in 1778, which would make it one of the first in the county, and it celebrated its 127th anniversary at the pub in 1905, by which time numbers had fallen to such an extent that there were too few members to form the usual procession to Cardigan.

The Sloop was also a meeting place of the local seine-net fishermen who no doubt spent many an evening grumbling into their pints of home brew about everything from the weather to the various Fishery Acts which curtailed their salmon-catching activities. David Davies was landlord from 1858 to 1865; a widow named Mary Davies held the licence from 1871 to 1891, when she was 80; and Ann Thomas was licensee in 1894. From 1900

An early view of St. Dogmael's High Street.
(Picture courtesy of the Teifi Netpool Inn)

The former Sloop Inn still bears its old name

to 1913 the landlady was Mrs. Mary Lewis, and during her time the local vicar, the Rev. Mr. Hughes, led calls for the Sloop to be closed on the grounds that it was 'totally unsuitable as a public house, being nothing more than a cottage'. The closure move failed, but Mrs. Lewis called it a day a few years later, not bothering to renew the licence in 1913.

Nautical names were popular in the village and the **Ship** was open from 1823 when the landlord was George Richards. He died in 1844 and his widow Ann Richards was in charge from 1844 well into the 1850s; she appears as 'retired publican' in the 1861 census. By all accounts this pub was virtually opposite the Sloop, in the building now known as Amblestone.

Numerous beer-houses were to be found in this area in the 1850s kept by, among others, Elizabeth George, Mary Lloyd, Ann Rees, Thomas Gwynne and Louisa Jones. Frustratingly, their signs were not recorded by the census enumerators, nor by the compilers of the trade directories. Better documented is the **Red Lion** which was on the same side of the road as the Sloop, about half-way up to the junction. James Watkins was there in 1858 and his wife or widow Mary Watkins held the licence in 1867. She was followed by John Phillips in 1871 and subsequently by his son-in-law Peter Jones in 1875. He was a master mariner and while he was at sea his wife Ann Jones ran the inn, as she did in the years following his death in 1893. When she died three years later the pub closed for a few years, but had reopened under Captain J.P. Richards by 1904, in which year the Red Lion was sold at auction as a going concern, together with outhouses, brewhouse and a large garden. The purchaser was a Captain Wigley who obviously had no interest in running a pub and made no application for the licence to be renewed in 1905. The business became a draper's shop but still has echoes of its previous life, being called Lion House.

Further up the hill, virtually on the corner, was the **Mariners' Arms**. Ship's carpenter Thomas Evans was landlord from 1867 to 1881, although it was his wife Elizabeth who was usually behind the bar. Mary Griffiths was the publican in the 1880s and William Jenkins kept the pub and brewed his own beer from 1887 to 1921 when no application was made for the licence to be renewed.

On the corner itself was the **Sailor's Home** This kind of name was understandably very popular in the village, Elizabeth Evans keeping the **Sailor's Return** in 1844 and Richard Jones running the **Sailor's Arms** from 1844 to 1850, neither of which can now be identified. It was fisherman John Davies who ran the Sailor's Home from 1867 to 1871, while shipbuilder and innkeeper Thomas Evans was landlord from 1886 until his death in 1898, at which time the pub was put up for auction together with the fishing boat *Pinog* and an assortment of nets. John Davies was the landlord from 1901 to 1907 when the pub became an early victim of the redundancy ruling, being forced to close with Mr. Davies receiving compensation of £60. The owner of the property, Mrs. W. Williams, received a relatively high pay-out of £905. The building subsequently became Cross House, but was later demolished and a small seating area now marks the spot.

There was also a pub on the opposite corner. John Thomas seems to have opened the aptly named **Corner House** in the 1840s. Master mariner Evan Phillips held the licence between 1858 and his death in 1870 at the

The Corner House closed in 1939

age of 72 when the widowed Margaret Phillips took over; she was still there in 1880. John Phillips was the landlord between 1891 and 1906, during which time the property was substantially rebuilt, and Eleanor Phillips held the licence from 1907 to 1910. William Bowen was in charge from 1910 to 1920 and William Thomas Davies kept the pub throughout the 1920s, followed in turn by David Lewis and Annie Bowen. She was there in 1937 when the local police superintendent reported that the pub was 'fairly clean', but that the amount of trade 'can only be described as very poor, being practically nil except on Friday and Saturday nights when there is a little trade done'. This lack of trade presumably accounted for the fact that the pub closed in 1939.

A little further up the hill was the **Rose and Crown**. Peter Davies was maltster and postmaster in 1850 while his wife Elizabeth ran the pub; Davies himself seems to have been the landlord thereafter until at least 1871. Their son-in-law John Lewis was the landlord from 1873 to 1888, but as he was often at sea it was his wife who really ran the pub. Builder and painter Henry Owen Davies (a son of Peter Davies) was landlord from 1891 until his death in 1911, after which his widow Mrs. Mary Davies held the licence until 1922. Mrs. Elizabeth Rowlands took over the licence, although the pub seems to have been more or less disused by this time. However, as owner and licensee she received £300 compensation when the pub was closed under the redundancy ruling, the axe falling in June of that year. The pub was later demolished and replaced by Bethsaida Chapel vestry.

The **Teifi Netpool Inn** has long been at the heart of the village's salmon fishing industry; the green outside was once covered in 'standards' – frames

Salmon fishermen outside the Tivy – now the Teifi Netpool Inn.
(Picture courtesy of the Teifi Netpool Inn)

The Tivy was once surrounded by its own farmland.
Note the 'standards' for drying nets in the field below the pub.
(Picture courtesy of the Teifi Netpool Inn)

where the seine nets, dipped in tannin to preserve them, would be hung to dry
or be repaired. Shipbuilding was carried on at the Pinog on a reach of the river
just below the pub, and this was also where the salmon fleet was beached.
The nearby Teifi netpool, like the Cardigan netpool across the river, was one
of a number of prized salmon pools on the Teifi, and to ensure fairness, the

The Teifi Netpool Inn has a fine collection of memorabilia
recalling the salmon fishing industry

fishermen would draw lots each day to see who fished which pool. The draw took place at the Teifi Netpool Inn, where a bag of numbered pebbles was hung in the porch, and at the end of the day the catch would be weighed and sold at the pub, some of the fish going to the smokehouse next door.

The **Tivy** as it was then usually called, was run for over half a century by David Thomas who was the landlord in 1891 and who died in May 1949 aged 94, having seen the salmon fleet diminish from 20 boats to just a handful. It was a substantial place in his day, having five bedrooms and three attic bedrooms, a brewhouse and a cowshed; it was also surrounded by a large area of farmland, much of which was later taken for council housing. As the fishing industry dwindled, so did the pub trade, and it was reported in 1937 that 'the business done is very small except during the summer months when it is a little better'. It was also noted that 'the cleanliness of this house leaves a good deal to be desired'. When new landlord William Alban Williams took over from the deceased Mr. Thomas, one of his first moves was to apply for a full 'on' licence, the Tivy having previously been run as an old-fashioned beer-house; he also built an extension to the original building. Mr. Williams remained in charge until 1960 after which Margaret Williams and Mrs. Danville Grota both had periods in charge. Brian and Diane Miles were the publicans in the 1990s, while Brian and Val Ashford, who have been running the Teifi Netpool Inn since 2001, have been diligent in helping to preserve the heritage of the salmon fishing industry. The pub walls are covered with wonderful photographs from the hey-day of the industry, while also on display are a coracle and a pair of the immensely long and oddly bent oars that would have been used to propel the salmon boats. (The pub also boasts what is probably the only haunted pool table in Britain – but that is a different story).

Further down the river at Glant-eifon was the **Royal Exchange** where Anne Rees appears to have been licensee in 1861. Fisherman Thomas Davies moved from the nearby Ferry Inn to run the pub from 1871 to '81 with the help of his wife Elenor, while Richard Kirkham from Plymouth kept the pub from 1891

Fishermen would sneak into the Royal Exchange
by the back door for an after-hours drink

A rather battered poster advertising an auction sale at the Royal Exchange

until his death in 1902. Thomas Bowen was the landlord in 1906, handing on to Ann Staton who was in charge in 1908 when the magistrates came under pressure to refuse to renew the licence. The Rev. Mr. Hughes, scourge of the licensed trade, was again the one leading calls for the pub to be closed, while Constable Thomas deposed that he visited the premises from time to time as part of his duties, but rarely found more than two

*The Ferry Inn still looks much the same as ever from the front,
but has been extended greatly to the rear*

customers inside – 'usually the same two'. He also expressed concern that
the rear of the pub could be approached from the river bank and that people
could thus sneak in without being observed from the highway – a clear hint
that the Royal Exchange was more used by afterhours drinkers, especially
fishermen, than regular customers. The magistrates renewed the licence
for a year on condition that a six foot high wall be built surrounding the
rear of the premises; this didn't happen and the licence was withdrawn the
following year.

Next door is the **Ferry Inn** which David Rees ran in the early 1840s.
He died in 1845 and the following year Elizabeth Rees was ejected from the
pub, despite claiming in court that it was her property. Doing the ejecting
was one John Rees and he was in residence in 1851. Catherine Mathias
was licensee in 1861 and in 1867 the landlord was Thomas Davies. He
moved to the Royal Exchange and Elizabeth Jones was in charge in 1871
followed by Evan Jones in 1875. David Rees, coxswain of the Cardigan
lifeboat, held the licence from 1881 to 1914. During this time the pub was
the lodge of a branch of a Friendly Society known as the Ancient Britons,
whose parades through the village in full regalia and led by the Llanfyrnach
Miners' Brass Band always drew crowds of spectators. John James and
Thomas Morris then had stints in charge, while Stephen Morgan ran the

The Webley Arms as it used to look.
(Picture courtesy of the Webley Arms)

pub and brewed his own beer between 1919 and 1940. 'The house does a fairly steady trade', it was reported in 1937. Elizabeth Morgan took charge in 1940 and remained until 1947.

Her departure signalled a turbulent 20-year period in the pub's history, during which time no fewer than ten different licensees came and went. Only Esther Lewis and Barbara Bowen, who each lasted four years, stayed for any significant period, while William Kingsley Thomas became bankrupt in 1965 after two years in charge, blaming the opening of the caravan club at Poppit for taking his trade away. David Owen fared rather better in the 1960s, while big changes to the pub took place in 1972 under partners John and Pamela Goldstone and Tony and Rosemary Wordberg. They built a 60-seater restaurant at the back of the original inn, since when decked terraces have been added to take advantage of the river view – the same view that would have been enjoyed by the coastguards who once kept an eye on the river traffic from the Watch House next door. David John Kendall was licensee for 15 years before leaving in 2002 to run a pub in Lampeter, and the Ferry became an S.A. Brain and Co. house in January 2005 when the Cardiff brewers took over the west Wales inns previously owned by Innkeeper Wales. Like all the pubs in the village it has a fascinating collection of local memorabilia on the walls, mainly posters and bill-heads from the hey-day of the river trade.

*The original Webley Arms can still be identified at
the heart of the later additions*

Beautifully situated, the **Webley Arms** near Poppit evidently takes its name from the Webley Parry family of Noyadd Trefawr. It was run by David Davies from 1844 to 1850, followed by Samuel Owen and then John Davies. The freehold of the inn came up for auction in January 1862 when Davies was the tenant. Prospective buyers were informed that 'a great number of vessels are always moored exactly opposite to the door of the Inn and the Webley Arms is much resorted to as a marine residence in the summer months'. Master mariner Joseph Williams was in charge in 1871 but by 1881 the licensee was his widow Elizabeth. By 1885 the licensee was William Harper and the pub boasted 'a first class covered-in skittle alley', while in the summer months Mr. Harper entertained trippers in a 'well-appointed refreshment tent, 40 feet long' on the nearby sands. The enterprising Mr. Harper remained in charge until 1904 and may have been the one who began to extend the property which has changed greatly over the years. Lewis Davies was the landlord in 1906 and there was another John Davies in charge, brewing his own beer, between 1910 and 1920. David Davies was the landlord from 1923 to 1927 and he was succeeded in fairly quick succession by, among others, H.C. Miles, Daniel Davies and Harry Hurst. The arrival of Martha Daniel in 1941 put an end to the comings and goings; she was in charge until 1958 when Eric and Lily Daniel took over, followed in the 1970s by Mr. and Mrs. C. Reece. Islwyn Bowen became landlord in the 1990s and still owns the pub, while the licensees for the past five years have been Simon Regan and Sandra Holloway.

On the way to Penrhyn Castle coastguard station was the **Sea View,** superbly sited overlooking the Teifi Estuary. Mary Morris was the landlady in 1881 but the pub closed a couple of years later to enable Mrs. Morris and her seafaring husband John to enjoy a peaceful retirement. Evan Jones revived the pub in 1898, and he still held the licence in 1921 by which time it was a Swansea Old Brewery house. David Morgan was the landlord from 1921 to 1928 when the pub was forced to close under the redundancy ruling; the compensation payout was £120. It is now a youth hostel. There also seems to have been an inn called **Tivyside** near the Sea View in 1891 kept as a sideline by local river pilot William James.

CHAPTER EIGHTEEN

Villages along the A478

BRIDELL, BLAENFFOS, CRYMYCH etc.

The main road south from Cardigan to Narberth weaves in and out of Pembrokeshire and there were a number of hostelries along its length. Heading south from Cardigan, the first to be encountered was actually just in Ceredigion, the **Rhydygwin Inn** at 3, Rhydygwin near Troedyrhiw, kept by John Jones from 1861 to 1881 and later by Mary Jones. Jane Davies was the innkeeper in 1901.

Back in Pembrokeshire, the next stop would have been the **Penybryn Arms** which is still flourishing, despite determined efforts by the local Baptists to have it closed a century ago. Carpenter William Morris was the landlord of this crossroads inn from 1867 to 1871 followed by his widow Sarah between 1875 and 1891. Phoebe Williams was there in 1895 and she married Titus Morgan whose name was over the door from 1901 to 1904.

The Penybryn Arms, an attractive crossroads pub

Miss Sarah Williams was the landlady from 1904 to 1912 and it was during her time that the Rev. Glyndwr Watkins began a campaign to have the pub closed. His main objection was the annoyance caused to people attending services and eisteddfodau at the nearby Penybryn Baptist Chapel by people the worse for drink; he claimed that some of them had even wandered into the chapel and interrupted the songs and recitals. However the pub managed to avoid the magistrates' axe.

Sarah Williams was followed by Adeline 'Addie' Williams from 1912 to 1920, during which time it became a Swansea Old Brewery house. Benjamin Davies was landlord in 1920 while the long-serving landlady between 1921 and 1960 was Mrs. Mary Ann Davies. She was followed by her son 'Dai Penybryn' and his wife Winnie who were behind the bar from 1960 to 1982; when they retired Dai was given a clock by Cardigan police as a gentle hint that his timekeeping had not always been accurate in the past! Vaughan Davies was the landlord in the 1980s and Malcolm and Cath Allan were behind the bar in 1998.

Last orders at the Bridell Inn was called many years ago

Half a mile further south, next to the parish church, was the **Bridell Inn** which seems to have been opened in about 1780 by David George. For some reason the inn features only intermittently in the licensing records, with Thomas George of Bridell being licensed to keep an ale-house in 1795 and Louisa George evidently being in charge in 1819. In January 1839 the freehold of the Bridell Inn was offered for auction at the Black Lion in Cardigan. Prospective bidders were informed that the inn had been in the occupation of 'David George, auctioneer, deceased and now of Louisa George and her tenants'. As the auction notice in the *Welshman* newspaper declared:

> The dwelling house, which has for many years been used as a public house, adjoins the high road from Narberth to Cardigan. The farm buildings which adjoin the dwelling house are commodious and well arranged and suited to a large farm.

Unfortunately there is no indication who purchased the freehold of the farm and ale-house, but Margaret John was the innkeeper at the time of the 1841 census. Louisa George was back in charge by 1851, described in the census as a 69-year-old tavern-keeper. She was being helped by her nephew John Richards and it was his mother, an 80-year-old retired farmer named Elizabeth Richards, who had charge from 1871 to 1875.

Farmer John Davies held the licence from 1881 to 1909, followed for three years by Addie Williams, who appears to have then moved to the Penybryn Arms. Benjamin Davies was licensee from 1912 to 1920 when he too followed the well-worn path to the Penybryn. William Jenkins took over and was still the landlord in 1926 when the inn was considered 'surplus to requirements' by the magistrates; it closed the following year under the redundancy ruling and is now Bridell House, the adjoining coach-house having been converted into Bridell Cottage.

The crossroads at Rhoshill once boasted two pubs, one of which was kept by Thomas Jenkins in 1851. Perhaps this was the **Foundry** which was kept by blacksmith William Davies between 1867 and 1914. Mrs. Sarah Ann Morris was the landlady from 1914 to 1924 when Anna Morris took over. She became Mrs. Benjamin Morgan the following year and was still in charge of the pub in 1968. It was later run by her daughter Sally and her husband Norman Wright. Sadly this friendly little country pub closed in the 1990s.

*The Foundry at Rhoshill with the smithy still in operation
in the background.*
(Picture courtesy of Cilgerran Language and Heritage Committee)

The Foundry closed in the 1990s

Diagonally across the road at the northern end of Bronwydd Terrace was the **Bronwydd Arms**. Simon James was the landlord in 1867 followed by the widowed Eleanor James in 1871, while Abel Isaac kept the pub from 1875 to 1881. William Samuel was licensee in 1890 and Rebecca Samuel had charge in 1894; it seems to have closed by the turn of the century.

Moving further south, the **Cilrhiw**, **Kilrhiw** or sometimes even **Kilrhue Arms** stood to the north of Blaenffos, on the Boncath junction; like the majority of pubs along this route it stood on the western side of the road. It is thought to have served as a 'half-way house' on the stagecoach route and John Owen was the publican in 1841. Farmer David Thomas seems to have been the landlord in 1851; he was certainly the licensee from 1861 to 1891, after which the Cilrhiw appears to have closed.

Blaenffos was once one of the main settlements on the road from Cardigan to Narberth; it had a pub kept by David Jones from 1812 to 1826, while Robert Marsden was landlord of **Bwllch Inn** at Clover Hill on the southern edge of the village in 1823-24. The arrival of the railway and the rapid development of Crymych a mile or so to the south stole much of the thunder from Blaenffos, so that nowadays it is a small ribbon village through which the traffic whizzes by along the A478. In Victorian times it was the passing trade along this road and the drovers' trails which kept the village pubs busy – especially on Crymych market day – and there were four of them in the village at one time, plus a well-established shebeen.

Three of the pubs were in the northern part of the village, close to the village square (a 'square' in Pembrokeshire being a crossroads). One of them was the **Kilwendage Arms** kept by William Morris, innkeeper and butcher, in 1851. Thomas Luke, grocer, draper and victualler, was there in 1867, a blacksmith called Thomas Griffiths had charge in 1871 and Daniel Morris was there from 1875 to 1891. The pub stood on the lane leading off the square towards Maencoch and a ruined building seems to be all that remains.

Across the main road was **New Inn**, a farm-cum-pub occupied by the Thomas family. Henry Thomas and his wife Mary were the innkeepers in the 1870s, the widowed Mary carrying on into the 1880s; the pub was closed and empty at the time of the 1891 census. In recent years it has been the New Inn garden centre.

Blaenffos is dominated by its Baptist chapel, and the surfeit of pubs in the village was a cause of great annoyance to chapel members who campaigned long and hard for their closure – successfully, too, because the axe had fallen on all the pubs by 1925. Of particular annoyance was **New House** which was just off the square, directly opposite the chapel. A plaque on the adjoining coach house states that Asa J. Evans built the property in 1860 and Thomas Harris was landlord here in 1867. Thomas Luke, formerly

The former New Inn at Blaenffos

Chapel-goers helped bring about the demise of New House, Blaenffos

of the Kilwendage, held the licence from 1871 to 1908, when he left to run the post office nearby. David George took over, followed in 1914 by Elizabeth Walters. She hadn't been there long when local chapel minister the Rev. Aaron Morgan stepped up the campaign for the closure of the pub which he had begun several years earlier. 'It is within 50 yards of Blaenffos Baptist Church,' he told the magistrates. 'It is nearer still to the graveyard, which to many is very objectionable'. The magistrates finally agreed and quashed the licence, paying £40 to the licensee.

The **Rhos** was further from the chapel, so it lasted a further decade. William Jones held the licence from 1867 to 1881 and also ran a grocery business. His wife (or widow) Mrs. Elizabeth Jones was there from 1891 to 1895 and Benjamin James was the owner and licensee from 1901 to 1924. It was in that year that the redundancy committee decreed that the Rhos Inn was surplus to requirements and refused to renew the licence. A healthy pay-out of £550 must have cushioned the blow somewhat for Mr. James. Now called

This was once the Rhos at Blaenffos

Rhoslyn, the property adjoins the village store, its outbuildings and coach house having been attractively renovated. Just to the north of Rhoslyn, again on the main road, there once stood a cottage shebeen known far and near as The Black.

Crymych is a much more recent development than Blaenffos. It stands in a gap in the Preseli chain, between Frenni Fawr and Foel Drygarn, and before there was ever a village here it had become a convenient collection

The Crymych Arms, possibly the only building in the village
to pre-date the arrival of the railway

point for the cattle drovers preparing for the long drove east. It appears that the **Crymych Arms** opened in the 1860s to cater for the drovers, and also for the coaches on the Narberth to Cardigan road. When the railway arrived in 1875 the pub gave its name to the nearby railway halt, and eventually the small town that grew up around the station became known as Crymych. Thomas Harries was licensee from 1871 to 1875, William Thomas was there in 1891 and Thomas John was landlord from 1895 to 1901 when Mrs. Rachel John took over. The landlord from 1905 to 1926 was Captain John James. The pub was sold that year and the new licensee was James Harries who remained landlord until 1956. William Thomas was landlord from 1956 to 1960, followed by John Howells, formerly of London House, who was there until the mid 1970s. Geraint Jones was licensee in the 1980s and Bill and Meima Evans have been in charge since the 1990s.

The last days of the London House as a pub

London House seems to have been opened in the railway boom by James James who was described in 1881 as 'shopkeeper and farmer, London House'. Whether it was also a pub from the outset is unclear, but Mr. James was certainly the pub landlord from 1901 to 1914. From 1923 to 1926 the landlord was William Peter Evans. John Isaac was mine host in the late 1930s, followed in turn by John Harries and David Jones. John Howells held the licence throughout the 1950s before moving across the road, being succeeded by John and Dilys Thomas. Following her husband's death, Mrs. Thomas remained in charge until about 2001, after which the pub closed; it is now a private house.

It is many years since this building at Pentregalar went by the sign of the Union

A couple of miles south of Crymych, in the fork of the road at Pentregalar, stood **Tymawr** where farmer, innkeeper and open air preacher James Davies, or 'Shams Dafi' as he was known, was the landlord for a number of years from 1823. According to E.T. Lewis in *Llanfyrnach Parish Lore*:

> He kept a very orderly house; he was also a pillar of nonconformity. The inn at this period welcomed notabilities, where they dined on their way to Cardigan.

By 1851 the hostelry was known as the **Union** and was run by James Thomas, farmer, licensee and brewer, and records show that in the 1860s local tenants of Lord Kensington would troop to the pub on rent day to pay their dues. Thomas was still serving in 1875, but the census of 1881 makes no mention of the property still being a licensed house.

Further south again, another roadside inn was the **Travellers' Rest** which was mentioned in the *Welshman* newspaper in 1855 when it was up for sale. Described as 'formerly Brynhowell', it was a 45-acre holding on the fringe of Llanfyrnach Common, 'late in the occupation of John Evans and now Mr. Dan Davies'. Davies was a stonemason and it was his wife Anne who held the licence from 1851 until the late 1850s. Daniel Luke and his wife Eleanor were in charge by 1861, but there is no sign of the inn on the 1871 census. Instead, the oddly-named **Stamber Inn** appears in roughly the same location, run by agricultural labourer Thomas Lewis. How long this remained a licensed house isn't known.

CHAPTER NINETEEN

East of the A478

CILGERRAN, BONCATH, ABERCYCH, LLANFYRNACH etc.

Beautifully situated on the south bank of the River Teifi, and overlooked by the ruins of a Norman castle, Cilgerran has long been famed as a centre of coracle fishing. According to one visitor in Victorian times:

> The coracle, a kind of portable boat, is in general use – almost every cottage door being furnished with this indispensable requisite which is carried on the backs of the men or women to the water's edge.

In medieval times Cilgerran must have been a settlement of some note and Speed listed it as one of the chief market towns in Pembrokeshire, the market being held in Castle Square. It later enjoyed a few decades of prosperity following the establishment of an extensive tinworks at nearby Penygored in the 1760s, which gave work to upwards of 200 men. However by the turn of the 19th century the tinworks was on its last legs and the little township was suffering accordingly, causing J.T. Barber to note in 1803: 'The town of Kilgerran is diminished into one street, thinly inhabited by labouring farmers and fishermen'. It was also diminished in the number of ale-houses it possessed; in 1779, when the tinworks was flourishing, there had been six, run by William Davies, James Edwards, Margaret John, Charles Mason, Maud Edwards and John Lewis, but by 1805 that number had been halved, and for the next 20-odd years there were never more than a couple of pubs in the village. One of these was the **Soldiers' Return** which was run by Richard Joshua from 1811 to 1825, except for a two-year period when Joseph Davies was in charge. Mary Joshua took over briefly, but there is no mention of the pub after 1826. It is believed that the dwelling near the Square known as Norfolk House was once the Soldiers' Return.

The **Kilgerran Castle** appears to have been run by Owen Evans as part of his general store; it was open in the late 1820s. John Finch was landlord of the **Letters** in Cilgerran in 1835 but it too seems to have been short lived.

('Letters' was once a fairly common name for pubs, but few still survive; the 'letters' on the sign would often be ABC). As with the Kilgerran Castle its position cannot be determined.

From about 1830 onwards the fortunes and population of the parish began to revive, due mainly to the growing importance of salmon fishing and slate quarrying in the locality. A writer in 1850 noted:

> Slates of a good quality are obtained in the vicinity of the town, and every burgess having by charter an undisputed right to open a quarry many cargoes are annually exported from the port of Cardigan.

The quarries were all along the river, and the slates would be moved downstream in shallow-draughted lighters. The arrival of the Whitland and Cardigan Railway made transport of the slates even easier, as well as bringing tourists – especially salmon fishermen – to this beautiful corner of Pembrokeshire. And as the town's fortunes improved, so did the number of hostelries, most of the pubs in the village being along High Street, the site of the busy livestock fairs in May, August and November. These fairs were very well attended and the number of animals being offered for sale was prodigious; one visitor in 1804 marvelled that all the fields for three miles around the village were full of cattle waiting to be sold on fair day, when they would line the village street from end to end. Drovers and cattle dealers came from many miles away to purchase livestock for the English market and the village pubs must have done a roaring trade.

John Bowen was landlord of the **Kilgerran Arms** from 1830 to 1836 when the local Leet Court was held here, but by 1843 he was running the **White Hart** and he was still there in 1852 having survived a very nasty incident. At the height of the Rebecca Riots in the 1840s it became necessary for troops to be billeted at local inns. This proved far from satisfactory. As Lieut. Col. Love complained to the Home Secretary, it was ridiculous for his men to be accommodated 'in small, detached public houses, the resort of the people whose irregularities they were sent to suppress'. One of these public houses was the White Hart, and in 1843 it was the focus of a particularly violent episode involving a number of these troops of Marines. Following a brawl with a party of locals further down the street, the Marines retreated to the White Hart, hoping to obtain reinforcements from other troops billeted at the inn. When landlord Bowen shouted down from an upstairs window that the house was empty of troops, the Marines began beating down the front door. As the *Carmarthen Journal* reported:

> Bowen then proceeded downstairs to expostulate with them and to beg of them to leave, when one of the Marines named Hornet, by the request of Sergeant Lord, shot him.

Three of the Marines were later arrested, while Bowen recovered to carry on running the White Hart for a few more years. Where it actually stood is open to speculation, there being numerous John Bowens mentioned in the relevant census returns, not one of them described as publican or innkeeper. Equally, the location of the **Panalltrihney Arms** cannot be determined. William Thomas was the landlord from 1844 to 1858 and may have been a cooper by trade. The tongue-twisting pub name comes from Panalltrihney house, once the home of Major John Phillips and now known as Alltyrheiny.

Moving through the village from the western end, the **Cardiff Arms** still stands near the start of High Street. The name apparently derives from the home city of the first landlord, and it is thought that the pub – like the small hotel opposite – might have been built in readiness for the arrival of the railway. If so, the speculators were in for a disappointment, because the station was eventually built at the other end of the village. Thomas Mason was landlord of the Cardiff between 1880 and 1891 and his son William Mason followed him from 1893 to 1907. In that year he was twice charged with serving on a Sunday, the charges being dismissed both times; perhaps a higher judge then intervened because he died soon afterwards. His widow Mrs. Ellen Mason ran the Cardiff between 1908 and 1930. She was still brewing her own beer up to the mid-1920s, but poor health meant that the pub was often closed during the latter years of her time there. By 1931 it had become a James Williams house and several different tenants had charge in the 1930s, including David Lewis (formerly of the White Lion, Aberporth),

A traditional coracle hangs outside the Cardiff Arms in Cilgerran

Elizabeth Underwood and Daniel Oliver. Miss Annie Thomas was licensee from 1939 to 1953 and it was a Felinfoel house by the time Bryn and Mair Jones took over in 1955; they were still there in the 1980s. Bryn and his second wife Hilda then had a further ten years in charge, followed by the current licensees Glen and Heulwen Jones.

Moving east, and on the opposite side of the road, there was once a heavy concentration of pubs on either side of the lane leading down to the river at Dolbadau. The first of these, now called Ty Llew, was once the **Black Lion** where the landlord from 1835 to 1844 was Thomas Thomas. The local petty sessions were held here in the 1850s and Mary Davies was landlady from 1850 until her death in 1853, having moved from the Red Lion. Thomas Evans, whose family ran the Castle Inn on Cardigan Bridge, took over and held the licence until around 1868. The widowed Margaret Evans was in charge by 1871 and William Sambrook was the licensee from 1875 to 1880. For a short time in the 1880s David Davies and his wife Martha ran both the Black Lion and the nearby Angel, and it was their daughter Margaret Ann Davies who was licensee of the Black Lion in 1891, aged 19. George Reed (ex Castle) ran the Black Lion from 1902 to 1912, but it was his wife, Mrs. Mary Ann Reed, who was the landlady from 1912 until

The Black Lion closed in 1930

her death in 1925. Their daughter Sarah Evans was licensee from 1926 to 1930. The pub was deemed surplus to requirements by the magistrates in 1929 and forced to close the following year under the redundancy ruling – though not before the owners and licensee put up a fight. Compensation was assessed at £475.

Just past the junction, on the corner, was the **Red Lion**. Thomas Edwards seems to have opened this pub in 1822 and he was still there in 1828, while a stonemason named John Owens kept the Red Lion from 1830 to 1835, possibly followed by John Edwards. The inn then closed for a few years before a local maltster named Mary Davies reopened it in April 1843, advertising in the *Carmarthen Journal* that she had gone to considerable expense in repairing and furnishing the inn. Her aim was to cash in on the growing number of visitors attracted to the area, both by the romantic scenery around Cilgerran Castle and by the excellent sport the river offered to anglers. Those who stayed at the Red Lion in 1843 were assured of 'excellent and well-aired beds and a good table at moderate charges' as well as 'superior home-brewed ale, draught and bottle porter'. Richard Richards and George Merryman were among those who succeeded Mary Davies, but the Red Lion seems to have undergone another period of closure before local grocer John Jenkins reopened it in the 1870s. The Red Lion had closed for good by 1880 and a private house known as Pentre stands on the spot.

Next door but one was the **Angel** where clogmaker William Jones was landlord between 1858 and 1871. Carpenter David Davies was in charge from 1874 until his death in 1884. In the 1880s this was the registered office of the Tywysoges Ann Lodge of the Independent Order of Ancient Britons – a Friendly Society with a typically daft name; it also had a good deal of stabling

There have been no customers at the Angel for over a century

which made it popular on market days. The widowed Mrs. Martha Davies was the landlady from 1884 to 1891 and her daughter, Miss Mary Davies, was in charge in 1895. Thomas Griffiths was there in 1901, followed by Margaret Griffiths from 1902 to 1904. The following year the tenancy of the inn was being advertised as available; there being no takers, the freehold was offered for sale at auction. Again there was little interest, the property being withdrawn when it failed to reach its reserve. The Angel never re-opened and is now a private house called Angorfa.

Two doors from the Angel was the **Castle** where William Jones, formerly of the Angel, was landlord from 1874 to 1891. Thomas Lloyd was there in 1895, when the pub housed the Castell Cadarn Lodge of Ancient Britons, and George Reed was the keeper of the Castle in 1901. David Davies ran the pub from 1902 to 1905 when there was no application for the licence

The Castle stopped serving in 1905

to be renewed. It is now a private house called Lyndhurst.

Further along and across the road, the **Pendre** was built of local slate and stone, and there are fine flagstones on the floors of the bar and lounge. It was the George family pub and several generations served behind the bar. Thomas George was landlord between 1864 and 1867, the widowed Mary George, maltster and publican, was there from 1871 to 1891 and her son, William George, was the landlord from 1895 to 1912; he too was a maltster. Mrs. Mary Ann George ran the pub from 1912 to 1932 and, like every other publican in Cilgerran at the time, she brewed her own beer. Ethel Beynon was licensee from 1932 to 1937 followed by Elsie Sandalls who had a decade in charge. During this time the local magistrates recommended closing the pub

The whitewashed Pendre in Cilgerran in the early 1950s.
(Picture courtesy of Cilgerran Language and Heritage Committee)

216

under the redundancy ruling; however, for once the recommendation wasn't acted upon and the pub was spared. Reg Popplewell was licensee from 1947 through to 1968, followed by Ralph Andrew, Vic and Marge Griffiths, Deborah and Geoff Makin, Colin and Carol Dark and the present licensees Jeff and Helen Jones.

Mary and Reg Popplewell ran the Pendre from the 1950s to the 1970s.

(Picture courtesy of Cilgerran Language and Heritage Committee)

The ancient ash tree was still very much part of the picture at the Pendre when this photo was taken in 2004, but the trunk was discovered to be hollow in 2008 and the tree had to go

Also in High Street was the **Tivyside** which appears under various spellings including Tivie Side. Louisa Mitchell or Michael kept the pub from 1844 to 1858. There was also a short-lived pub called the **Commercial** in Castle Square which in 1891 was run by a 60-year-old widow called Mary Michael. Apparently it is the house facing you as you turn from the square towards the castle itself.

To the east of Cilgerran is the hamlet of Cnwce. William Thomas and his wife Hannah were innkeepers here in 1841, presumably of the **Drovers' Arms** which was the village pub at the time. Labourer William Nicholas was the landlord from 1844 to 1867. As quarrying developed locally, so the **Masons' Arms** opened in Cnwce to serve the slate-workers. David Griffiths was licensee from 1858 to 1861 in which year he was made Portreeve of Cilgerran, but he died soon afterwards and his widow Mrs. Hannah Griffiths was the landlady until 1895. Enoch Thomas, a carpenter by trade, was the landlord from 1901 to 1906 and Mrs. Mary Thomas ran the pub and brewed her own beer between 1906 and 1916. Mrs. Hannah Thomas and her husband William – a cooper by trade – were in charge from 1916 to 1951 when Lily Davies took over. She became Lily Kean the following year and departed soon afterwards, and Mrs. Elsie Brand was there from 1954 to 1968. More recently the pub has been run by Ritchie and Mary Ray, followed by Barbara Wainwright between 1990 and 2007 and the current licensee Francine Barber. Retaining many of the features from the days when it would have been crowded with slate workers, this attractive little pub is known locally as 'Y Rampin' or 'The Ramp', the nickname coming from the adjacent 'incline' – a tramway leading down to the slate quarry, now used as a footpath.

An old tramway runs from the back of the Masons' Arms down to the quarries

218

The Royal Marine has not seen active duty for 150 years

Not too far from Cilgerran, on the road to Rhoshill, was the **Royal Marine**, a pub-cum-smallholding where Daniel Griffiths was landlord in 1835. When it closed isn't known, but it stood at the junction with the lane to Alltyrheiny, a property still known as Marine Lodge.

Of the village of Boncath, B.G. Charles had this to say in the *Place-names of Pembrokeshire*:

'Boncath' or 'bwncath' is a buzzard. The original name, later abbreviated, may have been Tafarn y Boncath, an inn name, perhaps with a buzzard as its sign.

According to Mr. Dillwyn Miles, the first of the benefit societies to become established in Pembrokeshire was the True Briton Society. This was formed in 1772 and its members met every month at **Tafarn y Boncath** when they were expected to contribute sixpence for the fund and tuppence for beer. Since Martha James ran the only ale-house in Boncath between 1782 and 1812 it must have been this place. The name had been anglicised to **Boncath Inn** when Mary Evans was the landlady from 1817 to 1828 and Thomas Evans was the village publican in 1829. John Owen was in charge by 1840 and his wife Mrs. Elizabeth Owen was landlady from 1861 until 1880 when the following advert appeared in the local press:

To be let by TENDER and entered upon at Michaelmas 1880, that old established Inn called BONCATH INN with about 40 acres of land, capable of immense improvement, in the parish of Llanfihangel Penbedw in the county of Pembroke, now in the occupation of Mrs. Elizabeth Owen.
This old established full licensed inn is situate close to the site of the proposed Railway Station at Boncath.

Farmer Thomas Harries was landlord from 1881 to 1901, duly welcoming the first train in 1884, and his daughter Miss Sarah Harries ran the pub from 1902 to 1920. John Harries (probably her brother) was the landlord

An early postcard view of the Boncath Inn, which is thought to have given its name to the village

from 1920 to 1943. Roberts Breweries Ltd. of Aberystwyth acquired the pub during the war and it was run in the 1940s by E.A. Rees, Wynford James and Mrs. Lorna James who was there until 1956. Mrs. Margaret Powell was licensee from 1956 into the 1960s, during which time the ownership of the pub changed hands again, passing from Roberts Breweries Ltd. to Hancocks which had swallowed up the Aberystwyth concern. Tommy Powell was

Still a popular village local – the Boncath Inn

licensee in the early 1970s, followed in 1977 by Hugh Davies who died tragically in a road accident outside the pub in 1982. Eric and Betty Davies took over, keeping the business going until 1998. The Boncath Inn has changed hands a number of times since, winning a CAMRA 'pub of the year' award during the time that Marcus Reed was in charge. It was bought at auction by local couple Glyn and Ann James just before Christmas 2009 and they are running it as a classic Welsh country pub, full of interesting photographs and memorabilia of village life. The pub's resident ghost confines herself to wandering about upstairs and doesn't bother the drinkers.

Diagonally across the square, but in a different parish, stood the **Boncath Tavern.** It was probably opened by shopkeeper Thomas Rees in the early 1860s while blacksmith and innkeeper Meshach James was there from 1871 to 1880. By 1889 Mr. James' widowed daughter Hannah Evans was licensee; in that year she married local farmer David George and

The Boncath Tavern stood across the square from its rival

they ran the pub for the next ten years. Hannah died in 1899 and the pub expired with her, Mr. George apparently happy to concentrate on farming.

In 1795, David Evans ran a pub in the nearby farming village of Newchapel, while from 1807 to 1812 Theophilus Thomas ran a pub in the village. No name is given, but it appears to have been the **Newchapel Inn** in the centre of the village. Old Theo was followed by David Thomas between 1819 and 1828 and by Margaret Thomas in 1841. By 1851 she had become Margaret Charles and she was still in charge of the Newchapel Inn in 1871 when she was 80. Her daughter Sarah and son-in-law Evan Elias had taken over by 1881 and by 1895 the pub name had been changed to the **Ffynnone Arms** with Elias still in charge, the new name honouring the local manor house of the landowning Colby family. (There is a suggestion that the original cottage pub was rebuilt on the present scale at the same time). The landlord from 1901 to 1919 was David Jones followed for a few years by Mrs. Anne Jones. Herbert Thomas kept the pub from 1923 to 1932 followed by Evan Rees. Jack Evans took over in 1937, buying the pub from the Ffynnone estate in 1947, and following his death in 1955 his widow Mrs. Elizabeth 'Tish' Evans carried on as licensee for another 20-odd years. Her sons Alun and then John succeeded her behind the bar, running the pub until about 1988. Since then this fine, stone-built hostelry has changed hands a number of times and has even gone through periods of being closed,

The attractive Ffynnone Arms in Newchapel

but under new licensees it is looking smarter than ever and appears to have a bright future.

The former **White Lion** on the roadside in Abercych isn't easy to identify these days, having become a private house called Tegfan. It was the Davies family pub and from 1867 to 1875 Hannah Davies was licensee. Between 1881 and 1895, when wood-turner John Davies kept the pub, it was handy for workers at Forge Cych mill and woollen factory. It was also very popular with fishermen who had easy access to the river nearby. Anne Davies

Last orders were finally called at the White Lion in Abercych in 1928

was in charge in 1901 and Thomas Davies was the owner and landlord from 1903 to 1912. In 1909 the pub escaped being closed under the redundancy ruling, despite the best efforts of James Jones of Waunisaf, Boncath, who gloried in the title of Chief Ruler of the Abercych 'Tent' of the Independent Order of Rechabites, the 'Tent' being located in the school near the pub. Catherine Davies was licensee from 1912 to 1916, while the licence-holder from 1916 to 1927 was Mary Williams. Miss Annie Davies was in charge in 1928 when the White Lion was finally forced to close under the redundancy ruling. Miss Davies received compensation of £40; owner Mr. James Davies received £260.

Moving along towards Pontseli is the **Penrhiw Inn** which originally stood across the road, on the south side of the junction. John Gibbons was landlord from 1867 to 1875 and William Davies was in charge in 1881. David Owens was landlord between 1901 and the First World War when James Davies took over. He remained in charge until 1942, after which the pub was run by Rachel Davies until 1951. David and Florence Jones, John Jenkins and Joseph Williams all had spells in charge, before Thomas Jeremiah took over and ran the pub from 1963 until the mid-1970s. It was at this time that the old pub was demolished to improve visibility at this dangerous junction. Mr. Jeremiah retired and the licence was transferred across the road to the former village Post Office and shop which was converted into a pub and run by Steve Entwhistle. (The old pub ended up being reduced to hard-core for the car-park of its replacement). Popular with anglers, the new Penrhiw has been run for the past 14 years by David Woodthorp.

The Penrhiw was formerly a post office

The Nag's Head at Pontseli now takes up the whole of the terrace

John James ran a pub at Pontseli in 1784. This could have been the attractive and historic **Nag's Head** at the bottom of the hill, which was kept from 1807 to 1824 by David Jenkins and from 1825 to 1828 by Ann Jenkins. The pub also served as the local smithy, and it appears that William Davies was blacksmith and innkeeper in 1841. In about 1850 the first ever sitting of Cilgerran petty sessions took place at the inn, and it continued to act as the courthouse until the magistrates moved to the Sessions Room in Newchapel in 1908. Blacksmith Joshua Evans was landlord from 1851 to 1867 and his son Josiah, another blacksmith, was landlord of this Clynfyw estate pub from 1871 to 1917.

It is said that Josiah was a skilled metalworker and that he invented a special iron plough which was used with great success in America and Australia, although he seems not to have benefited financially from his invention. Despite his long tenure, he had little interest in running the pub which came as an inconvenient adjunct to the smithy, only keeping it open at the behest of the landowner; indeed, he was known to drive noisy drinkers out of the bar if he felt they were disturbing the studies of his two young sons, James and Herber. (It obviously helped their careers, because James went on to become an important civil servant at Somerset House in London and Dr. Herber Evans became one of the most famous preachers in Wales). While Josiah was landlord the pub had a Biblical quotation in Welsh over the door; translated it read: 'Be wise as the serpent, harmless as the dove'.

William Finch Jones ran the pub and brewed his own beer from 1918 to 1924, being followed by Alf Thomas. David Morris took over in 1928 and kept the Nag's Head until 1955 when he was in his 90s. It was in about 1950 that Mr. Morris became part of the legend of The Giant Rat of Abercych. For months people living along the Cych Valley had been terrified by sightings of a large rodent, three-foot long, and there were fears that the area was about to be over-run by a new breed of super-rat. Digging potatoes one evening, the 88-year-old Mr. Morris cornered the fearsome beast and dispatched it with a garden fork; it was later stuffed and put on display in the pub, where it still has pride of place. Experts later determined that the creature wasn't a giant rat after all, but a luckless coypu that had escaped from captivity.

David Morris' son Gwyn took over in 1955 and remained in charge until his death in the 1980s. Until this time the pub was relatively small and basic, with a bar one side of the front door, a parlour the other side, and beer served in a jug, straight from the barrel. When new owner Alan Jones of the Llanboidy Chocolate Factory bought the pub in about 1990 he also bought the neighbouring buildings in the terrace, formerly a shop and workshop, so that the Nag's Head now occupies the whole block. The pub was extended without losing any of its character, and the adjacent buildings were converted into a pub restaurant and – for a time – a brewery which produced the pub's own Old Emrys beer which is still available, but is now brewed off the premises. Samantha Jamieson has been licensee since 1996, her regulars including the Carreg Las team of Morris Dancers.

From 1851 to 1861, Anna Jones was licensee of the **Bridge End** pub further up the wooded Cych Valley, not far from Llancych House, while her husband William worked as a farm bailiff. The Bridge End seems to have closed in the 1860s. Not far away, and close to the parish church of St. Clydai, was a property known as the **Larch** or **Large** inn. Various references exist to this property in Victorian times, none of which suggest it was still a pub at this time.

Confusingly, there were two inns called Lancych Arms in Clydey parish in the latter part of the 19th century, both of them owned at one time by H.A. Jones-Lloyd of Lancych House and Pembroke Dock. In September 1860, a new licence for the sale of malt liquor was granted at Cilgerran petty sessions. This was for the **Lancych Arms** in the tiny woollen mill village of Star where the first licensee was David Davies. For some obscure reason the name of the pub had been changed to the **Ship** by 1871, but it had reverted to its original name by 1880 when David Davies' widow Mary Davies was in charge. She was still in charge in 1891, but by 1895 the pub had passed to her daughter Mary Ann Davies and her husband Enoch Davies. Enoch appears to have died in 1902 and Mary Ann retired in 1909, after which the pub never re-opened.

The village itself seems to have taken its name from a much earlier ale-house called **Star**, and B.G. Charles has identified a reference to the Star as early as 1734. It is said that early Methodists met in secret at the pub to avoid persecution. Methusalem John was landlord from 1779 to 1807 and David James was landlord from 1810 to 1828. In December 1835 a victualler from Star named John James was jailed for three months for his part in a poaching raid on the Dyffryn pheasant preserve; the poachers were described as 'idle, dissipated, worthless midnight plunderers'. Nathaniel James was the land-lord of the **Cross Inn,** Clydey, from 1793 to 1828 (although the records are sketchy). This seems to have been Cross Inn farm, south of Star. Ann James was there in 1841, but it may not have been an inn by this time. David Lewis was licensee of the **Red Cow** from 1779 to 1784 and William Hughes was landlord in 1807; it was near the village of Henfeddau.

Once a popular pub, the Lancych Arms at Henfeddau is now a farmhouse

The other **Lancych Arms** was actually in Henfeddau, on the road from Llanfyrnach to Trelech. Nowadays this is a fairly insignificant farming hamlet, but at one time it boasted regular livestock fairs, with sheep and cattle penned in stalls from one end of the village to the other. James Hughes was an ale-house keeper in Henfeddau in 1795 but the sign of his inn is not recorded. The Lancych Arms appears to have been opened in the 1860s by John Thomas, who turned his farmhouse into a pub, and by 1879 it was being run by Morris Morris and his wife Anna. Philip Morris was licensee from 1891 to 1914, after which it was run for a couple of years by John and Emily Main. A description from about this time noted that there was a holding of 34 acres attached to the pub which had three rooms on the ground floor used for drinking purposes, four bedrooms and a cellar which doubled as a dairy. Philip Morris was back in charge in 1918, but by now the shadow of the redundancy axe was hanging over the pub. A police report in March 1920 observed:

> The district is thinly populated and the fairs held at Henfeddau are fast disappearing. There is not much traffic on this road and the Wolfscastle Inn, 1,024 yards distance, would meet the requirements of the neighbourhood.

Later that year the Lancych Arms in Henfeddau was duly closed under the redundancy set-up, Philip Morris receiving £10 of the compensation pay-out of £50. The building still stands at the western end of the village, but nowadays it is a farmhouse called Troedyrhiw.

The Pant-y-Blaidd was once the Wolf's Castle

Just up the road (1,024 yards, to be exact) and narrowly in Pembrokeshire, is the **Pant-y-Blaidd** – a rare example of a Pembrokeshire pub with a Welsh name. However it began life as the **Wolf's Castle,** the 'castle' presumably referring to a nearby tumulus. Phoebe Morris ran the Wolf's Castle from 1871 to 1881 and her daughter Mary had charge from 1891 to 1901. Elias Davies was there from 1907 to 1914 followed by Mary Davies and then Sophia Jones. In 1922 the licence passed to David James of Crymych, and he was landlord until 1932, having built an extension in 1927 to house an extra bar. In 1925 he was granted an extension of opening hours for Pant-y-Blaidd races, despite one magistrate objecting: 'There are enough evils there without public houses being open. They are ruining body and soul'. Oliver Jones took over in 1932 and was still there in 1957 when he handed over to Reg Bullock, formerly of the Swanlake at Jameston, who spent the next decade in charge. When Lynda Evans became licensee in 1966, one of her first moves was to change the name to Pant-y-Blaidd. Harold and Carol Bibby took over the pub – plus seven acres and a car repair garage – 24 years ago, and their son Harry is the current landlord. Although one of Pembrokeshire's most isolated pubs, the Pant-y-Blaidd continues to enjoy a steady passing trade and a loyal following from the local farming community.

A couple of miles to the north is Tegryn, where Thomas Davies and his wife Elizabeth ran a pub from 1841 to 1861; he was a slate-worker and the name of the pub isn't recorded. However by 1871 another, younger, Thomas

The Davies family outside the Butchers' Arms

Davies was running a pub in the village, and because he was a master butcher it followed that the pub was called the **Butchers' Arms**. Arthur Davies, blacksmith and victualler, was there in 1891 and William Davies was in charge from 1901 to 1923 followed by his wife or widow Mrs. Sarah Davies who carried on serving for another four years. Margaret Zillah Davies took over in 1927 and was there for 40 years; her sister Alice ran the local school at roughly the same time. Dan Nicholas took over the Butchers' in 1967 and he was followed by brothers Richard and Harold Butler and their respective wives Maureen and Norma in the 1970s; they made a number of alterations and improvements to the original pub. Subsequent licensees have included Derek Hendrickson, Peter and Liz Granfield, Scott and Lorraine Heron, Tim and Kerry Palmer and the present incumbent Christopher Bowen. Thought to have been opened as one of a 'chain' of pubs along the drovers' route to Carmarthen from Crymych and Cilgerran, the Butchers' has one special claim to fame – it is the highest pub in Pembrokeshire.

Pembrokeshire's highest pub, the Butchers' Arms at Tegryn

Although its pub, the **Lamb** has an agricultural name, the nearby village of Hermon was for many years a quarrymen's settlement, the slate quarries at nearby Glogue being among the largest in the county. The quarry closed in 1926, but the pub still boasts a 'quarrymen's cwtch' where the slate-workers would gather for a pint. The first recorded licensee was a carpenter and farmer named John Jenkins who ran the pub with his wife Elizabeth from 1841 to 1875. It was a notably well run house and in the 1860s was the venue of the Court Leet and Court Baron of the manor of Llanfyrnach-ar-Daf. By 1881 William Jenkins had taken over, farming 20 acres, brewing his own beer, and acting as publican at the Lamb, while John and Elizabeth Davies were there in 1891.

The Lamb at Hermon has been much extended over the years

Theo Evans was the landlord of the Lamb from 1901 to 1910 followed by his wife or widow Mrs. Sarah Evans who remained until 1924. David Evans then ran the Lamb for ten years followed by David Thomas who was still there in

Inscribed flagstone at the Lamb

1940. John Evans was in charge during the 1940s followed by Henry Bowen in the 1950s and Bill Vaughan in the 1960s. George and Joan Jones who ran the Lamb in the 1970s built a large extension on the rear, partly to serve food and partly, it is said, to cater for the Sunday influx of drinkers in the days when nearby Carmarthenshire and Cardiganshire were 'dry' on the Sabbath. The pub subsequently changed hands a couple of times and was even closed for a period before being reopened by Mebs Phillips in the 1990s. Current licensee is Nick Street who has plans to restore a 'lost' feature of the pub. This is an inscribed slate flagstone from the days of John Jenkins and his son William pronouncing them to be 'licensed brewers and retailers of ale and spirits'. Banished to the backyard during the renovations of the 1970s, this beautifully inscribed flag-stone could soon be given a place of honour inside the pub itself.

As a justice of the peace for Cemais in the 1580s, the antiquarian George Owen of Henllan once tried a thief who stole a drover's purse at an inn near Llanfyrnach. Much more recently, in the 19th century, the village was the centre of an important lead-mining enterprise with ore being transported to Cardigan by horse and cart for shipment. The Whitland to Cardigan railway passed through the village in the 1870s making transport easier, although by this time the mineral deposits were becoming exhausted and drainage problems caused the workings to be abandoned in about 1890; considerable remains of the industry can still be seen as well as a terrace of back-to-back houses for the key mineworkers. There were two innkeepers in the parish in the 1760s, John Griffiths and Thomas Morris, while Josiah Hughes was an ale-house keeper in Llanfyrnach in 1795.

The New Inn at Llanfyrnach was once the haunt of thirsty lead miners, but closed during the First World War

William Lewis kept the **New Inn** at Llanfyrnach from 1805 until his death in 1840 and Hannah Lewis, an 80-year-old widow, was there in 1841. Ben Williams and his wife Anna ran the pub in the 1850s and early '60s, with the widowed Anna running the pub with the help of her daughter Mary from 1871 to 1875. Thomas Evans, a lead miner by day, was licensee from 1881 to 1891, Morris Morris was the landlord in 1895 and a butcher called George Jones was licensee from 1901 to 1915. The pub was on the edge of the village on the lane leading past the church and it seems to have stopped serving at about this time; the licence was finally withdrawn in 1920. The building became a private house known for many years as Cartref, although more recently it has become Brookmans.

Bibliography

Much of the information in this book has come from old newspapers, in particular the *Welshman*, the *Carmarthen Journal*, the *West Wales Guardian*, the *County Echo*, the *Teifiside Advertiser* and the *Haverfordwest and Milford Haven Telegraph* and its successor the *Western Telegraph*. The various trade directories have also been of great assistance, particularly those published at various times by Slater, Kelly, Pigot and Hunt.

General

Ale and Hearty, Alan Wykes, 1979.
British Brewing, Gavin Smith, 2004.
Drink and the Victorians, Brian Harrison, 1971.
Farmhouse Brewing, Elfyn Scourfield, 1974.
The English Pub, Peter Haydon, 1994.
The English Pub, Michael Jackson, 1976.
Kilvert's Diary, Francis Kilvert, pub. 1938.
Man Walks Into A Pub, Pete Brown, 2003.
Pigsties and Paradise, Liz Pitman, 2009.
Prince of Ales – The History of Brewing in Wales, Brian Glover, 1993.
The Pubs of Leominster, Kington and North-west Herefordshire, Ron Shoesmith and
        Roger Barrett, 2000.
Victuallers' Licences, Jeremy Gibson and Judith Hunter, 1997.
Welsh Pub Names, Myrddin ap Dafydd, 1991.

Pembrokeshire

The Ancient Borough of Newport, Pembrokeshire, Dillwyn Miles, 1995.
Cilgerran Community in Photographs, Cilgerran Heritage Committee, 2007.
Cwmyreglwys Church and Churchyard, Rex Harries and Rhiannon Comeau.
Descriptive Excursions Through South Wales and Monmouthshire, E. Donovan, 1804.
Discovering Pembrokeshire Country Pubs, Richard Jago and Nigel John, 1981.
Eglwyswrw District – History and Memories of a Community, edited by Beatrice
        Davies, 2009.
The Footsteps of Our Fathers, Peter Davies, 1994.

A Guide to Pembrokeshire Inns and Pubs, Michael Fitzgerald.

The Gateway to Wales, W.J. Lewis.

The History of Haverfordwest and Some Pembrokeshire Parishes by John Brown, revised and extended by J.W. Phillips and F. Warren, 1914.

The History of Solva, F.W. Warburton.

The Inn Crowd, C.I. Thomas (publ.).

The Last Invasion of Britain, Commander E.H. Stuart Jones, 1950.

Llanfyrnach Parish Lore, E.T. Lewis.

Looking Back, John Miles Thomas.

The Mariners of Newport, Pembrokeshire, Dillwyn Miles, 2006.

Memories of Letterston, Evan Raymond.

Nicholson's Cambrian Travellers' Guide, 1840.

North of the Hills, E.T. Lewis, 1972.

Old Haverfordwest, W.D. Phillips, 1925.

Pembrokeshire, the Forgotten Coalfield, M.R. Connop-Price, 2004.

Pembrokeshire Life (various issues).

The Pevsner Guide to the Buildings of Pembrokeshire, Thomas Lloyd, Robert Scourfield and Julian Orbach, 2004.

Pilgrimage – A Welsh Perspective, Terry John and Nona Rees, 2002.

The Place-names of Pembrokeshire, B.G. Charles, 1992.

Porthgain and Abereiddi, Peter Davies, 2007.

Pub Walks in Pembrokeshire, Laurence Main, 1994.

The Railways of Pembrokeshire, John Morris, 1981.

The Solva Saga, Eric Freeman, 1958.

Solva – An Introduction to Village Life, Jean and Paul Raggett, 6th ed., 2003.

Spit and Sawdust, G. Nelson Edwards.

A Squint at St. David's, George Harries, 2003.

The Streets of St. David's, George Middleton, 1977.

Street Names of St. David's City, Francis Green, West Wales Historical Society Transactions, Vol. XIII.

St. David's and Dewisland – A Social History, David W. James, 1981.

St. David of Dewisland, Nona Rees.

Treasury of Historic Pembrokeshire, Francis Jones, 1998.

Twr y Felin Guide to St. David's, Henry Evans, 1915.

Wales' Maritime Trade in Wine During the Later Middle Ages (Maritime Wales, 1992), K. Lloyd Gruffydd.

The Welsh Sunday Closing Act 1881 (Article in The Welsh History Review, December 1972), W.R. Lambert.

The Western Telegraph 'Then and Now' Series.

The Journals of the Pembrokeshire Historical Society.

West Wales Historical Records, Vol. VIII.

Index

In the following index all pub names, old and new, are indexed – where there has been name changes they are cross-referenced and shown in brackets. 'Inn' is not normally used in the title (apart from 'New Inn'). To avoid confusion the town or village is shown. Page numbers in bold type indicate the main entry for that inn; those in italics refer to illustrations.

The Pubs of Haverfordwest, Milford Haven and Mid-West Pembrokeshire

by Keith Johnson

As ever, the history of the local hostelries of an area provides the background to a host of great characters, strange events, amusing incidents and intriguing buildings. The tales are many: a dentist in the mid-1800s who sought customers in the pubs, carrying out his operations on the spot; bodies found walled up in one pub, believed to be those of sailors who died of fever; and a fox that sought refuge on the roof of a pub used by the local hunt.

(304 pages, over 200 photographs and other illustrations £9.95)

The Pubs of Narberth, Saundersfoot and South-East Pembrokeshire

by Keith Johnson

This covers all existing hostelries in almost, but not quite, the old Narberth Hundred licensing district, along with many that have come and gone. It also includes details of the use of south Pembrokeshire coal in the wider brewing industry and information on the Narberth wine merchants James Williams.

(208 pages, many illustrations £9.95)

Neolithic Sites of Cardiganshire, Carmarthenshire & Pembrokeshire

by George Children and George Nash

From chambered tombs the authors extrapolate to create a picture of Neolithic society, dividing the 37 remaining sites into five groups which they believe may have formed Neolithic territories. This book is a useful guide for anyone interested in exploring the sites, and an intriguing read for anyone interested in the origins of mankind in south-west Wales.

(148 pages, 84 black and white photos, plans & maps £7.95)

Castles and Bishops Palaces of Pembrokeshire

by Lise Hull

This guide covers all the county's castles, from mighty Pembroke and enriched Carew to the lowliest motte or ringwork, together with bishops palaces. General chapters tell the county's military history from 905 to the Civil War, after which each site has an entry detailing construction and history, location and access arrangements.

(240 pages, over 100 black and white photos and plans £7.95)

Around & About
South-West Wales

by Graham Roberts

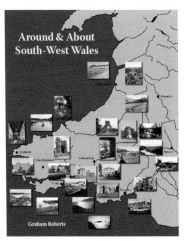

Ten road-based tours cover Pembroke-shire, Cardiganshire, Carmarthenshire, parts of Glamorgan and a large part of Powys. Starting from seven different localities the tours vary from 25 to 100 miles in extent and cover a range of spectacular scenery, many well and less well known historically or architecturally interesting buildings, several towns, a good handful of villages, many beaches, a clutch of prehistoric sites, gardens open to the public, nature reserves and much besides. Developed from a knowledge of the area gained over many years, the tours will lead you to places which you would otherwise have needed time to find out about as visitors – even some long-standing local residents may be surprised and carried away by what they have missed out on seeing to date.

Paperback, 288 pages, 300 photographs
(ISBN 978 1904396 74 1)   £12.95

Also from Logaston Press

The Civil War in Pembrokeshire

by Terry John

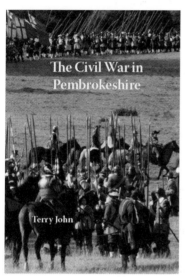

When the Second Civil War began in 1648, some contemporaries believed that it was due to the actions of Major-General Rowland Laugharne and Colonels John Poyer and Rice Powell. Until that time these three men had been adherents of the Parliamentarian cause, if for different reasons. Laugharne appears to have been a man of deep convictions and beliefs as to how society should function, whilst Poyer was an abrasive character who was quite possibly out to feather his own nest and often took great risks (though it must be borne in mind that much of his 'character' has come down to us through the words of his enemies). Least known is Rice Powell, who seems to have been a family man perhaps swayed by the actions of others.

This book explores the background to the Civil War in Wales, the lives and characters of the three main protagonists, and the events of both the First and Second Civil Wars with all the ebb and flow of march and counter-march, siege and battle – at Carew, Pembroke, Tenby, Haverfordwest, Pill fort, along the Milford Haven waterway, Newcastle Emlyn, Cardigan, Colby Moor, St Fagans, Cardiff, Laugharne Castle, Carmarthen, Roch, Picton Castle and elsewhere.

Using many personal letters and records of the time, Terry John provides a very readable account of complex and intense times full of men and women of principle and many a (male) rogue.

Paperback, 192 pages, with 35 black and white illustrations
(ISBN 978 1904396 90 1)   £12.95

Also from Logaston Press

The Story of the Milford Haven Waterway

by Sybil Edwards

This book, a major revision of that first published in 2001, focuses on how the Milford Haven waterway has shaped and developed the fortunes of the settlements along its shores, from the arrival of early man through to the present day.

Trade developed with the arrival of the Romans and from the Dark Ages that followed emerged the multitude of Welsh Kingdoms that often fought with one another. Into this feuding mix arrived the Normans, Flemings and English. In due course, trade with Ireland led initially Pembroke and then Haverfordwest (as well as Tenby) to develop into thriving ports, safeguarded by their own castles. Along the shores a multitude of small sailing craft were built. Yet not all was calm. The waterway with all its creeks and inlets was also a haven for smugglers and even piracy. Of all nationalities, the pirates occasionally raided the offshore islands, sometimes brazenly sold stolen goods on the quaysides, even stayed in the homes of their friends.

Sea-borne trade, initially in agricultural produce, quickened when local mines started producing quality anthracite, and when lime kilns established along the waterway required a constant supply of lime with which to make fertiliser. Ships grew in size and battle waged between various settlements to become the main dockyard, a contest won, eventually, by Pembroke Dock, though Milford became the main fishing port, supported by Neyland. Various schemes for the fortification of the waterway to protect what became a main naval dockyard saw a flurry of forts, towers and barracks, their design often rapidly overtaken by changes in military technology. More recently the waters have served the need of oil supply, and most recently Liquified Natural Gas.

Paperback, 224 pages with over 140 black and white illustrations
(ISBN 978 1906663 10 0)   £12.95

Fishguard Fiasco

by John S. Kinross

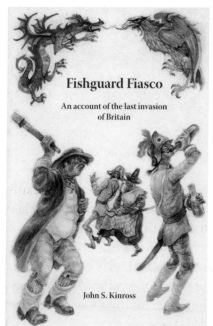

Why choose to land an invading force at Fishguard and then surrender with hardly a shot being fired on either side? The range of possible options given to the commander of this force from Revolutionary France, the American William Tate, suggests that it was seen more as a chance to offload a prison population on the English. If they should happen to burn Bristol, or raise the Welsh in revolt, or act as a flying column up the Welsh border to join with French and Irish forces landing in Liverpool, having successfully freed Ireland, then so much the better. As it was, the force landed at Fishguard, the ill-fed French troops feasted on all the food they could find to hand and washed it down with copious amounts of alcohol. Coupled with lack of decisiveness by Tate to make the most of his surprise appearance, this left them in no fit state to face the hastily assembled bands of Yeomanry and Militia, backed up, at least in the popular imagination, by scythe wielding Welsh women in their national costume, which the inebriated French supposedly took for additional regular army units.

Paperback, 128 pages paperback, with 40 black ad white illustrations
(ISBN 978 1904396 68 0)   £9.95

Pembrokeshire
another year, another day

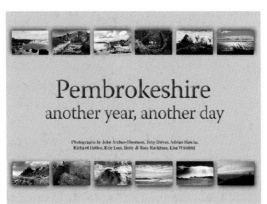

Photographs by John Archer-Thomson, Toby Driver, Adrian Hawke, Richard Hellon, Eric Lees, Betty & Tony Rackham and Lisa Whitfeld

In 2007 Logaston Press published *Pembrokeshire: a year and a day*, a selection of the work of a number of local photographers. This second volume, which is to a larger format and on heavier paper, adopts the same style, the photographs being arranged so that they broadly run from early morning in winter through the soft light of spring, the stronger light of summer and the varied colours of autumn, to conclude with a series of winter sunsets: 'another year, another day'.

This volume includes the work of eight local photographers whose images capture the county in many moods and weather conditions. Their chosen subjects include many stretches of the county's coastline, several historic sites, the Preseli hills, the Gwaun Valley, Tycanol and Pengelli woods and a variety of flora and fauna, including some below the surface of the sea. The quality of the images is undeniable, and many deserve a long and lingering look; and as a group they present a moving portrait of a beautiful county.

128 pages with 116 photographs, largely in colour
Paperback (ISBN 978 1 906663 34 6)   £12.95
Limited edition Hardback (ISBN 978 1 906663 33 9)   £20